T0374562

THE

PUBLICATIONS

OF THE

SURTEES SOCIETY

THE

PUBLICATIONS

OF THE

SURTEES SOCIETY

ESTABLISHED IN THE YEAR

M.DCCC.XXXIV

VOL. CLXXVIII

FOR THE YEAR M.CM.LXIII

At a Council Meeting of the Surtees Society held in Durham Castle on 7 June, 1966, Mr. C. R. Hudleston in the Chair, it was ordered that Mr. H. T. Dickinson's edition of the Correspondence of Sir James Clavering should be printed as a volume of the Society's publications.

W. A. L. Seaman
Secretary

THE CORRESPONDENCE OF
SIR JAMES CLAVERING

EDITED AND ARRANGED BY

H. T. DICKINSON

PRINTED FOR THE SOCIETY BY

NORTHUMBERLAND PRESS LTD.
GATESHEAD

1967

CONTENTS

Introduction

In many ways Sir James Clavering, 1680-1748, was a typical member of the lesser gentry in County Durham in the first half of the eighteenth century. He owned small estates at Lamesley and Greencroft, where he farmed with some success. As a country gentleman he was active at quarter sessions and in local parliamentary elections. Through his family connections however he had other and widespread interests. There were branches of the Clavering family at Axwell Park and Chopwell, and, by marriage, the Claverings were connected with many of the leading families in the north-east. James Clavering's mother, Jane, was the daughter of Benjamin Ellison, merchant. His sister, also Jane, married Thomas Liddell, and a son of this marriage became the first Lord Ravensworth. James's first wife was Catherine Yorke of a prominent Richmond family. Some of her letters to him are in section five of this volume, while sections two and three contain letters from her brothers, Thomas and John Yorke. After Catherine's death in 1723 James Clavering married Elizabeth, daughter of Lionel Vane of Long Newton. These were not James Clavering's only important family connections. The senior branch of the family, the Claverings of Axwell Park, had married into the Middleton family of Belsay, and the Mallabar and Fenwick families of Newcastle. It was from the senior branch of the family that James Clavering inherited his baronetcy in 1738, when he became the sixth baronet on the death of Sir Francis Clavering of Axwell. Even more important were the marriage alliances of the Claverings of Chopwell. Mary, daughter of John Clavering of Chopwell, became the second wife of William, Earl Cowper and Lord Chancellor of England. Her sister, Anne, married Henry Liddell, the "governor" and one of the leading figures in the coal-trade. Anne's letters to James Clavering form the first and most important section in this volume. The two sisters' young half-brother, John or "Jacky" Clavering, on the death of their father, was heir to valuable land and coal-mines. James Clavering was one of his trustees and this led him into correspondence with Anne Clavering about the management of Jacky's affairs. It was through these important family connections that James Clavering became interested in both national politics and the coal-trade. His interest in the Court scene and Westminster politics was passive, in that he learned the latest gossip and news from Anne Clavering and later from John Yorke. But as a trustee for Jacky Clavering he had to become actively engaged in the expanding coal-trade, though this seemed to have been against his inclination. In fact he appears to have found the cut-throat nature of the coal-trade more than he could manage. This contrasts strongly with the professionalism of William Cotesworth and Henry Liddell.

The letters in this volume illustrate the several interests of Sir James Clavering, and, as such, they are not uniform in their intrinsic importance or in their value to readers. The letters from his wife, Catherine, may perhaps be of little interest beyond the eccentricity of her spelling. Other letters are of general social and economic interest. They deal with the family affairs, health, education, and recreational activities of fairly typical members of the lesser gentry of this period. The most significant letters, as might be expected, deal with politics and the coal-trade. The letters dealing with national affairs are mainly among those written by Anne Clavering and John Yorke, in sections one and three, though there are political references in all sections. Those from Anne Clavering deal mainly with politics in the reign of Anne, when her brother-in-law, Lord Cowper, took a leading part in national life. From this relationship and from her London vantage-point, Anne could inform James Clavering of the Court and parliamentary scene. Some of her letters, especially those on the Sacheverell trial of 1710, are of first-rate importance. Indeed, Anne Clavering clearly had a keen mind and ear, and both a passionate interest and a definite whig bias in politics. At this period she has few rivals as a female commentator and it is unfortunate that her letters are not more numerous. There are fewer letters by John Yorke on political matters, but particularly interesting are his letters referring to Walpole's excise scheme. Among the useful letters on the coal-trade are many of those written by Anne Clavering and those letters in section four. Naturally they do not give a coherent picture of the coal-trade, but they form a useful addition to the work of writers like the late Professor Edward Hughes. The reader particularly interested in the coal-trade should also examine copies of James Clavering's out-letters, in his letter-book in Newcastle University Library. This letter-book deals principally with James Clavering's business interests and it is hoped that it may be published by the Surtees Society.

The present volume contains the extant 214 original letters to and from James Clavering in Durham University Library. These are unbound and uncatalogued, except six letters (those numbered 18, 165, 167, 171, 185 and 214), which are bound in a volume of Sharp's material on Durham City and County elections 1650-1831. This is also in the University Library (Ms. 942.81.E7.). In arranging the letters a strict chronological sequence has not been followed. Instead the letters are grouped in sections, largely according to who wrote them. One advantage of this method is that the sections with the more numerous and more important letters come first. With this method Anne Clavering's letters are in the first section, followed by the letters of the Yorke brothers, and so on. Moreover since nearly all the letters are addressed to James Clavering, and we do not possess his replies, there is a greater coherency if all the letters by one particular writer are in sequence. In this way a particular theme can be followed more easily than if the letters were interspersed with those from other people of an entirely different type. Even this arrangement does not disturb the chronological sequence too much since the first three sections, the largest and most important, are very nearly in chronological order.

In order to present a clear and coherent text the letters have been subject to a little alteration. All the letters are published *in extenso* except that, after the first letter or so in each section has established the pattern, the concluding compliments and signature have been omitted. This also applies to the address, but when the letters are sent to a new destination then the new address is printed. The original spelling has been kept throughout, except that common abbreviations, which would present an untidy printed text, have been expanded. Thus "yt" becomes "that", "wt" becomes "what", "Ld" becomes "Lord", etc. Where it has been necessary to expand other abbreviations and initials, or to explain unusual words or spellings, the additions have been enclosed within a square bracket. Some of the letters were written without punctuation, and others have only a succession of commas in very long letters. Punctuation has been added only where necessary, to promote clarity and avoid ambiguities. An attempt has been made to identify every person mentioned in the letters and to give a footnote reference in every case. This has not always proved possible, though it is hoped that all the important people, and those mentioned frequently, have been identified.

In conclusion, it is a pleasure to record my appreciation of the help I have received in producing this volume. Professor H. S. Offler and Mr. C. Roy Hudleston gave every assistance and encouragement. Mr. Hudleston also helped to identify some of the more obscure individuals mentioned in these letters. Dr. Doyle, keeper of rare books in Durham University Library, first drew my attention to these letters, while the library authorities gave me permission and facilities to edit them. Mrs. Eleanor Yorke answered many queries about the Yorke family. The editing was completed while I was fortunate enough to hold the Earl Grey Fellowship at the University of Newcastle.

H. T. Dickinson, Edinburgh University.

ABBREVIATIONS.

The following abbreviated forms have been used for references in the explanatory notes:

A.A. *Archaeologia Aeliana.*

Boyer's Annals. Abel Boyer, *The Reign of Queen Anne digested into annals.* II vols. 1703 sqq.

C.J. *The Journals of the House of Commons.*

D.N.B. *The Dictionary of National Biography.*

Foster. *Alumni oxonienses* . . . 1500-1714, and 1715-1886, ed. Joseph Foster. 8 vols. 1888-1891.

G.E.C. G[eorge] E[dward] C[ockayne], *The Complete Peerage.* Revised edition. 1910 sqq.

Hodgson. J. C. Hodgson's Durham & Northumberland pedigrees in Newcastle Central Reference Library.

Hughes. Edward Hughes, *North Country Life in the Eighteenth Century.* 1952.

Hutchinson. W. Hutchinson, *The history and antiquities of the county palatine of Durham.* 2 vols. 1785-7.

Letter-book. James Clavering's letter-book in Newcastle University Library.

L.J. *The Journals of the House of Lords.*

Luttrell. Narcissus Luttrell, *A Brief Historical Relation of State Affairs.* 6 vols. 1857.

Parl. Hist. William Cobbett's *Parliamentary History.* Vols vi-viii. 1810.

Sharp Mss. Sharp's pedigrees in the Dean and Chapter Library, Durham Cathedral.

Surtees. R. S. Surtees, *The history and antiquities of the county palatine of Durham.* 4 vols. 1816-40.

S.S. The publications of the Surtees Society.

Venn. *Alumni Cantabrigienses.* ed. J. and J. A. Venn. Part I to 1751. 4 vols. 1922-27.

The Claverings of Axwell.

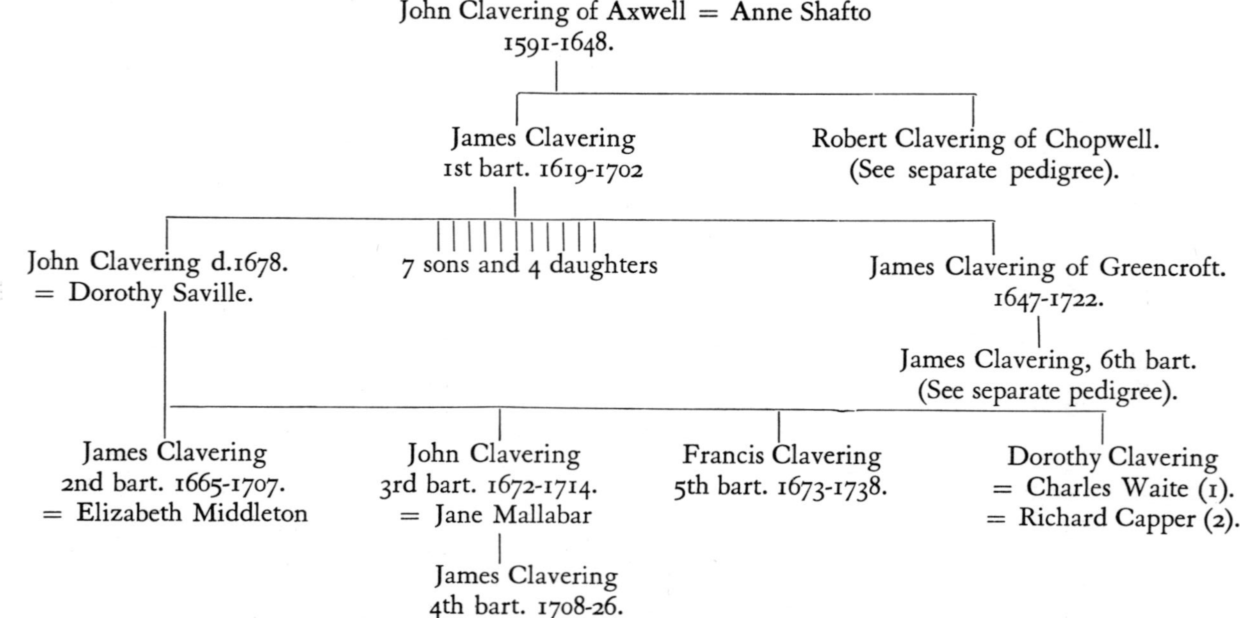

John Clavering of Axwell = Anne Shafto
1591-1648.
James Clavering
1st bart. 1619-1702
Robert Clavering of Chopwell.
(See separate pedigree).
John Clavering d.1678.
= Dorothy Saville.
7 sons and 4 daughters
James Clavering of Greencroft.
1647-1722.
James Clavering, 6th bart.
(See separate pedigree).
James Clavering
2nd bart. 1665-1707.
= Elizabeth Middleton
John Clavering
3rd bart. 1672-1714.
= Jane Mallabar
James Clavering
4th bart. 1708-26.
Francis Clavering
5th bart. 1673-1738.
Dorothy Clavering
= Charles Waite (1).
= Richard Capper (2).

The Claverings of Chopwell.

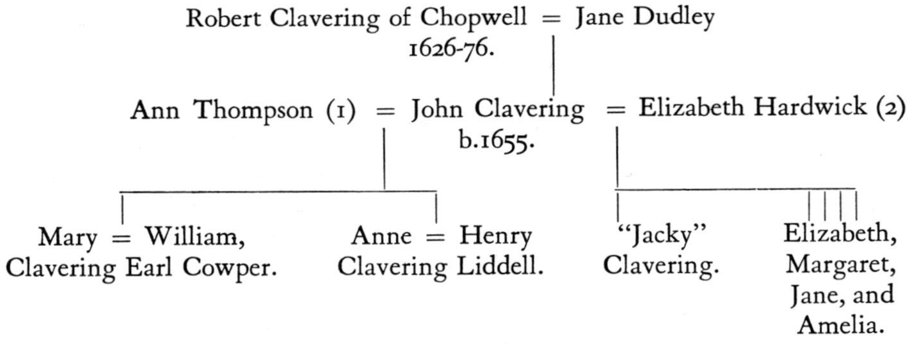

The Claverings of Greencroft.

James Clavering = Jane Ellison

Catherine Yorke (1) = James Clavering = Elizabeth Vane (2)
6th bart. 1680-1748. d.1747.

Jane Clavering = Thomas Liddell

Elizabeth, Anne Isabel, and Alice.

4 sons and 2 daughters died as infants.

Thomas 7th bart. 1718-92.

George

John

I. LETTERS FROM ANNE CLAVERING

1. London. May 15th, 1708.

Sir,

Nothing but the indisposition I have been in could have prevented my returning you thanks for the favour of yours, but since the receiving your Letter I have been confined to my bed [a] great part of the week, by a rash which now thank God is almost gone; Jacky[1] came to town of Thursday and our friends in Lincoln Inn Fields took a whim to goe lye one night in Hertfordshire, and were but to return late the night my boy came. However I sent to forbid his coming here least he might gett any desorder which young creatures a[re] subject to; however my Sis[ter][2] brought him with her to see me yesterday morning. He's very well but I find is not yet reconciled to Eaton. He told me he had writ to you the first Saturday of the month, and beg[ged] I would from him tell you something about his gold he left behind him; to which I replyed yes, but did not understand what he ment; if it be of consequence I shall hear of it again. So will you I make no doubt. His wigg becomes him very well, and he's pleased with his watch.

This [is] now time to wish you joy of the Election. I am glad the Lord B[ishop][3] is sensible. Theare are whiggs enough in the County to make one member of P[arliament]. But had it not been for shame I could have been in a predigious ill humour that Mr. M— interest was not so good as the D-ke[?]. Had those Copes but lost the making off their bossom snake for a representative I should never had ail'd anything but old age, tho' by that I should have

[1] John or "Jacky" Clavering was the son of John Clavering of Chopwell, by his second wife, and half-brother of Anne Clavering. Born 1698, M.P. 1727-34 and groom of the bedchamber to George II. *Surtees*. At this time he was at Eton, but visited Hertfordshire during the holidays.

[2] Mary Clavering, who had recently married William Cowper, the Lord Chancellor. She was later lady-in-waiting to the Princess of Wales. See *The Diary of Mary, Countess Cowper*, ed. Spencer Cowper. 2nd ed. London 1865.

[3] Nathaniel Crewe, 1697-1721. Bishop of Oxford 1671-4; Bishop of Durham 1674. Staunch Tory and a former favourite of James II. Son-in-law of Sir William Forster of Bamburgh.

lost a great deal of sweet conversation I now have the prospect to enjoy next winter att the B[ishopric] of D[urham]. Thomy was so fond of the conquest he'd made that imediatly he frankt a letter to town not considering it could not goe and was putt out again att the post house. Yet methinks I am concerned to find so good a commander as Sir B[ellasyse] dirst not stay to attack (tho' but with a few men) those who pretend to no skill in war tho' often to judge of battles; if Lord Terawly[4] should hear that he retires to his castle for security upon the approche of the enemy without making the least defence, he might justly say 'twas not so when we were att Port St. Marys, but it shews the Court had reason to putt him in disgrace. But I will leave these worthless folks and proceed to the Keelmen. You, I thought, had made a plain storry, and I had joyned with you in opinion, but since I see a letter from a K[eelman] of the town to excuse that and lay the thing upon the fitters, for now that rabble were gone to work; att this I was a little surprised, and could not forbear asking if they rowed the Keels to the barr and back again for diversion, being all the ships were gone to load att Sunderland. This, with the late proceeding of that corporation to the troops from Ostend, are contradicted and the storry only raised by some enemys to town. But what is the greatest jest to me, the noble Earl's friends say you all of you mistook him that day he invited you to dinner; he never designed to lett up Lord Lumley[5] "O," quoth I, "that's a pretty air. Now he's shewed his teeth. But how could so many mistake the same storry, and Mr. Carr[6] ingage himself, if it never was mentioned". "No," they said, "he named some such thing without design to vex our neighbour, and he being jealous took what he said in jest to be earnest". "That may be," says my Aunt, "but I will be the one as soon as the other." And perhaps all was jest for Nany made an inquiry after the comission that was passing and it proved one for no body till he spoke ever heard it mentioned. So I don't wonder after all this that they endeavour underhand to ruin the instert [? interest] of the person who so rudely

[4] Charles O'Hara, 1st Baron Tyrawley, c. 1640-1724. Distinguished army officer, who had fought at Landen, Cadiz, Vigo and Almanza. At Vigo he had attacked Port St. Mary with troops under Sir Henry Bellasyse. See note 56.

[5] Henry, Lord Lumley. Eldest son of the Earl of Scarborough and M.P. Arundel. d. 1710.

[6] William Carr; coal-merchant, head of Hostman's Co., Mayor of Newcastle 1702, and M.P. Newcastle 1690-1710, and 1722-34.

refused a first vote. Lord Halifax[7] dos not understand the opposing of a good vote when he might have opposed a Tacker.[8] I hear little news. Sir J[ohn] Bucknal[9] and Colonel Plumer[10] design to petition against Freeman[11] and Halsey,[12] which pleased my Sister. Last night I was told that Lord Griffin[13] would this day be called to know why sentence might not pass upon him, and that Lord Duke Hamilton[14] would be made a Peer of Great Britain, being [sic] he has changed his principle as one might see by his bail [supported by] four great gromelsotions [sic] whiggs, who are angry not to be more regarded. I approve of the thing but would have Lord Belhaven[15] made one also for then he and Lord Havers[ha]m[16] will make the house spend many a pleasant hour. Collonell M—[17] is to be Lord Dover and all's well. If you have seen the female Granadeer and the ballad made of that man's wife to the tune of the Dame of Honour, you must have been diverted. This [is] now time to conclude and assure you Sir, I am

your most humble servant
A. Clavering.

[P.S.] I beg my service to your spouse. I can't find out the second Ba[ronet] that went in prosession with the monks when some C[hurchmen] walkt for a show. The clergy will hang me if they can but I shall always keep out of there clutches. Just now I have had a visitt from Frank C[lavering],[18] but he came not in. My Aunt's your servant. My Uncle's out of town.
[No address.]

[7] Charles Montague, Baron later Earl of Halifax, 1661-1715. Chancellor of the Exchequer temp. William III, and member of the Whig Junto.

[8] Those extreme Tories, who in 1704 had attempted to "tack" the Occasional Conformity Bill to the Land Tax.

[9] Sir John Bucknell, a London merchant, knighted 1685 and died 1711. Former high-sheriff of Hertfordshire and M.P. Middlesex.

[10] William Plumer 1687-1767. M.P. Hertfordshire temp. George II.

[11] Ralph Freeman, Tory M.P. Hertfordshire 1697-1721.

[12] Thomas Halsey, Tory M.P. Hertfordshire 1695-1705; 1708-1715.

[13] Edward Griffin, first baron. A Jacobite who was arrested after the abortive 1708 invasion attempt. Sentenced to death, reprieved, but died in the Tower 1710.

[14] James Hamilton, fourth duke, 1658-1712. Arrested 1708 as a suspected Jacobite, but released through Whig influence.

[15] John Hamilton, second Baron Belhaven, 1656-June 1708. Arrested as suspected Jacobite 1708.

[16] John Thompson, first Baron Haversham.

[17] Colonel Henry Mordaunt?

[18] Francis Clavering, 1673-1738. Fifth bart. 1726-38, succeeded by James Clavering.

2. London. May 29th, 1708.

Sir,

Yours came safe to hand of Monday last, and had I not been prevented should sooner have returned you thanks for it, as also for the concern you are pleased to express for my indisposition. I thank God I am perfectly recovered of it after keeping house 15 days. I have att the request you made sent you both ballads; the latter, with some verses made by Mr. Walsh[19] (before his death) upon the same occassion, were given by the D[uche]sse of M[arlborough][20] to some ladys since the reconciliation betwixt her and bed-chamber woman; which convinces me 'tis a politick part only they play. The Queen has gott the gout in her foot, which misfortune has prevented Mrs. Temple's[21] marriage this week; it not being proper to ask the consent of the Queen now, but next week it will certainly be. I cannot agree with the town to think it a good match, but she has prospects, att a great distance, for an estate, but the Gentleman's own estate is but small. How Segnior Carnaro[22] will bear this I can't judge; when, for her refusing to live in Italy with him, he kept his bed three days. By the concern that others show upon the same account we ought to look upon C[arnaro] as a jest, for Mr. Windam[23] has already rub[be]d off the death of his beautifull mistress. Lord Longville's[24] sister [has] come in for maid of honour in Mrs. Temple's room. Last night I heard of the removal of Lord Chief Justice[25] [who is] to be made a Baron, and that Sir Jo[seph] Jekyll[26] was to succeed him in [the] office of C[hief] J[ustice]; Sir James Montague[27] to be Chief Justice of Chester, Sir Thomas Parker[28] [to be] Attorney Generall, and Mr. Ayres[29] Solicitor

[19] William Walsh, Whig M.P. 1698-1708. Died 1708. *Foster*.

[20] Sarah Churchill, favourite of Queen Anne and the wife of the great duke. At this time she was being ousted from favour by Mrs. Masham.

[21] Maid-of-honour to Queen Anne. Married Mr. Littleton in 1708. *Luttrell*, vi.

[22] Francisco Carnaro, ambassador of the republic of Venice 1706-10.

[23] Probably one of the several Wyndhams, who were M.P.s during the reign of Queen Anne.

[24] Talbot Yelverton, 1690-1731, 2nd viscount Longueville 1704, and Earl of Sussex from 1717.

[25] John Holt, 1642-1710. *D.N.B.*

[26] The great Whig lawyer and M.P. 1697-1738. He was not made Lord Chief Justice.

[27] Whig M.P. 1695-1713; Solicitor-General 1707 and Attorney-General 1708-10.

[28] Whig M.P. 1705-10; Lord Chief Justice 1710-18. Created Earl of Macclesfield 1721. *D.N.B.*

[29] Robert Eyres, Whig M.P. for Salisbury 1698-1710. Appointed Solicitor-General 1708.

[-General]. This is to imploy the minds and heads of idle people, and I look upon it all as spoke without grounds, for Lady Holt[30] has not personal interest enough att Court to make this alteration, and till then I believe her Lord will be continued in his place. They have also turned out Lord Little Chamberlain,[31] but this they always doe upon all occassions. After this groundless news I fear 'tis to[o] true to tell you that Lord Windsor,[32] having gott himself and Shipen[33] chose for B[r]amber, and being himself chose elsewhere, designs in the last place to bring in the great and valiant Cesar,[34] who I hoped might have retired this winter for the sake of his health. The election of Rutlandshire is carried as wisht, and the E[arl] of N[ottingham][35] has turned off all his tenants, and putt out of offices all who were suspected to be for Mr. Sherrard.[36] I am glad Sir Arthur Kay[37] lost his att York. Lord D[owne][38] is upon peace and behaviour. I wish you Wednesday well over. A certain Lord I perceive is mightly carressed amongst your magistrates. Has he gott a lease of the lives of some that he's busling 3 years before hands?. My Lord[39] and Sister I hope will return tonight. Jacky and his neice are both well. I showed him what you said and unfortunatly, as he was att breakfast with us yesterday, in came Mr. Freke,[40] but Jack never moved from my elbow the time [he] staid, nor could not be prevailed upon to give his consent to the match, tho' I told him he was the first proposer of it. I am called of to the Park therefore can only beg a humble service to my Cosen and return you my uncle and aunt's, who give you many thanks for your repeated assurances to assist them in their affairs and subscribe myself Sir, . . .

A.C.

[30] Anne, daughter of Sir John Cropley. Married John Holt 1675 and survived his death in 1710.

[31] Henry Grey, Marquis (later Duke) of Kent, 1671-1740. He did not lose his place until 1710.

[32] Thomas Windsor, an Irish viscount and son of the Earl of Plymouth. Tory M.P. 1685-7 and 1705-11.

[33] William Shippen, the celebrated Jacobite M.P. 1707-43. *D.N.B.*

[34] Charles Caesar, Tory M.P. Hertford borough 1701-15 and 1722-3.

[35] Daniel Finch, second Earl of Nottingham and a former Tory Secretary of State.

[36] Philip Sherrard, c. 1680-1750, Whig M.P. Rutlandshire 1708-10.

[37] Sir Arthur Kaye, Yorkshire squire and Tory M.P. for the county 1710-26. *Foster*.

[38] Henry Dawnay, third Viscount Downe, 1664-1741. Tory M.P. 1690-1701 and 1707-27.

[39] William Cowper, Whig M.P. 1695-1705, Lord Keeper 1705, Lord Chancellor 1707-10, created baron 1706 and earl 1718.

[40] Rev. Thomas Freke, pastor of the dissenting chapel in Smithfield. *Hughes*.

[P.S.] I should be undone had I seealed [sic] this, and not from the above said, wish our neighbour and all you his friends success of Wednesday.

To James Clavering Esq. of Lamesley near Newcastle upon Tine.

3. London. June 10th, 1708.

Sir,

I hope 'ere this you have received a letter from little John who left us last Friday and returned to Eaton in the coach with Mr. Bragg.[41] I gave him a strickt charge to remember the first Saturday of the month. The day sevennight he dined with Lord B[arnard][42] and, as he told me att his return, my Lord ask[ed] him if he was not his tenant in a lead mine, to which the child sayd, "Yes". "Then," replied my Lord, "If we can but agree Master, I hope we may be landlord and tenant as long as [we] both live". "Indeed," says Jacky, "Sister, I carried myself very well. I did not laugh, but drunk the healths of my Lord, Lady, Mrs. Vane,[43] and Mr. Wm. Vane,[44] but not the mad-man's, tho' he was the eldest son". I am not in the least surprised that the magistrates should treat my neighbour so rudely. 'Twas what I expected. There letter makes out what is said in town upon that score, that they could never forgive Mr. H[enry] L[iddell][45] making himself governor of the Hoastmen's compagny, that there (in the letter) they plainly point att. I have vanity enough to think I could return an answer to it, to Mr. Carr's advantage, but to vex the souls of the rest. They certainly lye under great obligations to him, but there was no occassion in espousing his interest to affront the other. However, I am glad it was not in their power to turn him out. After all the proffers they made severall letters were writ to the high sheriff of Durham to beg of him to oppose Sir H[enry Liddell][46] and,

[41] Jacky Clavering's tutor.

[42] Christopher Vane, 1st Baron Barnard. *Surtees.*

[43] Lucy, second daughter and coheiress of William Jolliffe. Married William Vane 1703. *Surtees.*

[44] William Vane, second son of Lord Barnard. Whig M.P. temp. Anne, George I and George II. Created Viscount Vane 1720. *Surtees.*

[45] Son of Sir Henry Liddell, 3rd bart. He later married Anne Clavering, the writer of these letters. *Hughes* and *Surtees.*

[46] Sir Henry Liddell, 3rd bart. Whig M.P. Durham City 1689-98 and Newcastle 1700-10 *Hughes* and *Surtees.*

as I hear, the like to Mr. Davison[47] of Beamish, but both declined. Lord Wm. [Pawlet][48] was plain with more than one person. He, we say, gave J.O.[49] the lye, which is not usual from one gentleman to another. "So," says I, "but my Lord considered him as an attorney and consequently a— and as the piper's son of Berwick". In the Print Sir H[enry] had the preheminence. The magistrates doe me a great deal of honour in telling of my good judgement in the matter of elections. I did not know I had any interest in that town, but suspition is sometimes as bad as fackt, and as they are a parsell of worthless fellows I despise what they can say and shall continue my old opinion to lett them talk of me till they are warye [weary] and then they of course will quitt the subject. Who is your sheriff and representative that did not sign the epistle? My neighbour will treat with respect those who never diserved it from him. I have scarce any news. Mrs. Hales[50] comes in maid of honour upon pretence that Mrs. Yelverton[51] is too young. The Queen still has the gout and dos not goe to Windsor till next week. Sister Cowper has been out of order these 3 or 4 days. Of Tuesday I governed and sent for Dr. Morly,[52] but he not being att home then, she never would speak with him since, she being better. Therefore you know [she] means [it] was not proper. It was violent pain in her head that came att a certain hour so violently that by the screams she gave one would have thought her upon the rack. She was much better last night and spoke of coming abroad, which I could not consent to. I thank you for your letter and am Sir . . .

[P.S.] I beg my service to my Cosen. My aunt's your servant. My uncle left us to goe a horse hunting.

[47] Probably William Davison, 1673-1735, son of Timothy Davison, a merchant and former Mayor of Newcastle. *Surtees* and *Sharp* No. 12, Vol. II.

[48] Lord William Pawlet, second son of 1st Duke of Bolton. Whig M.P. 1689-1729. *Hughes* and *Letter-book*.

[49] ? Samuel Ogle was a barrister and M.P. for Berwick at this time.

[50] Miss Hales of Hertfordshire married Thomas Coke, the Vice-Chamberlain. She was the sister of William Hales, M.P. 1709-17. *Luttrell*. vi.

[51] Sister of Talbot Yelverton, Lord Longueville.

[52] Either Christopher Love Morley, an eminent physician (*D.N.B.*) or Dr. Charles Morley, a commissioner of the sick and wounded. *Boyer's Annals*, i, 52.

To James Clavering Esq., of Lamesley. To be left att the Post House in Durham.

4. London. June 26th, 1708.

Sir,

Yours of the 18th instant came safe 2 post agoe, for which my thanks are due. My sister, I thank God, is now perfectly well, and give me leave to tell you that you misinterpreted my meaning about her, and when she denies anything of that sort I am apt to believe she speaks truth. She's realy a slow hussif, and, I fear, designs, before she has another little one, to spoil this girl, for that I think is often the fate of the first child. I dined in Lincoln-Inn Fields of Thursday (it being my Lord's birthday) and then spoke to her about the putting some friends into the Commission of Peace joyned with the Ma- t's [Magistrates?] as you mentioned. I understood [from] her [that] she had writ to you about it to tell you she feard it was not in my Lord's power but that she would inquire after it, and see what was to be done, that she might not be unjustly blamed by them a second time. The revolutions which attends the brains of those men are not a little surprising. Can they, after all the abuse putt upon my neighbour, ever think of treating him? Is it out of respect to him, or to have the world say that they are true and zealous friends to the Government, and as my Lord of D[urha]m dos, take this way of convinsing unbelievers they Drink the Protestant Succession?

We still in this part of Great Brittian complain of Lord W[illiam] P[awlet] who we say gave himself to much Liberty of Speach when amongst you, and carried the jest so farr as to call the Mayor a Blockhead or some such like thing. Methinks the quarrell att Durham has but an ugly aspect. Some are so kind to that velvet head J[ohn] T[empest][53] to say 'twas polisy in him to gett the useless General to dispatch his B[rother] for the advantage of his spouse. I have charity enough yet to look upon that as malice, but at the same time the ground of this quarrell must be laid at his door. How can any man have so mean a soul as to make himself a meer tool to the high-Church? With my consent, if Nicholson[54] should drop, both the Sir and Brother ought to swing that there may be

[53] John Tempest, 1679-1737 a former M.P. for County Durham. *Surtees*.

[54] James Nicholson, wealthy merchant, former mayor of Hartlepools and M.P. Durham City 1708-10. *Surtees*.

no more Jack Halls.[55] Did the General's second ever see or understand the use of a sword in such like cases? Woud he not be of more use to him with a good oak stick? However if this quarrell is to have no end Sir H[enry] B[ellasyse][56] should be advised rather to fight with sword and pistole upon one of the breed of the horses the Lord Lieutenant[57] has had ever since the revolution; being he thinks 'tis honourable to fight upon such foolish reasons.

The caracter [which] has been given of your pupill ever since his return to Eaton, must make up for his diffects whilst in town. The discipline of the school I perceive keeps the young man in aw, and in my thoughts the resolution you took of his remaining there some time without coming to London will be no small advantage to him. Cosen Smithson[58] seems inclined to have me goe next week with her to make him a visitt. If so in my next [I] can give you a fuller account. Doll[59] leaves us of Monday next for Newcastle. I do not hear she yet has disposed of her liberty, tho' I fear will to[o] soon, so you'll first have the oportunity to wish her joy. We have no news in town but a parcell of weddings which have long been on the stocks. A Ball there was last Tuesday given by Lord Dorsett[60] to his admired Collier;[61] a handsome intertainment, a great deal of good humour and gayaty was amongst the whole compayny.

My uncle and aunt are your servants and bid me return you many thanks for your concern in there affairs, and that if you think it convenient should be glad you would lett Mr. Poyen[62] accompayny you to Durham when you go to speak to D[avid] D[ixon][63] and if they can be any way serviceable to you in town begs of you to be

[55] John Hall, draper and merchant of Durham.

[56] A Lieutenant-General and M.P. 1695-1708 and 1710-15, part of the time for Durham City. *Surtees.*

[57] Richard Lumley, 1st Earl of Scarborough, 1650-1702. Lord Lieutenant of Durham and Northumberland.

[58] Elizabeth Clavering of Newcastle, who in 1707 had married Charles Smithson, attorney of Carlisle and Newcastle. She died 1721.

[59] Dorothy Clavering, sister of James, John and Francis Clavering, 2nd, 3rd and 5th barts., and cousin of James Clavering, 6th bart. Born c. 1671, died 1754. She married (1) Charles Waite and (2) Richard Capper of Bushy, Hertfordshire. *Surtees.*

[60] Lionel Cranfield, 7th Earl and later 1st Duke of Dorset, 1688-1765.

[61] Elizabeth, daughter and co-heiress of Lt.-Gen. Walter Colyear or Collier. Maid of honour to Queen Anne. Married the Earl of Dorset in January 1709.

[62] Daniel Poyen, principal agent for the Tyneside mine-owners, like the Liddells. *Hughes* and *Letter-book.*

[63] David Dixon, an attorney of Durham and an executor for some of the Clavering family. *S.S.* cxxiv and *Letter-book.* He died 1728 and appointed James Clavering one of his executors and trustees. *Raine* Ms. 40.

so free as to command them. I beg my service to my Cosen and am Sir . . .

[P.S.] Pardon me if I give you the trouble of returning my service to my neighbour[64] and thanks for putting his name [on] the direction of your letter.

5. London. July 27, [1708.]

Sir,

Pardon me that I have not sooner given you joy of your nephew, but the sudden journy my Lord Chan[cellor] and [my] sister took into Kent (from whence they returned last Sunday) made me differ [i.e. defer] writing sooner, being desirous to inquire into the affair you mention. If by the copy of the abstract there is the power wee hope for, you need no longer doubt of seing a great alteration, and the sooner that can be done and the better. Had you not formerly given me a hint of a designed invitation I should have been under a great surprise. Was his partner present? You also mention the high Church's diserting a velvet head has [i.e. as] Sir H[enry] B[ellasyse] stiles him, and that he seems desirous of coming unto the name of an honest man by joyning with those of good principle, but since the loss of him is no great shock to that party you ought to have some great proof of his repentance 'ere you admitt him.

The news here has a very low ebb. The weddings in the Devonshire family has occasioned some discourse. Lord James[65] has a faire prospect to be unhappy. We impatient ourselves for news from Flanders, but I am one of those who thinks that the dam'd Duke of B[erwick][66] has been an ugly thorn to us by his counsell to perplext Vandome;[67] but time will lett us see more clearly into that affair. I therefore can only dayly pray for a second success upon them, for such another slight skirmiges as the Jacks [i.e. the French] call it, would send the children into France. However what has been done has not a little sett the brains of witty men to work in making ballads and ridiculing the Princes of the Blood; but as they all do, I must not quitt this subject without praising our young

[64] Sir Henry Liddell.

[65] Lord James Cavendish, son of 1st Duke of Devonshire. Whig M.P. 1701-10 and 1715-41.

[66] James Fitz-James, 1670-1734, illegitimate son of James II and marshal of France.

[67] Duke of Vendôme, 1654-1712, marshal of France and victor over Stanhope at Brihuega in 1710.

Electoral Prince[68] who has done that which has not imprinted a mean thought of him in the heart of the English. My uncle Manson[69] left us last week and went into Yorkshire. In 14 days time I believe my aunt gos to Bath; and after the thanksgiving I shall take a turn into Hertfordshire, w[h]ere my Lord, sister and family goe tomorrow. This [is] high time now methinks to conclude, considering this will take you from more agreeable conversation being as I doubt not att Durham. My aunt's your servant. So am I to your spouse and give me leave to assure you Sir . . .

[P.S.] I find I must wait the sitting of the Parlmt for the explination of your new title. Don't you know your kindsman Sir W[illiam] Thornton[70] is a prisoner to the French? That is often the fate of travelers.

6. Hertingfordberry, Sept. 2d, 1708.

Sir,

Yours of the 10th and 17 of Augt. came both safe to my hands. I beg a thousand pardon for not answering them sooner but if you give me leave to make the true apologye, yiu will not find me so negligent [in future.] For the time I stayed in London I was so hurry'd about my aunt's affairs that I had not time to doe some small ones for myself and since I came here, which is now 19 days, have had but this opportunity to send directly to London, and I am unwilling to take any other method for fear letters shoud be lost. I can send you no news, but what you will find in the Prints. We hope to be masters of Lisle, but whether the French yet will attempt the relief of it or only look on, that nobody can judge. Our thanksgiving service att Pauls was an incomparable one. I hope you will give it a reading. Did our ghostly father doe the same in his diocese, or did his lady's indisposition prevent his study? I am concerned good lady she should be in so ill a way as to give him the least hopes of a third wife; which now putts me in mind to give you thanks for your proferr, but I have an aversion to the gown, so must lay those vain thoughts far from me. I wish my sister and I had been att London that we might have served both you and your friend with a spinett, but if the beginging of the next month when we goe to town will doe you any service you may command us both. Your pupill att Eaton is well. My sister had a

[68] The future George II, 1683-1760, who distinguished himself at Oudenarde.

[69] ? The Monson family of Broxbourne, Hertfordshire.

[70] Sir William Thornton, barrister and Yorkshire knight. *Venn*.

letter from him last week. Be not angry with him. He serves you as the rest of his friends, which give me cause to hope his time is better imployed. I have given my aunt an account about D[avid] D[ixon]. She's infinitely obliged to you for your trouble about that affair, but I was always of opinion that you would never be the wiser by speaking to him. As Lord Barnard goes not down this summer his creditt, I hope, is saved upon my bro[ther's][71] account, for I hear that when that bussiness was mentiond to him he said that he should not medle, others might ackt. Your Durham Assizes gave us good diversion. A certain High Church man and myself laugh heartily att Beau Eden's[72] duelling. These young men! Well, for his sake if ever I have a son, Paris he shall never see, without it be the general education for young men. For one amongst a thousand to have that advantage of education makes so much emulation amongst the rest, that those things he has been [taught?] by seing the world give others an oportunity to expose themselves by shewing their ignorance and ill nature att once. Should Sir R[obert] E[den][73] [have] died, where could that young barronett meet with a person suitable to him? Would he not do better in the Senat house that the foreman of the Grand Jury? But that person, though I mention him, yet time will not lett me inlarge. Wherefore I referr it to the next oportunity, and beg leave to tell [you] I was not a little pleased Sir R[alph] C[arr][74] was fined and that my neighbour gott the suiet. You tell me in that letter that when I order you will transmitt the names of those to be joyn'd to the bench, which I shall not disapprove of. Have you look over the abstract of the Charter to give the least hope? If so, whenever you please, I doubt not but you will find this family ready to serve you upon this occasion, who are your servants. My sister as soon as she [has] a spare moment will write to you, but country wifes have always matter of great importance to take up their time. I am called of, Pardon a bad pen and what other faults are in this from . . .

[P.S.] I beg my service to my cosen. May I wish you both joy or refer that till you are grown a grave fatherly man.

[71] Jacky [or Dudley?] Clavering.

[72] John Eden, 2nd bart., c. 1680-1728. Tory M.P. Durham county 1713-27. *Surtees*.

[73] Sir Robert Eden, 1st bart. Many times Tory M.P. Durham County 1679 to 1713. *Surtees*.

[74] Sir Ralph Carr, 1634-1709, merchant and former Mayor and M.P. of Newcastle. *Surtees*.

7. Hertingfordberry. Sept. 23d, [1708.]

Since I have an opportunity of sending my letters by the [Sealours?], I can't lett it pass without returning you thanks for yours dated of the 10th, as also to assure you I am heartily concerned to hear your spouse has had so great an indisposition especially att this time. I live in hopes your next will give me an account of her perfect recovery (and that she's in no danger of parting so soon with her little one) which I sincerely wish her. Doll write me she spent some days with you. How do you approve of our new Kindsman?[75] I am a perfect stranger to him [torn.] For her sake I wish he may prove better than was expected; when one has foolishly parted with their liberty one has need of all the comforts one can, and in that state I fancy all are often too few. I expect the above said lady in town soon. I suppose her stay att York will not be long. 'Tis well if she comes safe up from thence. I hear that robbing is come fashion. She will there meet with the news of the long expected match betwixt Mr. Bourchier[76] and Mrs. Bellwood, a dapper couple. I have sent my play fellow the willow ribon upon that account. I hope it will come safe to his hands. You have surely heard of the match Lady Kay's friend and companion made now in less than a month time att Bath. He pretends to an estate. That is he formerly had one. His children are in this country with their mother's relations and to her, poor woman, tho' a vast fortune, he was the most ill natured beast in the creation. He's a great liar. I remember him when I was there. Perhaps upon second thoughts that may have first been occasioned by his poetry, for that dos often require lofty flights and expressions. But what is still more amazing is that the lady she's with had no hand in making the hopefull union.

You tell me that when my neighbour comes to town he will have the originall charter perused (which I shall have related over a pott of tea. I am obliged to you for acquainting me therewith and do assure I will for the future be more civill than when he persude his Godson). I see no cause of fear in that respect. All I hope will goe well and 'tis what all honest men will approve of. I heard some whig Lords lamenting the loss of the place. I am told the young senator I am for promoting has gott a rival. I won't say who because my author

[75] Presumably Charles Waite, the husband of Dorothy Clavering.

[76] John and Ralph Bourchier were nephews of Elizabeth Clavering, Anne's step-mother. *Letter-book*.

is not very good. Indeed he's no poet, no ill-natured beau, but an attender att the Senate in the Torry corner, where the great Hercules with his club will be introduced. Sure should that happen and some farsess again played in the House it should be the marriage-hater match and he play the part of Solon and Tom Titt that of Byass. I hear he has built fine stables and coach-house what he dos design. 'Tis now to late for what he projected, for I am of opinion that when the troops went northwards upon the sham invasion, he design baking for the whole army and those outhouses were to keep his firing dry. My imagination dos not much stand towards him. I am out of humour and so shall be till I know the fate of Lille. This post, that Earl's[77] troops have took with the defeat that Cadogan[78] gave La Motte,[79] has given some small hopes, but how long that will continue I almost fear to know. I can but fancy Bouffleurs[80] fears the surrender least the same fate should attend him as did att Namur. Therefore if a Prisoner he will be one on honorable terms, but some extraordinary things suppose he thinks out to be the last action of a man's life. I dare answer if we fail in this siege it will breed ill blood among us and give occasion to cry the battle of Oudenarde was no compleat victory, nor Earl's descent no great hurt to the French, for which I have often wisht I had had the hoisting of the beast, tide in ropes, from the one ship to the other, and then I could have assured him he should never have undertook an affair again where his worthless person should have been exposed. He may say, lett those who love fighting have enough of it for my part I don't. However this putts me in mind of Wager.[81] Are you not a great admirer of his since he has took the comission from his two captains, Windsor and Bridges?[82] I dare say they two were brought up under Sir George Rook,[83] and after all we in great mercy when they come into England shall make them Griffin I fear. Did it not shew to much

[77] Major-General Thomas Erle of Charborough, M.P. 1678-1718.

[78] William Cadogan, 1672-1726, Quarter-Master General to the Duke of Marlborough and later ambassador to The Hague. *D.N.B.*

[79] Comte de la Motte, 1672-1731; defeated by General Webb at Wynendael and disgraced after the surrender of Ghent.

[80] Louis-Francois, duc de Bouffleurs and a Marshal of France, 1644-1711.

[81] Admiral Sir Charles Wager, Whig M.P. 1710-11 and 1713-22. *D.N.B.*

[82] Captains Edward Windsor and Simon Bridges were court-martialled on 23 July by Admiral Wager for not doing their duty in the late engagement with Spanish galleons in the West Indies. *Luttrell*, vi, 351 and *Boyer's Annals*, vii, 194-7.

[83] Admiral Sir George Rooke, Tory M.P. 1698-1708, and the Tory hero of Vigo, Cadiz and Malaga. *D.N.B.*

barbarity in my temper I could wish for less mercy and more justice. The Queen comes to Kensington of Tuesday which will occasion this family to remove to town for a few days. If I goe up with them I think they shall drop me that [I] may gett myself settled against my Aunt returns from Bath. Your pupill is well tho' he never writes to anybody, but I don't doubt but when Christmas draws nigh I shall be made a staking horse of to gett him a release, which I assure you I shall and doe oppose. My sister and Lord are your servants. I beg my service to my cosen, and am Sir . . .

[P.S.] What is your neighbour Mrs. Johnson[84] a doing she dos not gett a husband as well as other Kiblesworth ladys? Pardon all faults in this for our good lady and servants are att family talk by me and I am almost deaft with them.

8. London. Oct 16th, 1708.

Sir,

Yours of the second from Richmond had not laid unanswared so long (especially when I was almost in town a forthnight without my aunt) had I not been desirous of having you att home 'ere I ventured to write, which by this time I hope you are, tho' you made no mention how long a time you would spend abroad. I heartily rejoyce to hear your spouse[85] has her health so well. When she has occasions for things usefull for one in her condition I hope you will lay your commands upon my sister and self who will both use our utmost endeavours to serve you, as I hope we shall doe cosen Liddell soon. Our friends in Lincolns Inn Fields came of Wednesday and are all well. If you would not judge me very partial I could tell you my niece is one of the finest girls I ever saw, and since we left Hertfordshire has gott 3 teeth. My sister writes this night to Jacky to lay her commands upon him to write to you, if that will have any effect. I could wish he were not so great a humourest but I fear 'tis not without cause Mr. Brag makes those complaints; for by what I hear from other hands the whole school are weary of him. I write to my two sisters att Greencroft this last week. I hope they have received my letters. You seem to desire the name of Lady Kay's compagnion att Bath. It was Mrs. Ann Beaumont a person of £300 fortune, who married one

[84] The Johnson family of Medomsley and Ebchester. *Hodgson* and *Letter-book*.
[85] Catherine, daughter of Thomas Yorke of Richmond. *Surtees*.

Rudgers, a piece of a poet as to lampoons, panegyricks &c., as also poverty, for that part of his estate, which is not settled upon his first wife's eldest son, is morgaged to John, Duke of Malborough.[86] That name makes me think of the siege. What say you now? These delays I hope make you sencible I did not see more difficultys than were real tho' it then made you intertain ill thoughts of me. However I am resolved to hope the best and don't doubt but Prince Eugene will do his best to redeem his last year's fault tho' some will not allow that. If any misfortune is yet to happen att that place I shall goe almost melancholy mad, for the loss of poor Monsr. D'Auverquerque[87] has not a little seized upon me; he was a truely valuable person and one who will be genarly lamented by all honest people, as well as his family, tho' the town are malitious enough to say that when the news came to his lady she bore it with Christian patience and said she ought not to regret att anything the Lord does; but I can't give creditt to this storry, or, if true, so farr from thinking his death is but a month to soon (for that also is laid to her charge) that I could wish he coud have spent the years over again; but since that can't be we must content ourselves in deploring this death (as he sett us the example) for a faithfull friend. I see some compagny yesterday who regretting the want of news from my neighbour. The last letters from thence having given an account of some indisposition he was under. The country I fear grows to cold for him and tho' the Parliament is putt of to a longer time yet he ought to consider the weather and ways will be dayly worse, which can make travelling no pleasanter. However lett him putt of those thoughts as long as he will. The Speaker I desire may not be chose without him. That affair lyes dorment yet to see how the world wags, but I'm told if Sir R[ichard] Onslow[88] be baffeld there he will be made a baron and I perceive there yet remains one difficulty; that is, if the Whigs will turn as they did last year and not keep firm one to the other or rather all to the Court, they will indangour a Torry ministry. 'Tis late so I quitt this subject and all other least I loose my supper and shall only beg you will pardon the faults of this (for my aunt and I are both writing upon table which is loose and consequently plays prettily)

[86] John Churchill, 1650-1722, Duke of Marlborough.

[87] Field-Marshal Auverquerque or Overkirk, the Dutch commander at Oudenarde and Ramillies, died October 1708.

[88] Sir Richard Onslow, 1654-1717, Whig M.P. 1679-1716 and Speaker of the House of Commons 1708-10. *D.N.B.*

and give me leave to present my service to my cosen and assure you I am . . .

[P.S.] My aunt A.[89] is your servant. I had almost forgott to beg you will secretly tell your sister Nancy[90] I have the 3 books of Grand Cyrus, by aunt Ward's[91] leave, to read and that I will take great care of them, as also that I am her servant.

9. Oc[tober] 19th, 1708.

Sir,

By my letter last post you will soon believe I was not easy in my mind, and if I therein said [anything] amiss I hope you will pardon it. My surly temper continued the next day for tho' I dined att our friends in Lincolns Inn Fields, yet none of us durst send for to know the confirmation of what came the night before. Had I had the good fortune to sitt up of Saturday night till twelve doubtless I should have danced when the Tower guns went of, but as I was in some concern (as you know) I had so fatigued my thoughts so much that I almost believe it made my sleep more even than usual. However as I had incurd your displeasure by comunicating my fears to you, I dare not slip this post without assuring you I have laid aside all cameris and do now heartily rejoyce att our good news. I am glad we have gott the town and doe not question the cittadell by one means or other [will be ours.] Sure you will all own P[rince] E[ugene] can doe when he's rewarded with glory. That's all he covetts. Lett the only slip be now buried and letts consider we took part in the undoing so well a designd thing. 'Tis too difficult for me to tell you whether the Ladys are more overjoyed att the surrender of Lille, or att Sir Dicky [torn][92] safe from so tedious a siege. Captain Moyser[93] is not so [torn] it may be the news he brought yesterday morning might be as great a cause of joy to them, but in my own sentiments the reducing of Minorca is no dispisable thing. Now we can winter in the Mediteranian, which perhaps may give an awful thought to some of the Italian Princes and do no service to his Holiness, for an heritick

[89] ? *Anne* Clavering, sister of Dorothy Clavering, or Jane Clavering, who may have married an *Allanson*. See note 215.

[90] Ann Clavering, sister of James, died unmarried 1750. *Surtees*.

[91] Grace Ward, née Clavering, younger sister of Ann's father. *Surtees*.

[92] ? Sir Richard Allen, M.P. Dunwich.

[93] Captain Moyser, aide-de-camp to James Stanhope, returned to England in 1708 with the news of the capture of Minorca. *Luttrell*, vi, 362.

fleet is enough to terrifye the Devill. I would, if I could avoid it, pass the seige of Leffingen[94] by in silence; for should I enter into the resolution and conduct of Duke Ven[dôme] in the taking of that strong place my paper would be little to hold a 5th part of the praises are due to him. You see he satt down before it with his army in form, made trenches, saps and all in little to resemble P[rince] Eugene, only the church yard not having so many out-works, nor so great a garison, by the assistance of one of our men the 1100 that defended the church-yard and village submitted to be made prisoners. O, I repine like true English that Ven[dôme] escaped us so narrowly. He'd been pretty compagny for Count Tallard[95] this winter. Methinks we could not have hoped for so great a redicule upon them as this is. It often makes me think of King James taking Buda upon Hounslow heath. If our poets make a ballad I will send it you. In the meanwhile be content Major-General Earl is in a safe skinn in Ostend, and we are so hemed in that the French must either fly before us or fight. I will add no more least I prevent your wishing the continuation of success in your turn. So shall only subscribe myself . . .

[P.S.] I salute your spouse.

10. London. No[vember] 20th, 1708.

Sir,

Yours of the 26 of October now lyes before me which I am realy ashamed to look upon and should be att a great nonplus to answer were not my excuses just. When I received yours my aunt was then very ill and under my care, my uncle was in Yorkshire, and Dr. Ratcliff[96] out of town. 'Tis certain the bath did not agree with her as usuall, and this last indisposition of hers was the Colick. She kept her chamber about ten days, and when she began to get downstairs then went of[f] our Lord High Admiral[97] and since his death I have been buying mourning and shaping as much, I am sure, as any other shop-keeper. So much I am possitive I have cutt out that I have

[94] At Leffingen Vendôme inflicted 1,000 casualties on Major-Gen. Erle. *Luttrell*, vi, 362.

[95] Camille d' Hostun, duc de Tallard, 1652-1718. The Marshal of France captured at the battle of Blenheim in 1704.

[96] John Radcliffe, 1650-1714, wealthy and eminent physician and sometime Tory M.P. *D.N.B.*

[97] Prince George of Denmark, 1653-1708, husband of Queen Anne. *D.N.B.*

not time to cutt my own linen out and what's worse I am weary of the employment. The old saying, I may vouch, is true, to spur a free horse to death. My sister has this moment sent to tell me she's received a commission from your spouse and if I will goe and assist her she will call of me. So I must leave of and prepare to gett ready against she comes. Adieu.

Sir, att my return home att two a clock, I mett yours which my neighbour had send me. I am sorry I am so great a stranger to your spouse as that she should believe I can think it any trouble to serve my friends. You see by the former part of this I did not stand upon ceremony. Your affairs are bespoke. I think [they] are handsome and are what I hope you will like and not think dear. If you both approve of them we shall be extreamly satisfyed. I wish my cosen a happy moment and I hope she will use these affairs often. My neighbour came to town of Saturday last. You say his indisposition made you part with him uneasily. He yet has some remains of his cold but looks well and is very chearfull. I see him of Monday and then I told him by his stay in the North I began to fear the Speaker would have been chose without him. But he answered imedaitly that tho' he was ill he durst stay no longer for he was sure, if he had, to have mett with a reprofe from this family, and, as he suggested, so it was, for in a civill way my aunt reproved him for his visit to Lord Sca[rborough]. This has so farr made an impression on him that hearing my aunt's cold was no better when I was abroad, he came and insinuated himself so much into favour as to undertake to cure her if she would throw of her nurses (which were my uncle and self). You shall be judge. Is this fair prosedings? Have I not reason to complain for I design it loudly att our next meeting? Mr. Nic[holson][98] I hope will answer the character his friends give. I have desired my neighbour to advise and protect him, but it was before he used me thus ill. As to publick affairs I hearr none good. 'Tis by the generallity of people believed the French will sitt down before Brussels. However I keep to my former resolution. Whenever the cittadell of Lille is took I will have a bone-fire. Have we had any loss by the late promotion think you? I can but say I am pleased when I think and hope our new Lord President[99] had his head preservd to

[98] James Nicholson, recently elected M.P. for Durham City, who did in fact prove to be a Whig.

[99] Lord Somers, 1651-1716, a former Solicitor and Attorney-General and Lord Chancellor. *D.N.B.*

make the other party ones more smart. His advancement is a dreadfull thing. The other two the torrys would have submitted to if he had been but dropt. Yet methinks altogether it looks well, as also that her Grace of M[arlborough] is coming again into favour. I should if I had'd power chose an impeacht Earl for the Lord High Admiral,[100] but, as it is, I must be content tho' he is not so himself. We talk of an Irish barronett that's almost mad for Mrs. Hailes, the maid of honour. He profers her to stay in England, to have a thousand pound a year joynture, and desires nothing but her person. Don't this look well? Yet 'tis to be feard in prosess of time he will agree with the opinion of her old lover, Mr. Ash.[101] My paper will lett me add no more save my best service to your spouse and once more assure you I am . . .

[P.S.] This night I write to the Esq. att Eaton. I forgott to tell you I hear Lord Little Chamberlain is to have a blue garter and the marquiss of Dorchester[102] to have his place.

11. London. Dec. 9th, 1708.

I give you many thanks for your kind offer of being mediator betwixt my neighbour and me. The difference was easly adjusted by reason of a good sermon I heard the bishop of Sarum[103] preach upon this subject and his discourses out of the pulpitt have always a great influence upon me; and so that day it had upon Mr. Freeman of Hertfordshire, who never in his life made sister Cowper a bow but then. I have [torn—seen?] my neighbour about the business of the [torn] of the Charter which has so long been [torn.] He told me it was promissed him as yesterday, so I expect he will soon lett me have it. I wish that, and whatever else is for the establishing of his interest in that vile corporation, was done, tho' now there's no election he seems to be lookt upon with civility by some. I have rejoyced as much as you could att our late good news of Saturday. I had my bonefire, which alarmed the whole square, and I may venture to say gave as much uneasiness to my neighbours as either yours or

[100] Admiral Orford (Edward Russell), 1652-1727. The Whig victor of La Hogue and impeached over the Partition Treaties. He was not made Lord High Admiral until 1709. *G.E.C.*

[101] Probably Edward Ashe, M.P. Heytesbury 1695-1747.

[102] Evelyn Pierrepoint, c. 1665-1726, later Duke of Kingston.

[103] Gilbert Burnet, 1643-1715, famous Whig bishop and historian.

the healths you drunk to your kind friends; but as the light my fire made was extinguishing, a gentleman, who lives not many door of[f], light his, which I was glad to see, and shall never be easie till I am of his acquaintance, tho' he's a married man. What a reprimende shall I have from our ghostly father (who, with his Dolly,[104] came to town last night) when I see him, for Mr. Forster[105] spent that same evening with us, and declared Lady Ann's care of Prince Eugene's glory should be printed and sent over to him. Also he would tell it [to] all his acquaintance in town. If my Lord should once break silence upon that subject our discourse I dare say would be diverting. The Queen comes to chapell of Sunday and of Monday, sees compagny for the first day, and so will continue the week. For one hour in the evening she's to lye upon the bed with one curtain open, to have 2 candles in the room, and two sticks upon the fire. The new opera is to be of Tuesday and [the] new Italian[106] has indeed a most glorious voice. I heard him of Tuesday last in Lincolns' Inn Fields, where he was brought by Lord H[alifa]x, and Lord President was amongst us. I find that same person a great thorn to the High Church, tho' they endeavour to carry things fare, for the morning after he was declared P[resident] severall people came to his levie, who had never made him one civill visitt since he had been Chancellour. The Pope and Emperour, I find, are about an acomodation but as the Germans, in my thoughts, are always making rediculous agreements so they doe in this. But what will you say if it be true Prince Ragotky[107] has took a flight into Poland to joyn the Crown General and oppose Stanislaus? That, [it] may be hoped, [will] prove a means to continue the war between the Czar and King of Sweden. This is all the news I have to relate save one alteration I heard of att St. James, which is a new bed-chamber woman. Poor Mrs. Feil[ding][108] not been well, so not capable to serve, and in her place comes in one who is to marry Dr. Moore,[109] Lord Droigheda's son and cosen to one of the clerks of the closett, as

[104] Dorothy, daughter of Sir William Forster of Bamburgh Castle, and second wife of Bishop Crewe. She died in 1715.

[105] ? Thomas Forster, M.P. for Northumberland 1708-16, and a leader of the Jacobite rising of 1715.

[106] Nicolini Grimaldi, famous opera singer, who visited England 1708-17, with his group of eunuchs.

[107] Francis Rakoczy, 1676-1735, Prince of Transylvania.

[108] ? Wife or sister of the Hon. William Fielding, Whig M.P. Castle Rising 1705-23.

[109] Son of Henry Hamilton-Moore, 3rd Earl and 5th Viscount Drogheda.

also a crony of M[rs.] M[asham.][110] 'Tis now high time to bid you adieu when I have returned the services of this family to yourself, and beged mine to cosen, and leave to assure you both I am . . .

[P.S.] Xmas draws nigh [and] I have often letters from Eaton. Your spouse's affairs will sett forward next Monday I hope.

12. Lon[don.] Dec. 18th, 1708.

Depending upon my sister to give you an account of the things we were commissioned to buy for your good spouse I thought not scarce of it. Of Tuesday we had a fright which indeed must plead both her excuse and mine, for returning from breakfast att cosen Shafto's[111] my aunt's coachman att St. Giles church begun to run with an other coach throw all carts, wagons, and whatever else was in the street, till we came to Drury Lane. Both coachmen being called to, pulled by the string, but nothing would doe because our fool though[t] there was a point of honour in the case, but my sister did screem to that degree that the whole street must have been raised had we not been upon the full gallop. Since this she's been ill and out of order, but owns nothing of what you suspect. This night is well att the opera, but going to see Jacky this evening he told me she ones orderd him to write to you, and again forbid him, saying she would doe it herself of Tuesday, but I, fearing that to late, was resolved to give what intimation I could, tho' very imperfectly. The box went from hence of Monday, by whom or to whom directed none of her servants could tell me; only this information I send you, that if there comes a box to Mrs. Mitford,[112] or else-where, with a white satin quilt and pillows trimed with gold, and a child sute of French lace, they belong to you. I hope my cosen will like them. I see my neighbour yesterday morning. He's well again. However my aunt and I both scolded him for going to the house without occasion so soon after his illness. If he plays the fool with his health 'tis not the fault of his friends for att this house he often has a lecture. When I see him next [I] shall discourse him upon what you mention and you

[110] Abigail Masham, née Hill, bedchamber-woman, who ousted the Duchess of Marlborough as Queen Anne's favourite. *D.N.B.*

[111] Mark Shafto, 1662-1723, high sheriff of Durham or his eldest son Robert, later Whig M.P. Durham City 1712-13 and 1727-30. *Surtees.*

[112] ? Wife or daughter of Ralph Mitford, Newcastle merchant and colliery owner. She is mentioned several times in these letters.

may be assured we shall both assist you as farr as we can. That house of commons is the life of him and I fancy att his death he will be buried under the Speaker's chair. When I was visiting this afternoon I heard of some weddings, some whereof has long been the subject of visiting days, viz Lord Sherrad[113] and the eldest Mrs. Brownlow,[114] and the Earl of Dorsett[115] and Lord Newport[116] for the younger sisters (what will Mrs. Collier say think you?); Lord Berkshire[117] and the Mrs. Grahme that was spoke of for the Duke of N[orthumberland];[118] the Earl of Scarsdale[119] and Mrs. P. Squire; the Duke of Grafton[120] and Lady E. Tollmash.[121] Some of these I dare say are true. Last Sunday I mett Lord Sc[arsda]le visitting his Mrs., and in the room Tom-titt, Jenny Sq[uire.] He and I had most [of] the discourse, which was intertaining to the rest, and since then, as I hear, he says he was to blame in not being civiler to me. 'Tis the first time I dare say he ever ownd himself in the rong. Now I have almost filled my paper I must answer the two last lines of your letter, by which I perceive you have yoked me, and take my word without any reason. That old castle requires ten thousand pounds by way of repairs, which I leave you to judge if I have that to give. I have [been] disposed of to so many men I never see, that this does not surprise me. A torry and I, you may yourself thing [i.e. think], would never do in one family, for as we now meet but seldom we dispute always about publick affairs, and last night I suped with him att my Lord of Durham, and Mr. Hugings'[122] going to the gatehouse was the subject of our discourse. 'Tis late and I am almost

113 Philip, Lord Sherrard, later Earl of Harborough 1680-1750. He, in fact, married Anne Pedley. See note 36.

114 In 1711 Miss Jane Brownlow, coheiress of Sir John Brownlow of Belton, Lincolnshire, married Lord Willoughby.

115 The Earl of Dorset married Miss Elizabeth Collier in 1709. See note 61.

116 Henry, Lord Newport, 1683-1734, was a Whig M.P. 1706-10 and 1713-22 and later 3rd Earl of Bradford. He appears to have died unmarried.

117 Henry Bowes (Howard), 1687-1757, Earl of Berkshire and later Earl of Suffolk. He married the daughter of Col. James Grahme, or Graham, of Levens Hall, Westmorland, in March 1709.

118 George Fitzroy, Duke of Northumberland, 1665-1716, illegitimate son of Charles II. He married his first wife clandestinely in 1686 and she died in 1714.

119 Nicholas Lake, 4th Earl of Scarsdale, c. 1682-1736, died unmarried.

120 Charles Fitzroy, 2nd Duke of Grafton, 1683-1757. Son of Henry Fitzroy, illegitimate son of Charles II.

121 Elizabeth Tollemache, sister of Lionel, 3rd Earl of Dysart.

122 John Huggins, head-bailiff of Westminster, was committed to Newgate for electoral offences in the recent contest between Sir Henry Colt and Mr. Medlicot. *Boyer's Annals*, vii, 271 and *Luttrell*, vi, 385 and 630.

asleep, but won't conclude till I have told you I hear your namesake complaind of for voting amongst the torrys, and upon inqu[ir]ing I find the party that had him last has his vote. I am glad your uncle is better. You say nothing of Lady Clav[ering's] big belly. That's what we speak of much att this distance, and since you say my praises eccho there, you've conversed with Roger Proctor[123] I dare say. Adieu. I am . . .

[P.S.] This family salutes you. So do I your spouse. Jacky charges me with his best service to you both.

13. Dec. 25th, 1708.

Sir,

My sister Cowper 'ere she left the town desired I woud ones be her Secretary, and beg of you and your good spouse to excuse her not writting. She has really never been well since that fright. However I hope that may not be altogether the occasion of her indisposition (tho' she'd have my head if she knew I said so much), and I am to say a world for her not giving you an account about the box, which was directed to Mrs. Mitford, but as compliments were always out of my rode I beg you will spare me the trouble, and imigane all that any one cou'd say on that subject I should say. Now must proceed to tell you Jacky is left in town during their stay in the country. He's so much improved in all respect that it would have been barbarous to have sent him down again, and I hope for the future we shall hear no more complaints conserning him. This day he's wholy spent with my neighbour. They have not been gone from hence above an hour, and had I had any paper then you should have had a frank. Mr. Gowland's[124] agent has never been with my good neighbour. 'Tis late. I must hasten when I have wisht you joy [of] the surender of Ghent, the evacuating Bruges, and the bringing in two whiggs into the House last Tuesday, att which I know you will rejoyce. I wish we may always have the like occasion to congratulate one another. Jacky charged me with duty to [you] and my Cosen whose servant I am, as also to yourself . . .
No address.

[123] Roger Proctor, merchant and alderman of Newcastle. He was a cousin of the Claverings. *Hodgson*.

[124] Ralph Gowland, senior and junior, were both Durham attorneys. The father died 1728 and the son, who was steward to Lord Scarborough, died 1749. See *S.S.* xciii, *Letter-book*, and letters 168-171.

14. Lond[on.] Feb. 19, 1708[/9.]

Tho' I have a letter to Ireland now before, about half writ, I am resolved it shall waite another opportunity to be finish'd that I may have time to return my thanks for the favour of yours of the 11th and 19, which came both safe to my hands; and to assure the Vaudois[125] I am concern for his cough and cold. I doubt not but the creeping so into the sick wife's warm room has tender'd you to much for the dreadful cold weather we have had of late, and in which I hope my cosen will see great alteration 'ere she gos out of doors. Whilst I think on, lett me return you my uncle and aunt thanks for your kind wishes. 'Tis an alteration everybody is pleased with, save the family who has lost the place, who thereby are ruin'd. The young Eatoner is well. I had a letter lately with some apologys for his silence, which he excuses by his exercises. In return to which, I told him I always was glad to hear from him, but I woud upon no score have him forgett his book, for without some learning he'd make but an indifferent figure in the world, and att last gave him a charge to write and give you joy of your son. Has he performed it? The family in Lincoln's Inn Fields are I hope well again and the big belly gos on again by providence and no care of the good woman's. When you hear from her she will then I suppose tell you what cosen Liddell's spinett cost, for she made me no answer. Yesterday I gave her the lead mine lease, to comunicate to her Lord. When I hear his opinion concerning the matter [I] shall not fail by the first post to acquaint you. All we Cla[verings] thank God have had a sensible proof of Mr. Dixon's esteem for us, which, in a short time now, I hope will be known to more than ourselves. It was Wednesday sevenight I was swore to the answer of your Bill and then Mr. Sanderson[126] told me the day following he would not fail to write to your Governour and proceed with all speed. Since then he made the same fair promises to my neighbour with the assurance he'd have the Bill and answer heard of Monday or Tuesday last, and then come and acquaint me (who was still angry). But now 'tis Thurs[day] [and] no news of Mr. Sanderson, which will fall heavy upon my poor neighbour, for I

[125] A native of the Swiss canton of Vaud and also the name applied to a strict Christian community founded by Peter Waldo in the twelfth century. Anne Clavering regularly addressed James Clavering as "Vaudois".

[126] Charles Sanderson an eminent London lawyer with a vast practice. A north countryman by origin, he was a friend of William Cotesworth and was connected with most of the local gentry and mine-owners. He is mentioned many times in these letters. *Hughes*.

shall certainly ferrit him about again upon this his honest cosen's way of proceeding. My neighbour I long to see, I own, to laugh att him for the Tuesday Elec[tion.] He, that morning, told me the Torry petitioner had been heard and had so fowl a cause he must be reject'd, but the jest of the Town upon it pleases me mightily for they say the rich rogues, the Whigs, were busy lending their money to the Government, whilst the poor rogues, the Torry, (who for a long time have deserved no bribes) having none to lend stuck to the Elec[tion] and brought in the Torry. Our friend was att the House to see fair play, which I am concernd att. It will make people believe he's disaffected. However what a noise abroad shall we make. To have so great a subscription so soon full, that above a million was reject'd; but when all come to be askt, after the Books were shutt, when it want'd six hundred thousand pound of being full, to give our High Allies the States of Holland leave to joyn with us. By a letter or two to your Governour[127] and my Steward[128] you will find I am turning stock-jobber, and yesterday the new subscription was riss 5 per cent which advantage I must be content with in case you cannot supply me with mony. The storry of our chief made my neighbour and self very merry; I wish I coud return it to you, but what one hears is so false that when you have told a thing you've nothing more to do than to contradict it; which putts me in mind of doing it to a former letter of mine wherein I told you the Vice-C[hamberlain][129] had ask the Queen's consent to marry Mrs. Hales. She now, by the permission of her friends, is treating a match with Sir Ro[bert] Maud, a teague, but the most people believe she married privately to Collonel Sidney.[130] I wish the former disappointed or a pair of horns on his head. He's dealt rudely with an agreable young woman in this neighbourhood. Lord Northampton['s] second dau[ghter], the Town says, certainly marries Mr. Gore[131] a citticen who has £5000 per annum. Your seal was safe. Madam B[lackett?] had not been in the office nor was I to hear any blockhead preach of the 31th nor of the 17th, and had I been in N[ew] C[astle] I shoud have given the vicar my room att church. One sermon (upon Divin-

[127] The "Governor" was Henry Liddell, later the husband of Anne Clavering.

[128] ? John Johnson, 1683-1746, of Ebchester, Lamesley and Medomsley. *Hodgson*.

[129] Thomas Coke, M.P. Derby 1698-1715. See note 50 and H.M.C. *Cowper* (Coke Mss).

[130] ? Col. John Sydney. *Luttrell*, v, 412, 576.

[131] William Gore, eldest son of Sir William Gore, married the daughter of George Compton, 13th Earl of Northampton. *Luttrell*, vi, 435.

ity) a week serves me, but some reviews I woud see oftener. I love truth. 'Tis well high time to conclude when I've desire you to return my best service to your spouse, and my namesake, and tell her that Mrs. Betty Rich has sent to desire her books for which I give her many thanks. I am, tho' I have fill'd my paper, in haste to goe visiting, therefore adieu, and believe me the Vaudois' most humble servant.

15. London. March 29th, 1709.

Upon a letter I received of Mr. Johnson,[132] by Friday's post, acquainting me that his men had yet no protections and that after so many fruitless request to the Mayor, who always gave a denial, he wated for orders either from you or me. This complaint (after I knew Mr. Burchett[133] had writ a sever letter to that magistrate, and that an answer thereto was returnd) did a little nettle me and amidst the rain of Sunday I convey'd my self to gett a partner to my sufferings, who was as much surprised as I (could) att it. Gave me Mr. Fenwick's[134] letter to read which Mr. Bur[chett] sent them. A full and an exact copy my neighbour received of me that night, and by this post returns it you. Such a saucy parentory letter form (sic) a man in authority is wonderfully new. In answer to it Bur[chett] had a letter of Sunday sent with Mr. Mayor's original (which he desired might be return'd). The Mayor's reasons were confuted in every paragraph and plainly told that since Lord H[igh] A[dmiral][135] had seem to decline joy[n]ing some justices with the Mayor in this affair. 'Twas grown so great an abuse not only to the private persons concern'd but the publick also, that the citty, who were always a party in an affair of this kind, were resolved to inquire into it. Now to back this answer to Mr. Burchett, you must draw up a petition of the coalowners, fitters, keelmen, &c, setting forth the particular losses they have all and severaly sustained by the refusal of Mr. Mayor; how many time you have all and severally been with your men to ask the protections; in what manner you were denied and

[132] John Johnson appears to have been Anne Clavering's steward. He is mentioned frequently. See also notes 128 and 195.

[133] Josiah Burchett, secretary of the Admiralty 1694-1742. *D.N.B.*

[134] Alderman Robert Fenwick, one of the ten large mine-owners who formed an agreement in 1708. *Hughes.*

[135] Thomas Herbert, 8th Earl of Pembroke, 1656-1733. Lord High Admiral 1690-92, 1701-2 and 1708-9. He was also Lord President 1702-8.

that your men were ready to take the usual oaths to qualifye themselves; what loss you have already had and what rong it will be to the publick as well as the private person if care be not took to prevent the like for the future; the answer to the riot he mentions and how 'tis not usual to punish offenders a year after the crime's committed; the answer to that misaplied charity he speaks of; and inquire, I desire, if none of those men concerned in the last year's riot have this year receiv'd protections, if they have lett us know in the petition who they belong to and why they were not denied it as well as ours; how this proceeding of the Mayor's has no president and how little regard he had for the letter from the Admiralty. This is what instructions I can give. Only every man must make his affidavit of the truth of this and not be nice, but has leave to agravate as farr as truth can reach. Compliments are of no use to us and if you will doe this nicely I promiss it shall be given in, either att the Councill board or Parl[iament.] Had we all this time had tools from you an end might have been made 'ere now. Your short affidavitts did not signifye one loose. Indeed you rongfully condemn my neighbour and self. It's your faults alone we are so slow. You give us hints of things and then leave us, as witteness that about the commission of the land tax. Do any of you now think that grievance can be redresst without a petition? Draw one up and send it with the former. The one will help the other. You can't say I have been idle, and I will clear myself of your aspertion as well as my neighbour. He deserves it not. He's realy vext I make mischief for him. Lett him aquitt himself of it when he can. Notwithstanding which, this morning he has told me I am the best solicitoress in England and I'll believe him, for he burries not his understanding in a coal-pitt. What I writ to your Governour of Saturday will still confirm you in your sentiments of that (worthless, I should say worthy,) Prelate Lord B[ishop.] Your answers I expect and then shall know what is to be done more than what has been already. I give you many thanks for your concern for my cold. I am perfectly well. [I] am summond to dress for visiting day which hastens me to assure you this family are your servants and none more so than . . .

[P.S.] Your spouse and my namesake I salute.
If what I have said is not full enough my neighbour's instructions and your own diligence in an affair of this nature will supply my want. 'Tis plain what has already been done has putt a stop to the

act for the making the mayor governour of the Keelmen's hospital. I wish us success in this, for as 'tis, I am in hazard of supplying Lord Griffin's place.[136] I have not time to tell you that storry of your Lord Leiutenant's son.[137] 'Twas about the voting for Meredith.[138] I write to Mr. Johnson this post, who I desire you will inquire of if it came safe. I suspect Bells. Adieu. My pen is very badd.

I'de like to have seal'd 'ere I'd given you thanks for the naming the 5 Justice. If that takes Mr. H[enry Liddell] I fancy will be the properer person, and sure your Go[vernor] won't decline for the apprehension of disobliging the neighbouring corporation. When you see him I desire you will lett him know an act must first pass 'ere I can tell him when I shall want more mony from him. If you mean the petition of Tim Tully[139] to his Bro[ther], this part of the town are strangers to it, and had not Mr. Liddell in Sir H[enry's] letter explain'd the matter we had remaind in the dark.

16. Lon[don.] April 14th, 1709.

By this last post came to my neighbour a very mild petition from the keelmen to the Queen. 3 affidavits took by Mr. Ellison,[140] one of Johnson's, one of his man's, in which he says most of his men had protections, whereas had it been inserted that some were, and the others refuse, the effect was the same, and then leave had been given to have took it in the worset sence, which would have been to us no disadvantage. But what I am most surprise att is that this justice should allow a man (Jackson)[141] to take an oath upon belief when he had no further to goe to be certain than to Mrs. Binks, and two several hands to the affidavits. 'Tis pots worse than that he sent formerly undated, which was took notice of, as I doe believe this will. Well I have an inclination to shame him and putt myself into the Commission of Peace and come and sitt amongst you. What we expect by the next post may, I hope, prove more effectual than what

[136] Lord Griffin, sentenced to death, had just been reprieved and ordered to be detained during the Queen's pleasure. See note 13.

[137] i.e. Lord Scarborough. See note 57.

[138] Thomas Meredith, M.P. Kent 1701 and Midhurst 1708.

[139] Son of the Rev. Timothie Tullie of Teesdale, he became a merchant and freeman of Newcastle. Born 1687, died 1737. *S.S.* ci.

[140] Probably Robert Ellison of Hebburn, 1665-1726, who married Henry Liddell's sister and who was a cousin of James Clavering. *Surtees.*

[141] Henry Jackson of Newcastle signed an agreement in 1711 with Sir John Clavering, 3rd bart., about leasing land in Durham. *A.A.* 3rd ser., v.

is already come, for I've yet exorted you to nothing but what Lord C[owper] order'd. No poor man ever freted more than he's done att your slow proceedings, and I dare be bold to say if this miscarrys, by your not making out what he promist to Lord H[igh] A[dmiral], he'll concern himself no more for us (nor can I ever ask him). Sir Harry's interest depends upon it, and I must freely tell you that had I forseen the nice consciences of the northern people I should have plead'd hard for the Governour to have accept'd of the trouble, which would have done him less harm than rubbing his inflamed leggs with Hungary water. Well he [is] a considerate man and throwing it into his head and stomach was the best way in the world to deliver him soon of a burdensome life. His slow amendment is a full proof of his good conceits. By my last you'll see I was not a little pevish, and should still have been so had not Mr. Barnes[142] letter divert'd my spleen, by saying, if the tools prove sufficient I doubt not but the Lady Ann will apply them dexterously. No letter from Johnson. I wish you joy of the Mayor's good graces and am . . .

[P.S.] This family salutes you. So do I yours.
I'de forgott Lord B[arnar]d who was by Sir H[enry] L[iddell] attended yesterday on our pupill's account. He did not sign the agreement, but inferred that one good turn diserved another, and that we should forgive Gibson his debt (what is it?). The perticular I reffer you to my neighbour. 'Tis so late I can scarce see. Adieu.

17. London. June 2d, 1709.

Had I not last post had as many letters of ceremony as I cou'd answer I had then writ to you to tell you that, of this day sevennight, Sister Cowper then told me she'd show'd yours to her spouse, and his answer was that he did not know what advice to give you in that matter. "That's well sister," said I, "for 'tis now 2 post to late to send any directions." What my neighbour did in this affair I don't know, but I perceive we lye a little thereby under your reproof. As to my own part for the future I assure you I shall not depend on the above mention'd person, but always ferret her about till I receive some answer. My neighbour came last night and deliver'd yours (for which my sincere thanks are due) and I woud have had him read it, but some chimera took him att that very instant that he coud not

[142] John Barnes, who leased land in Lamesley. *Hughes*.

read it, but he woud have it home with him. I fancy with a design to gett it by heart for he's not yet return'd it. However att night I will send for it, that tomorrow I may deliver it to my sister (who went into the country yesterday and returns today). Something you mention of a parson. Those are animals I have an advertion too, but as they are such as we must dispense with I will use my endeavours to procure him this preferment, if not already bespoke. Next post you shall hear more.

Is not this Lord B[arnard] a sort of a Plague of Egypt to us. I desire nothing more than ones to have an end with him, and for ever to add him in the Church litany. Mr. Saunderson came to me of Tuesday for that his Lordship calls the article betwixt us, which I desired might be intirely reject'd till Sir Harry[143] had received an answer from him of a letter he that post sent, which we may reasonably suppose will be near midsummer, so that of course this product of Sir J. Tillie's brain must be invalid. Sanderson also promist to writ this post to the Governour of further instructions as to our accounts. Lord Ch[ancellor] laughs at me and calls me lazy and I don't know what, that I have never been with our Master yet, nor heard of walking Chancery Lane in my pattens with a green bagg. And pray where lyes the fault that I proceed no faster? Our young squire[144] is come to town and extreamly down in the mouth. Whatever is the matter? I can judge nothing but the resentment of not coming up att Easter or not approving that my Lord and sister were gone out of town when he came. He was yesterday with his sisters, and run away from hence this day to goe with them to see my namesake and Mrs. Mitford, whilst I went up for some money, tho' I did, when I went down, design to have sent him, which he prevented. Travelling agreed extreamly with the young woman. Poor Betty[145] of Sunday went out with my sister to air, as farr as Kensington, without a hood, which gave her cold. She had a sore throat, a cough, a violent diffluction of rheum and some uneasiness in her breathing, and today, thank God, she's better. Peg's[146] a strong runt, which doe you call my favorite. They are both fine girls. The latter tells me she likes the family mightly where she is, but cannot reconcile

[143] Sir Henry Liddell.

[144] Jacky Clavering, who had four younger sisters, Elizabeth, Margaret. Jane, and Emilia.

[145] Jacky's sister, Elizabeth Clavering, born 1697 and died quite young.

[146] His sister Margaret.

herself to schooling. But whilst I remember lett me not forgett to give the Vaudois many thanks for the trouble of my Bill. This Bank[147] is resolved to have all our money before any peace can be concluded, which now I see no great signs of. 'Twill for a while please those Hell Hounds who stile themselves church-men, but I hope they may live to see that tirant[148] consent to by force to things not thought of when an accomadation was sett a foot in a friendly manner. I hear no other news spoke of save that Abigall[149] is more and more in esteem, and, from good hands I believe, I heard the former favorite never appear'd but when sent for. She's play'd her cards well, but I care not. 'Tis Johny[150] not she I think we ought to esteem. My paper will scarce lett me add my best service to your good spouse and assure the Vaudois I am . . .

[P.S.] This family salutes you. This day I have ended my baby cloths. The news of the Go[vernor's] indisposition from the little [torn] last night I doe believe given his Papa [torn.]

To James Clavering Esq., of Lamesley. To be sent by the Post Master of Durham.

18. London. June 9th, 1709.

Tho' 'tis very late yet I know the Vaudois will expect I shoud be as good as my word, and tell how farr we have transacted towards the parson. This morning my neighbour was with me when my sister came to call me out, so I desired him to make Madam a compliment for the letter he'd sent her concerning this man; which he did. She told us she did believe my Lord[151] was not spoke to by any for it, but that the Court of Chancery, Council, and Causeroom last night had so fategued him that he yet had not seen the letters, but this day he shoud, and accordingly after diner, much compagny being with us, she, tho' she coud not speak to my Lord, yet when she found some parsons wanted him, sent and bid Mr. Oaker lett Sir T[homas?] Allen know that there was a person recommended to that living in

[147] The Bank of England, which increased its subscriptions as the war of Spanish Succession progressed.

[148] Louis XIV, who rejected the peace proposals of 1709.

[149] Abigail Masham. See note 110.

[150] John Churchill, Duke of Marlborough. See note 86.

[151] Lord Chancellor Cowper had a great many lesser church preferments at his disposal.

case any spoke for it, and that when my Lord and she went out to air she'd acquaint him with it. The result you may expect by the next post. I had made a sort of a forfeiture of my word now had not my Lord surprised me this day with a letter from your mayor, signed by 8 other aldermen, to request his Lordship's favour in procuring J[ohn] D[ouglas?][152] the Queen's approbation, to serve by a deputy as town clerk. This is so unexpected a turn I could not omitt acquainting you therewith. Nothing more humble coud come from a vasal that theirs was, but, to make the obligation greater, he's found out that they and Sir H[enry] L[iddell] don't agree as to the power given by the Charter, for which reason, with the former concerning the parson, I shall tomorrow take the liberty to send my neighbour to wate on his good friend that he may be seen [to] solicite his own affairs. Time will not let me add more, but that for your diversion, now the peace is off, I have sent you the Royal Shuffler. Adieu. I salute your good spouse and remain . . .

[P.S.] My namesake dined with us in Lincoln's Inn Fields this day. She's very well. My sister will next post second you concerning your petition in her behalf.

19. London. July 28th 1709.

Sir,

Yours of the 16th is now before me and shoud sooner have acknowledged the favor thereof had I not waited to know your motion by a letter from your Mama to our girls yesterday. I perceive you are for Richmond,[153] where I hope this will meet you and your good spouse safely arrived. You surprise me att the constant attendance of our prelate and his compliments to my cosen G[eorge] B[owes].[154] That was, I believe, like the drinking of the protestant succession, more out of fear than liking. That gent, I hear, has him in aw, and when under that sort of hatch he has a constant sett of speechs. Your neighbours are all so much for the defence of the Church that I can easily believe those poor Palatins[155] will have no

[152] John [or Joshua?] Douglas, a Scotsman who made a fortune as a Newcastle attorney and bought coal-mines at Kenton. *Hodgson.*

[153] James Clavering's wife, Catherine, was a Yorke of Richmond.

[154] George Bowes of Streatlam, 1659-1724, brother of Sir William Bowes. Recorder of Durham city 1706. *Surtees.*

[155] In 1709 over ten thousand poor people fled to England from the Rhine Palatinate, where they had suffered from religious persecution and French incursions.

great help nor incouragement for you. The generality here grumble much att them, as forreigners come to eat the bread out of the mouths of our own poor. I shall be sure to observe those hints you give me of what you found in the accounts [of] 1708. I am impatient till 'tis arrived, for here we keep H[all][156] without business. I have not yet said anything to himself, but I shall, I believe, 'ere we part. For one thing I have remarked he speaks well of none, save sometimes of Wheat[ley][157] had two post agoe a letter from the Governour in relation to my aunt Newton[158] and the next post I think to write to her about it; being he says this scruple was never rais'd till her son-in-law came, and that you were willing to reffer it to Geo. Ledgard,[159] but however if she woud pay according to her own reckoning you woud leave to a referance the matter in dispute. In my last I think I told you she's willing to pay now £40 [or £70?] and find security for the rest. What say you? I have not one word of news for you. My sister is still on foot, which I am very angry att, for of Tuesday she was so much out of order that I putt of that post writing to you, in hopes of an opportunity to tell you she was in bed, but I now see no signs of it. Adieu. I find fixing my eyes long now I am a cold-bath patient dos not agree with me. Therefore excuse haste in the Vaudois . . .

[P.S.] This family salute you; so do I my cosen. I shoud make an apolegy for my paper but I've not a scrap more in the house.

I had almost forgott to ask what goods yet remain'd unsold of the girls for I believe sister Cowper may yet be a chapman for part of the plate when she knows what there is.

To James Clavering Esq. att Richmond near Borrowbridge.

20. Hertingfordberry. Augt. 15th, [1709.]

I've just time to thank the Vaudois for his letter (and to tell him he's brought me sixpence in debt to my neighbour, privelige being out) as also that we came to this place, of Sunday was senight, and that of Saturday last my sister Cowper was brought to bed of a son;

[156] ? Anthony Hall, attorney and alderman of Durham, who acted sometimes for the Claverings, or George Hall, who also appears to have been a steward for Anne Clavering. *Surtees* and *S.S.* cxxiv.

[157] Wheatley was a hostman of Newcastle. *S.S.* cv.

[158] Anne Newton was the sister-in-law of Elizabeth Clavering of Chopwell.

[159] George Ledgard successfully exploited Elswick colliery. *Hughes.*

she and it are both in a hopefull way, thank God. It was christened yesterday [and] call'd W[illia]m. Sir John Clavering,[160] my uncle Allanson[161] and myself were the Go[ds]hips. You must excuse hast att this time. In a post or two I shall give you a letter in answer to yours, but att present has only to beg my service to my cosen, who I hope is come home, and to assure that with this family I am the Vaudois' . . .

[P.S.] Who is young Mr. Vane[162] going to yoke himself to? My service to your Governour when you see him. Direct for me in Red Lion Square. It will come safe and no ways else. Adieu.

I hear no mention of Peace.

To James Clavering Esq. of Lamesley. To be sent by the post-master of Durham.

21. Augt. 25th, 1709.

My last was writ in so great hast that I've forgott whether I made any answer therein to yours dated from Greencroft and Lamesley or only gave you the account our good Lady was deliver'd. As I am still a sojourner with her 'tis but just she shoud be the first subject in my letter. Therefore I shall proceed to tell you that for near the 1st week she recover'd so very well one woud have been surprised. Since then the quite reverse, tho' now I hope I may venture to say she is, we hope, like to doe well. My Godson thrives most purely. My aunt and self talk of quiting this solitude next week for dear London, a place I beging to like as much as if I were deprived of living there. But 3 weeks is time little enough for us to remove houses in.

From the Governour you woud receive an account that Hall return'd home by Leeds to sett matters right with Atkinson,[163] who I plainly see is a steward. 'Tis most notorious to pay so much out of so small an estate and not to have anything to shew for the certainty thereof. I've in the foregoing project, I think, veryfied the old saying. Hall coud give me no account of what goods yet remain'd unsold in

[160] Sir John Clavering, 3rd bart, 1672-1714. Elder brother of Dorothy Clavering and cousin of Anne and James Clavering. *Surtees*.

[161] Probably Charles Allanson of Bedford Row, London. *Hughes*.

[162] Probably George Vane, 1685-1750, son of Lionel Vane of Long Newton.

[163] Charles Atkinson, hostman of Newcastle and fitter at the local collieries. *Hughes*.

any kind, only that those sold to Phill. Hodshon[164] was to cost our poor girls a law-suit this assizes. As to Lord B[arnard] I see no way we can deal with him if he consents not to the method Lord Chancellour proposed. By the decree the trustees are to treat with him, and the master to make the report to my Lord, so that when his honour [Lord] B[arnard] comes amongst you, you are to doe as seems most agreable to you for I joyn with the decree and leave it to you. I hope Mr. D[ixon's] anger against me will dayly increase. I give him leave if I gett but my boy's mony again and 'twill goe hard if I do not. I suppose he's to be swore as well as you to the accounts which diverts me that you shoud scarce look them over and yet be putt to your oaths. I'd a visit from my Beau Master 'ere I left Lon[don] and am ready att a sumance, whenever he comands me, to return that usuall compliment. I've heard no complaint of you. Yours was the last letter I received from the north, but what doe you mean by setting your foot on somewhat you say was erroneous? Our surprise was equal att my aunt Ward's return into England. I hope she's not come to spoile the good design I hear Mrs. Mitford said (when in town) was undertook to send your two younger daughters to their sisters next spring. 'Tis a vast expence they are att to have no education thereby. These poor things must, for there ages, meet with great difficultys in their learnings. Saturday I was alarm'd with a return of poor Betty's illness, and that very moment by order of my sister I sett pen to paper [to] beg of my neighbour to recomend her as a patient to Colebatch,[165] if in town, if not to Sir R[ichard] Blackmore;[166] for as we remember that was your request as to Johny when you left him. If you approve of any else lett me know. We skipt Rat[clif][167] for his negligence. If I hear she's worse or the d[oct]or has an ill opinion of her I shall imedaitly troop to town to look after her. I've no news to send you. I hear nothing spoke of but the Czar's generosity to the Swedish prisoners, save Count Piper,[168] who most believe will be retaliated on for poor Patkull.[169] The Czar's

[164] Philip Hodgson or Hodshon, hostman of Newcastle, who owned collieries at Jesmond. A Jacobite in 1715. *Hughes*.

[165] John Colbatch, the eminent physician, knighted in 1716. *D.N.B.*

[166] Sir Richard Blackmore, physician and writer. *D.N.B.*

[167] See note 96.

[168] Charles, Count Piper, principal minister of Charles XII of Sweden, who was at this time at war with Peter the Great of Russia.

[169] Johann Rheinhold Patkull, 1660-1737, a Swede, who had served the Russians and was executed by the Swedes in 1707.

peculiar mark of esteem to Gen[eral] Rensfield[170] is what was not expect'd; that att his own table, the day he gott the battle, he shoud ask him, why the King of Sweden coud be so unadvised to enter so farr into an enemy's country to fight so great a body of men with his handfull. He R[ensfie]ld shoud answer, 'twas against the consent of him, and the army, but that the King my master was resolved thereon and we have learnt to obey and love him so well to follow him even to distruction. If so, replied the Czar, give every man his sword, and you Gen[eral] R[ensfield] take mine (which he then took from his side) and wear it for my sake as a proof of my esteem to you for your fidelity to your master; and you shall all know the Moscovite have learned to be civilized as well as the art of war. What a turn is this to have the young hero swim over a river with 300 horses to save himself; and Piper stay to deliver himself prisoner of war. My paper will lett me add no more in praise of the Czar, so can only give the services I am command'd from family, and assure you I am to you and your spouse a real humble servant.

[P.S.] If you've any receit of your pupill's[171] they will be expected. I've this moment gott a letter from my neighbour and one from Mrs. Caverley[172] and Betty is now very well tho' she's been in great danger. 'Tis a convulsive asmat, Colebatch calls it.

22. London. Sept. 3d, 1709.

Yours by last post diserves the quickest return of thanks I can possibly give so this post I won't omitt assuring the Vaudois his last was very acceptable. I left the country of Wednesday and then all were in good plight; and so I found our little ones here. Poor Betty still looks pale and ill, but so much mended that one coud scarce believe it. She and Meg[173] were here all the day yesterday, the latter as wild and headless as ever, the former in love with her French and wishes to be mistress of it. She told me what care my neighbour took of her when she was ill. Good man, he's always ready to serve his friends. I am glad to hear thy 2 sisters are well and such fine girls. I own I

[170] Carl Gustav Rehnskjöld, 1651-1722, who was captured by the Russians at the battle of Pultava in 1709.

[171] Jacky Clavering.

[172] ? A member of the family of Sir Walter Calverley of Yorkshire, who was the father of Sir Walter Calverley Blackett.

[173] Margaret Clavering, sister of Jacky and half-sister of Anne Clavering, the writer of these letters. See notes 144-146.

dayly wish them here with these 2. Their expences are large to receive no advantage. I long to hear the success of your diner. Is the world in earnest run mad? Can anybody think of decoying people to do an absurd thing when 'tis plain all their other actions tend to the good and welfare of the infants? You've resolved on a good answer, I think, and stick to your points for I am ambitous to hear the world say that ours are the happiest orphans in the world. I've foreseen this project ever since the motion Mrs. Ellison[174] made, yet was surprised as I writ her Mrs. W.[175] of the journey and rout northwards. See how we mistake ourselves when she can think to make this pass on us as accidental. One or two letters I've had from her since her arrival, but all such matters I exp[ec]t are to be kept from me as a person who they are sure will never consent to any such demands. Your conversation with Mr. D[ixon] is to me very diverting. I doubt not but if 'twas in his power he would sett our youth att work with us, but we may say, as Mary in the scripture, we have chose the better and will not goe from it. I expect next week the account for the master about winning the new colierly. All the journalls and vouchers I sent Sanderson when I went out of town, that they might be laid before the master, who was to give Mr. D[ixon] a sumons to answer about his money. Then I'm sure he'll persist that we are in a wrong method, but his cosen Ann he knows was always mischievous. Had we had more of our mony in his hands 'twoud a been a greater charge to Jacky than bringing his accounts into Chancery. As to the house-goods, if I knew what plate there was, perhaps I coud help you to a chap-man for part if not all. What other stuff is left, in my thoughts, ought to be dispos'd of. It can be of no use to them. So if you find any fault in that article lett me know. The bill of perticulars I took from Hall and gave it amongst the rest. I never thought that affair well managed and so told Hall, both then and now when here. My neighbour's my witness and he denied he'd more to do with it than to receive the mony, tho' I sayd in that case as you doe. I joyn with you. A reformation in our servants woud be of great use. Why doe you not beging? If you allege faults and want a word of command you may receive it. I care not what they say of me. 'Twill be the old again, "now Madam Ann is come in we shall have no quiet". This bring to my thoughts a matter

[174] Elizabeth, daughter of Sir Henry Liddell, married Robert Ellison, son of Cuthbert Ellison. *Surtees.*

[175] ? Dorothy Waite, née Clavering.

I've yet not mention'd to you or my steward, which is that I observed, what of our coals, [which] are vented by other fitters, are brought to account? But no notice ever took that I hear of, of what coals ours vend for other owners, which as I am inform'd ought to be done. Another querry is, pray, after so many disputes how comes Milly to have the part of Bink's ship? There's £17 profitt sett down to her.

I've once more enter'd into the discourse with our councell about Lord B[arnard] from whom I received no incouragement, tho' I told what a rare thing it was these two last years. If my Lord will take, as I formerly writ you, a yearly part of the mine by way of rent then perhaps we shoud have leave for that; but he can lett no lease, take no fine, nor can we give any, were his terms more moderate than he att present mentions. They say an infant's mony ought not to be hazarded. The Court can't justly answer it, and if they coud, this may prove ill, then begings the young heir to rangle, if 'tis well, the thanks are, they were obliged to do so for their own creditts. 'Tis the answer I received, but you may sound my Lord when you see him. I told Lord Chan[cellor] of the joy my very good Lord of Durham expresst, that he, the best and civilest of all the fellows, had gott a son. He says he believes his joy unfeigned, and so do I, when I consider he loves all those who have him in aw.

Well I've now answerd everything in your letter so I proceed to tell you that the best return I can make you for it is to come to the agreable surprise we'd yesterday, by Mr. Mackey's[176] son, postmaster of Ostend; which was that after both armies had for 2 days cannonaded each other, and that we were joyn'd with that part of ours from Tournay, the Prince of Orange[177] and the Duke of Argile[178] enter'd the woods betwixts us and them, and after great resistance made them retire where they coud draw up in order of battle; and that they had after that this further advice that we had defeated them, tho' Bouffleurs came to serve as Villars'[179] aid-de-camp. I am

[176] John Macky, author of *Memoirs of the Secret Service of John Macky*, London, 1733.

[177] John William, Prince of Orange-Nassau and stadtholder of Friesland, who fought at Oudenarde and Malplaquet.

[178] John Campbell, 2nd Duke of Argyll, 1680-1743.

[179] Marshal Claude Louis-Hector de Villars, 1653-1734, the French commander at Malplaquet and the defender of the "ne plus ultra" lines.

impatient to the last degree for further perticulars, which I hope will be good, for I comfort myself with remembring that this very man sent us the news of Webb's[180] actions with La Motte 2 or 3 days before the express came. This may, for ought I know, be as great a cordial to the sick Governour as any the physicians can prescribe him. He love good news from Flandres and this will revenge poor Count Mercy's[181] defeat, which I yet mourn for, as I doe all accidents that befall our Elector's[182] army. As to domestick news nothing is spoke of but Lord Shaftsbury's[183] wedding, which was of Monday, to a relation of his own [with a] £3,000 fortune, which is so small for his estate [that] his friend Sir Jo[hn] Cropley[184] has gott the vapours upon [it] because he first see her att his house. The covetiousness of mankind! But why say I soe of him, that could oblige his sister to marry that beast Sir James Ash,[185] because of his estate? 'Tis plain he thinks of nothing but mony so may be allow'd to grieve that his friend, who needed no fortune, shoud marry to please himself. However this wedding is a surprise to the world, that so spleenatick a man shoud marry. This therefore renders it evident that neither that, nor vapours, nor any other melancoly, can secure one from thinking of that word matrimony. We see, one time or other, all folks are caught in that snare. I'm also told the great Dutch[ess of Marlborough] looses ground dayly. That all is done that possibly can to make her throw up her key, which the world says is design'd for Lady Hide.[186] A proper thing for her, who then may keep the councell-room door closer than last year. In the meantime whose hands think you we are most in? Pride and covetousness has been the ruin of that lady and woud soon be seen were it not for her husband. The town also talks that the Duke

[180] General John Richmond Webb, Tory M.P. 1695-1724 and the victor of Wynendael. *D.N.B.*

[181] Count Florimond-Claude de Mercy, 1666-1734, who served the Emperor in many engagements and was finally killed in action.

[182] George Lewis, 1660-1727, later King George I.

[183] Anthony Ashley Cooper, 3rd Earl of Shaftesbury, 1671-1713. In August 1709 he married Jane, daughter of Thomas Ewer.

[184] Sir John Cropley, 2nd bart., Whig M.P. Shaftesbury 1701-10 and a close friend of Lord Shaftesbury.

[185] Sir James Ashe, 2nd bart, 1674-1733. A London merchant and M.P. Downton 1701-5.

[186] Lady Catherine Hyde, sister of the Earl of Rochester and Lady of the bed-chamber to Queen Anne in 1712. *Luttrell* vi, 720.

and Du[ch]ess of Ormond[187] are come together again, and that he's discharged Lady Mary. Were it not for lengthing this letter, which is already to long, diverse excuse ought to be made for it. As 'tis I will conclude with my best service to your spouse and assure you, I am . . .

[P.S.] This family salute you. Pray send some money for your girls as soon as you can.

23. London. Sept. 15th, 1709.

I am surprised your guest shoud be thus long of breaking there minds upon so material a point, especially after so many fair opportunitys offer'd. 'Tis, I am satisfied, no chimera of your author or myself. Some such weighty afair as the care of one's own brother's children must have drawn one from the kindest friend in the world. Well I've turn'd this over and over and amongst our bairns and them I can't raise £300 per annum. This can never mentain them in meat, drink, close [sic], lodging, learning &c. So of consequence, were it as desired, Johny[188] coud not improve att so great a school. Wherefore to take him to his sister's and have a tutor for him at home were the best. Perhaps charges, his trustees think high. To salve which att fourteen chuse a new guardian. Why not D[avid] D[ixon?] He's been a good friend to the family. Then of nessecity must the bringing the accounts into Chancery be of no effect; but as you are resolved to grant no quarter I've rested easy on that subject. But the baseness of that man will always reign uppermost in my thoughts. I durst venture to swear he's been Wethearley's[189] chief councellour in his knavery. I'm not surprised att the account you give for this last seven or 8 years I've hated him as Old Nick dos the colier, tho' he's been thought so honest. I wish you success in your counter-design against him. Whenever you've an inclination Mrs. Guardian shoud raise herself she's att your service. Till then like fire I will conceal myself, to break forth with the more vehemence. I dare say 3 of us only wish to have matters acted with justice and honesty to our pupill, that he and we may both

[187] James Butler, 2nd Duke of Ormond, 1665-1745. He succeeded Marlborough as commander-in-chief in 1712 and turned Jacobite in 1715. His second wife, Mary, was a daughter of the Duke of Beaufort and lady of the bedchamber to Queen Anne.

[188] John or "Jacky" Clavering, who was at Eton.

[189] Edward Weatherley, coal-agent for James Clavering. See letters 156-8 below and *Hughes*.

be safe from all back friends. I hear the fitters have sign'd so that point I hope will be easy to you all for the future. I've order £40 of the mony you've return'd to be paid Mrs. Caverley, and when our country friends come we shall know what more they've occasion for. I see the girls today. They are both hearty and send you their duty. What did you with 2 different sett of people in the house att once? I pitty'd you on that score. If they are with you, I'm their servant. Matt. Smithson[190] is in my debt 2 letters. Did you make your chief rejoyce for the good news? How do you approve of perticulars? We are here grown weary of so good a subject to. It was candid with lyes and scandall in many thing to make it keep the better. The Dutchess of Beauford[191] is dead in childbed and I meet with none that can answer my query concerning the Duke so I must apply to Mr. Bickerstaff of the Tattler[192] to know whether his Grace shoud drink down his sorrow or refrain excess for some few days. We are here in confusion pulling down everything in order to remove into Bedford Row. I am call'd on again and again. My aunt has been ill ever since her return from the country. Yesterday was the first of her getting abroad. I've not time to read what I've writ and hardly as much as will give me leave to assure you this family are your servants, and that I am to your spouse and the Vaudois . . .

[P.S.] I made no bonefire because our sovereign order'd the guns to fire the first time since we wore black for the Prince of Denmark.[193]

24. London. Sept. 24th 1709.

I've now a quarter of an hour to spare before we remove into Bedford Row, which house we are to be in next Thursday; so I can't do better than thank the Vaudois for both his letters. The first thing that presents itself is the interpretation you putt on the narrative (as I remember) I gave you of Lord Shaftsburry's wedding. I never forswore entring into that state of life but am no nearer changing my condition that I know of than when I was seven

[190] ? A relative of Charles Smithson, the Newcastle attorney. See note 58.

[191] Rachel, daughter of the 2nd Earl of Gainsborough and wife of Henry Somerset, 2nd Duke of Beaufort, died in September 1709.

[192] Richard Steele, the writer of the *Tatler*, used the pseudonym *Mr. Bickerstaff*, probably on the suggestion of Swift.

[193] Prince George of Denmark, husband of Queen Anne, had lately died.

years old. But in case I were, if I but once reflect'd on Mr. Bickerstaff's Tattler of the Civil Husband, I am sure it woud break all resolution I coud make to change my way of life. That is so good an account of the married state that it ought not to be forgott. But I will leave this happy or miserable subject, being not so fitt for letters, and proceed to tell you I'm glad you've changed hands in your suit. Since that gentleman gives over accting for us I hope our servants make no more of those needless journeys to Durham, for besides the charge they've been dear journeys to us. I always understood that the lead was sold only in your name and that of my steward's. If so the cheat is upon the free-men, but in case D[ixon] is concern'd then undoubtedly you pay toll, as much as if it were in the name of the infant. As to Lord B[arnard] I always thought you or your Governour had been told that when he went to Lord Chan[cellor] to satisfye him about the refusal, he carried with him a new drawn copy of a settlement whereing he was only tenant in the mine for life, and deprived of taking a fine of renewal when our time was expired. This occasion'd our good Lord to tell him, as I've formerly hinted, that he might lett it by taking a yearly rent of part of the mine, but that for the fine his demands were so high, and a mine so uncertain, that his opinion was the Court would never consent to grant it for an infant. The reversion is lodged in one of the sons. I've forgott which, but that's no matter. The elder one can't deal with and the younger is so like the father that one woud have nothing to do with him. This is all that requires an answer in your first and as to the second I sincerly rejoyce the ladys are affraid to break their minds to you. Women ought not sure to ask the question first, but if love or despair forcess them to goe beyond the rules of decency for an example to others they ought to receive a denial. I durst not so much as name the girls in the letter I writ. I expect my Lord and sister in town tonight. He drops her as he goes to Windsor and calls of her in his return. I shall acquaint him with what you mention, but lett me tell you that last year we resolved on cosen Strother of Foberry for high sheriff the election year, but if the torrys are to name them doubtless they will then leave all honest men out. In my next you shall hear more on this head, and before I conclude a word to councellour Douglass.[194] 'Tis the return I always thought my neighbour woud have. I doe

[194] See note 152.

assure you no tutor ever took more pains to make his young charge polite than I have done to make my neighbour lay aside part of his civility to those monsters. I often coat [?quote] him the civill reprimand his friend Coatsworth[195] gave on that subject. But what will all this signifye? He's took a tour where the beau monde is and will certainly return with ten time the complaisance he used [to have]. Some time longer he must stay (not to perfect that accomplishment in him, but that will give him a greater habit, which we shall find difficult to break in this necessary point) for his room were yesterday but begun to be painted, and a little dry 'ere he returns is but fitt. Nay I expect he'll be full of complaints for the smell of paint may do his head no service. But who woud not be nice whatever one personally suffers. Att his return I shall call for Hall's inventary. I see our girls today. They are well. I paid them 40 pound of Jack's mony. They write for their things att Greencroft so I've decided they may be sent to Johnson, who I desire you will order to lett them be sent to misses att their arrival, with a note of the charge and they shall pay those who deliver them for the boxs Waters[196] sent Lord 2 months, because they'd nobody to send after the master. Don't fail when Mons is took to please your parson and beautifull daughter with a blaze. You whigs make great elluminations. May we often have those happy occassions and then lett the parsons say their worst. To do worse than other men is their dayly practice. Hang Dyer.[197] Monsr Bouffleur's letter, copied from grand Cyrus, make our victory more glorious than we ourselves do. I've not time to inlarge tho' I can talk of it hours together and never be weary, but time dos only allow me to beg of you to pardon the faults of this which I can't look over, and to beg my best service to your good spouse, and to assure this family salute you and that I am to the Vaudois . . .

[P.S.] Your next direct into Bedford Row. Cosen Liddell[198] is return their from Morelack.

[195] William Cotesworth (or Coatsworth), Whig M.P. 1701-15 and prominent merchant. *Hughes*.

[196] Harry Waters, son of Isaac Waters of Gateshead, was admitted to the Hostman Company at Newcastle in 1705. *Hodgson*.

[197] John Dyer, a Jacobite and non-jurer, who wrote regular newsletters, which were dispersed among the Tories. *Luttrell*, iii.

[198] Thomas Liddell, eldest son of Sir Henry Liddell, had married Jane, sister of James Clavering, 6th bart., in October 1707.

25. London. Oct 11th 1709.

Had I not been hurried of Saturday to a game att Bragg I had writ to a made inquiry after you, that I might once have turn'd the reproof of silence upon the Vaudois, but yours from Newton made amends. That I may not forgett I will beging with what came first in view, which is Hall's exact account of plate. He makes unsold the table of plate which you know sister Cowper bought. Besides is one bason, a large salver, a large tankard, a tea canister, 12 knives and forks, and six spoons, 3 porringers, 3 casters, 2 salts, a child's tumbler, a cup and a spleen tankard. Now the tea canister came with the table of plate to my sister. The large tankard, I think, was sold when the goods were selling. I see but two tankard sett down. Ask what that midling tankard waigh'd he sold to some of his acquaintance, att the canting, and who received the mony for the 6 spoons Dick Binks had and what we had an ounce? For as I remember there was 18 spoons mark J.E.C. and six old one J.A.C., but this Stevenson[199] can tell before you speak to Hall. The spoons I know Harry Waters was to have had att 5p. ounce, Britania plate. After I'd found his selling it for less than 5-6 which that plate always gives, tho' ever so ill used and all the fashion lost, and they return'd them back again upon his telling his mistake.

I don't know when this will come to hand. If you continue your resolution to goe to Raby I hope you expect no other advantage by the visitt than the redeeming the creditt of your family, which my Papa[200] lost for want of paying his respects to his landlord. Don't carry a large sumpter. 'Twill be needless and fright the ladys, who do not understand that word variety. The old tackle I hope he will purchase of us. Then adieu my very good Lord, and adieu the best of tenants.

What you tell me of the Mountagues[201] has not a little surprised me. If but bare compliments how will your Governour return them, and shoud the continuance convince one it was sincere, in what manner can he acknowledge the honour? There is but one way. I approve of your club for there you can never raise any combustion for who knows one, I judge, knows the whole six. Are you to be

[199] ? John Stephenson, merchant and common councillor of Newcastle. *A.A.* 3rd ser., V and *S.S.*, ci.

[200] John Clavering of Chopwell.

[201] Charles and James Montague, father and son, were kinsmen of Bishop Crewe and constables of Durham castle. They also owned coal-mines at Gibside. *Hutchinson*.

on politicks or private affairs. The latter I perceive has hither too been the subject, which I can but be pleased with, hoping you will overcome the difficultys of the waggon-way and salarys, which do not a little disturb me. My aunt Newton's affairs in our hands will be also best, least malice shoud avail with—to doe what woud prove to us of bad consequence. If I may advice, the Governour or Mrs. Guardian shoud move it. The prospect of a new seam has given me new life but no wining new parts of colierys without leave. I see Saunderson, since my last northwards, and the decree, commands a report to be made upon that occasion. My master's figary to Bath has putt a stop to our accosting D[avid] D[ixon], but he, Sa[nderson], assured me as soon as the m[aste]r return'd to town they woud proceed. I told him I granted no quarter for a reason I had, and more and more when I think of his vilany. The hearing of new things can't increase my avertion, but tho' Fen[wick][202] can't split on that rock Mr. D[ixon] and he consulted about, I hear of one, if true, will doe better, which is that some Dantzick ships are expect'd to unloade for them. If the coming of those vessells can but be hearof, or the bringing of any of those goods ashoar, will, I can assure you, be pye and roast to me. So be watchfull and diligent.

We shall excuse J[ohn] J[ohnson] from being a justice, being 'tis a pretence to excuse him for good and all for H[igh] Sheriff, and, if he were so, it coud be put of but for sometime. I said my account master shoud have no hand in the protection matter this year, but I did not know a Junto was to governern our fleet. Lord Pem[broke][203] retires to Wilton with his family, and a pention of £3000 per annum out of the Post Office during life. Lord Orford succeeds as head comissioner and under him Aylmer,[204] &c. Will the fleet suffer by the change think you? Tho' of the Junto,[205] who hate Volpone,[206] some do not like the change. That news was att Monsr. Spanheim's[207] of Sunday, and I suppose true. Mortality is the other point of our subject. The death of the Dutchesses of

[202] See note 134.

[203] See note 135.

[204] Admiral Matthew Aylmer, Whig M.P. 1696-1720. *D.N.B.*

[205] The leading Whigs, Somers, Orford, Halifax, Wharton and Sunderland.

[206] The nick-name given to Sidney, Earl Godolphin, 1654-1712, who was Lord Treasurer 1702-10.

[207] Baron Spanheim, ambassador-extraordinary from the King of Prussia.

Beauford,[208] Queensborough,[209] and Cleveland[210] are our entertainment. The first, as I told you, died of matrimony, the second of her own mismanagement, and the last as she lived and now revells with Portocarero[211] in the lower regions. The Duke of Gra[fton][212] has gott all she had to dispose of, which when Lord Quarrington[213] was sure of, he writ her a letter of all her prancks, which she read patiently, and when she'd done, ask where the devill the rogue had gott his intelligence. Since you laugh and make a jest of some amours I will be silent for the future. Why shoud not my neighbour think of entring the wholy state again when so great a fortune falls in way? Divert yourselves with your Governour. His papa shall be no more a jest to you tho' I coud tell more of his Bath progress. I'd an infinitt [sic] acquaintance there this last season. I am glad Jenny[214] recover'd. I'd from the house an account of her indisposition, and the letter I've this post answer'd in the same stile. Our northern widdows grow wanton and then merry, but she will stick hard I fear. Our High Priest I suppose is Doctor Phine. Betty has had a small return of her cough, but is well again. Johny improves dayly as his master told my uncle Allanson[215] last week when att Eaton, and tho' I never hear from the youth yet with the assurance of this I can goe through some difficultys for him with pleasure and satisfaction. So I believe we shall all. I've now answer'd all yours save the calling my neighbour a sad man, and the paragraph belonging to myself. The first I will pass by silently till I can discourse the gentleman: and for the other, now I'm out of Puss Corner, I hope I may meet with a mate. I've one in my eye, but allass the last time he was spoke of he was in Germany with his son and I don't yet hear he's return'd, which causes me no little uneasiness.

[208] See note 191.

[209] Mary, daughter of Charles Boyle, Lord Clifford, and wife of James Douglas, Duke of Queensberry, died 20 Oct. 1709.

[210] Barbara Villiers, Duchess of Cleveland, mistress of Charles II, died 9 Oct. 1709.

[211] Cardinal Portocarero, 1635-1709, Primate of Spain, who had had great influence over Charles II of Spain.

[212] Charles Fitzroy, Duke of Grafton, 1683-1757, illegitimate son of Charles II and the Duchess of Cleveland.

[213] ? Edward Henry Lee, Lord Quarendon, 1681-1713 or George Booth, Lord Warrington, 1675-1758.

[214] Jane, sister of James Clavering and wife of Thomas Liddell.

[215] ? Husband of Anne's aunt Jane, who was the sister of John Clavering of Chopwell.

I like our new habitation well were it not for two faults. The one is, we loose Georgy Vane[216] quite, and the other, yet worse, for I can't be a moment att the window, but you've such a superfluity of parsons passes you. 'Tis enough to make one mad. I enclose you three receit I desire you will give my steward for to give Hall, that, in due time and course, they may again be return'd me. This family salutes you. So do I your good spouse; and be sure you return my service to your late landlord, and the Hebburn justice as you call him. I am to the Vaudois . . .

26. London. Oct. 29, 1709.

The divertion I had in reading yours for Richmond diserves my best thanks. I never was more intertain'd than with the account you gave of your journey to Raby.[217] I did not believe there coud be room in the castle to lodge you. Nor coud I have thought that well bred Lord woud have show'd so much good manner to the Captain,[218] who, I suppose, has bid adieu to his honour. The reason of turning you out of his house was extra[ordinary.] Sure you will dispatch the Governour to pay his devoirs to the family. You seem to admire the neatness of the lady and that of your new neighbour, but their persons' charm me as much as their apparell. I've long been in raptures of the whole family and dayly give thanks that I've no more Lords to deal with. This proceeding must alarm the widdow, who, as I've told my steward, is the better match and then he must consider she's been a good wife formerly, and has paid him already part of her fortune. These are advantages he can't hope for in the young Chinese, for so Missy V[ane?] is call'd. And as I dare affirm that if my neighbour were a widdower within these ten days, he marrys none. He seems dead to his relations by his silence, which causes complaints against him. He's either secretly amongst you settling your Governour, who, the lady's friends say, has agreed to all demands or he's turn'd Owler for some statesman to France. If the latter, which I'm resolved to father on him att his return, we shall know much of the secretts of that Court. In the meantime I wish your Corporation would be adviced by me and

216 George Vane of Long Newton, 1685-1750. *Surtees*.
217 The seat of Lord Barnard.
218 George Liddell, 3rd son of Sir Henry Liddell. Later M.P. for Berwick.

take young R[amsay?][219] for alderman; and in a room full of the inhabitants of that town, I declar'd my thoughts on that score when I heard of H[all's?] death, tho' I said I remark that severally I hate the father, the son, and the whole Corporation, and yet wish them now success. Nay more att diner in this compagny one woud have given me some hare. I told 'em I durst eat none. 'Twas apt to make one dream of the devil, and, if true, I shoud be fright'd for I lye alone. "Oh," answers another, "for your reason I'll eat none. I shall dream of the devill's imps." "Do you know who those are?," said some. "No," replied they. "Then," said Lady Ann, "in few words I can tell you. 'Tis in what year you please, the M[ayor], Recorder, &c. of the Corporation last named." Don't I venture myself boldly? Now as to my girls 'tis true I bid them write for what things they had att Greencroft 5 weeks agoe, but now 'tis to late to send them up by sea so the way you propose is best, and what you might have done without asking leave. I hope you made a bonfire for my Prince's success. Your present to our friends I can assure you will be very acceptable for I can affirm that the good woman has not drunk a quart of malt liquor att home since all her Newcastle Ale was gone. I can say nothing as to D[avid] D[ixon] till the new owlers return, but the account you give me shocks me extreamly. I am heartily concern'd for you, and must beg of you to explain that matter a little more. Your news of Tom Titt is as surprising, and will be a loss to me. I shall want him to snarl att this winter, but why say I so, for I [am] sure Tomy Forster[220] will teaze us all to death about Dr. Ph[ine] and the York wedding. I vow I dread his coming to town now No[vember] draws nigh. When send you up your landlord Nicholson?[221] In return to your news I must tell you that when yesterday a visiting I was told my Lord Kent[222] shoud say all the maids were to be married and as an instance Mrs. Collier left the Court last week, but the man she marrys is not yet known. Some say Lord Dorsett,[223] others Monr. Hop,[224] but as the Court come to Ken[sington] next week she then leaves it. Mrs. Mas[ham] lyes in their of another girl. Miss Yelver-

[219] ? William Ramsay jnr., son of Alderman William Ramsay, was a Newcastle merchant and goldsmith. *Hughes* and *S.S.* ci.

[220] See note 105.

[221] See note 54.

[222] See note 31.

[223] See note 61.

[224] Jacob Hop, Field-Deputy and Treasurer-General of the Dutch Republic.

ton comes in maid in Mrs. Cook's[225] place. Miss Scarborough[226] is for the next vacancy, and I hear Mrs. D[olly] Walpool[227] has the third promise. 'Tis a pitty E. Sands[228] is dead. She might as well have come in. But I will quit these girls to answer your question as to the Juncto. I ment, as I said, his being of that sett made him disliked by some, but not me I assure you. I love not Vol[pone.] Now, by what I can pick up, by one and another, Lord Orford has another fault in the eye of those people, for a friend of his told me, the Queen had writ to tell him that he must not refuse the comand of her fleet. But tho' an express went to him of Monday last, and of Thursday he was expect'd, yet he won't come in as Lord H[igh] A[dmiral], only Head Comissioner, to name all under him, to putt out and in all officers of the Navy, and to doe what seems best to himself, and this with a promiss that the Navy shall be clear'd as soon as possible. Burchett, by this, must wink att his horns; they'll be his chief support. Sir J[ohn] Leake[229] will have a pention, and I believe you will find Aylmer sent abroad and your vacant flag given to that notorious Whig, C[harles] Cornwall,[230] which I sincerly wish; then I shall be pretty easy as to the Fleet. The protections you need not fear, but by the last I had from my steward he seem inclinable to try the present mayor, being loth to putt your friends to more trouble than you can dispence without. Which project I've told him I did not approve of. I thank you for delivering my receits. Our country folks, M[isse]s Stotes,[231] are all the noyse of the town. No man hears of them or sees them but sends to offer himself and estate. The ladys say they've £12,000 a piece, that you may justly suppose the beaus' estates are answerable, but betwixt ourselves I can tell you £400 per an. real estate is the greatest yet offer'd. Mrs. Frances is to have meritorious Shippen,[232] Mrs. Margett,

[225] See notes 50 and 51.

[226] Daughter of Mr. Scarborough, one of the Board of Green Cloth. Maid of honour to the Queen, she married Sir Robert Jenkinson, M.P. for Oxfordshire, in 1711. *Luttrell,* vi, 724.

[227] Sister of Robert Walpole. See J. H. Plumb, *Sir Robert Walpole,* i.

[228] ? Daughter of Edwyn Sandys, former M.P. Worcester.

[229] Admiral Sir John Leake, 1653-1720, famous for the relief of Barcelona 1706. *D.N.B.*

[230] Charles Cornewall, Whig M.P. 1709-10 and 1715-18. A naval officer since 1692, he was not promoted vice-admiral until 1717.

[231] Daughter of Sir Richard Stote of Jesmond Hall, Northumberland, who was a very wealthy serjeant-at-law.

[232] William Shippen, Jacobite M.P. See note 33.

Parson Tong[233] of Brancspeth, and Mrs. Mit., Sir A[lexander] Coming,[234] the youngest. Say not this from me, I desire, for I shoud be undone were it known; but I'm glad to hear this, for if Jacky lives till I'm seventy and makes me his executor, it will be my own fault if I marry not. My paper will lett me add only [the good wishes] of this family to you, and Mrs. Guardian's[235] to your good spouse . . .

27. London. Nov. 8th, 1709.

Yours last night I received, and must not only tell you I'm concern'd for poor Jenny, but that I am now turn'd nurse to dear Betty, who was well and with me when yours came to hand, but this morning I was [concerned] for she'd took one of her fitts of her ashma and sent for the Dr., but before either he or I coud come she was well again so he order'd her a vomitt. She continued well till above 4 a clock this afternoon, and since then has had little or no respitt. I again sumon'd the Dr., who, upon seeing her, laid aside the vomitt and had her blooded, which he hopes will be of more use. Some other things he's ordered her to take, which I hope may relieve, but my sentiments are [that] she'll not be cured. I am impatient to hear of poor Jenny and shall till the worst day is over and when, please God, she's recover'd and gott strength I beg you will command her to be well physickt. I read my neighbour your excuses and I can tell you Dr. Colebatch is angry att him. He's gott cold. Last night it lay much in his head, which I did not like, but his oracle says 'tis nothing but a cold and that, methinks, is bad enough. I've had one this month and for these last ten days I've kept house, but for an elopement I made the fifth to give thanks for the Revolution. Was I to blame in that when I'd my riding hood on? But in my return home I mett our neighbour, who chid me and bid me gett home and sitt in my hood by the fire-side; 'twas fitter for me. May I not return this compliment, think you, when he came abroad? My cough continues, and to appease Lord Chan[cellor] who for near a year and ½ has fancy'd me in a consumption; and now a cough has so confirm'd him in this opinion that I'm come to asses' milk; and last week I was whimsical enough to be of the

[233] John Tonge (1666-1727) rector of Brancepeth for 30 years, married Margaret Stote. *Surtees*.

[234] Sir Alexander Cummings, 1st bart., Scottish advocate and Whig M.P. 1707-22.

[235] Anne Clavering herself, who was a guardian for Jacky Clavering.

same thoughts, but though I am no better for his perscription yet I've argued myself out of my last week's folly. Other perticulars of your last I reffer for another post. You've read, I doubt not, the Saturday's *Gazette*, and consider how early your intelligence comes. The corporation has been nab'd. 'Tis so late I can add nothing but your girls duty to you and my cosen, and believe I am to you both . . .

[P.S.] I'd a letter half writt to my steward when I was sent for and now has not time to end it.

28. London. Nov. 12th, 1709.

When last I writt I was in a melancoly mood so coud talk of [nothing] but illnesses, but now my nursery is pretty well recover'd I must proceed to tell you I've diverted myself highly att the intelligence you promiss to give of the place appoint'd for the Dantz[ig] ships performing their guarantain. 'Twas a great change. I assure you the magistrate did not cry victory, they'd gott a great part in the Councill. Whoever you depend'd upon for your knowledge in that affair has not perform'd a faithfull part.

This morning I sent for Saunderson, who has promist me to goe this day to our master, to proceed against D[avid] D[ixon] with all expedition and to see if we can procure an order to prevent his ever calling for more of our moneys. Of Tuesday I shall have the answer when you, or my steward, shall have it imparted. Next I proceed to the civility of our good and well bred Lord B[arnard]. But why were not the tools praised before he came to Raby? He setts a noble example. I can't guess att your cosen, you say was prosecuted according to law, which you call Gally. I wish you joy of the prosecution of the Corporation, and of the death of your uncle. I hope you may end your affairs with less trouble now and much more to all your satisfactions. Cosen Clav[ering][236] writt to my sister Peg[237] two post agoe to beg woud lett my aunt Ward have money for some commissions. Now you know they've had no mony return'd them since they come. Forty pounds we cabaged from our pupill. This we've outrun so must desire you will return us some as soon as you can, as also some for Jacky; but sister Cowper has some of his in her hands so if my cosen will give herself the

[236] ? John Clavering, later 3rd. bart.

[237] Margaret, sister of Jacky and half-sister of Anne Clavering.

trouble to write to her she will with her order lett my aunt have what she calls for; but for Misses they are gott into Mrs. Calverley's debt. Had Betty been fitt to write she shoud have given this account herself, or Peg been att leisure, but she's att the dancing school practicing against Wednesday, which is Ball night. I've now being taking accounts and writting till I'm blind so must bid the Vaudois adieu . . .

[P.S.] My girls present their dutys to you. I shall be glad to hear Jenny is recover'd.

29. London. Nov. 26th, 1709.

I thought to have writ to the Vaudois last post, but just as I gott my paper ready the learned, bold and pious Mr. Sacheverel's sermon[238] came about so that I coud not forbear laying out that two pence and sitt down and read it, but I've gott no further than what I might have bought for three farthings. This is the real cause I writ not sooner to tell you Saunderson made me a promiss this day sevenight, that of Tuesday att the furthest, he woud attack your Bro[ther] Trustee, that we might know more of his sentiments concerning this foolish proceeding of ours in Chancery. Be you good boys now Madam Guardian is begun. I fear D[avid] D[ixon] will pretend to be from home, and be as dilatory in an answer as possible.

I've three letters of yours before me for which accept of my best thanks, and that I may not mistake I will answer them in order. I'm glad poor Jenny is so well recover'd. I wish Milly[239] as well over that disease. Ours here are now in perfect health. From our pupill I never hear, so believe him well. If you recomended the account of the Quarantian to Johnson, he kept it as a secret for I never heard one word of the matter from him, nor anyone else. The plague was a desirable evil woud it only have swept away the thirteen heads and their adherents, but that alone could not be. The Town Clerk shall hear I take his bawling to myself as he desired my interest with Lord Chancellour to procure his son the place. If I'm not aim'd att, perhaps half witts, to convince me, may name boldly. However I'll try. The coiners made a loud clamour

[238] Dr. Henry Sacheverell, who preached the famous sermon "On the Perils of False Brethren" in St. Paul's on 5 November 1709 and was impeached in 1710.

[239] Anne Clavering's half-sisters, Jane and Emelia.

here in town. The report is spread with zeal against you whigs. I am not a little pleas'd to find you bear their threats and aspertions so bravely. You shoud turn Governour for I plainly see that he, who bears that name, will not only make his Doctor's directions to him of no effect, but he'll worry my neighbour into the same misfortune. Can nothing one can say convince him he has not err'd; his power is not shooks by this action; his judgement not call'd in question by any of reason and justice? What then woud he be att when he regards the malicious aspertion of Belzebub's creatures, before the praises of honest men? The slander is so gross as will not bare. None of you who are living, nor my poor dear Papa, who is dead, will suffer in the least by it. Had none of you shewn resentments in the report before this, one might have laid hold of some who had given themselves an air in saying it, and tho' 'tis now a hard frost I'd with pleasure undertake a journey of 400 miles to see an Ald[erman] or any of the Corporation pillory'd. Why dos Sir Wm. Bowes'[240] memory escape? He was a friend to Baker,[241] and as they give convincing arguments to prove what they say, why leave out this? I shall laugh to see the scales turn. Baker, Hunter,[242] Hall of D[urham],[243] Potts,[244] nay even my tenant Squintavego, I'd part with, for a day of justice and to prove my sincerity, if I thought the latter had coin'd in the paper mill, I'd come and blow it up. However, good Vaudois, indeavour to bring your friends to themselves, for the teazing my neighbour with this att a time when he's uneasy about carrying publick affairs, and when Bowman[245] is walkt of, so much in his debt, in lieu of being supported; under this every letter must give new cause for the spleen. If it continues I'll write to Mr. Bickerstaff[246] to forbid the correspondence for some time, or else my neighbour, who justly may be said to be of the living, in a short time may be interr'd by the compagny of upholsters. I hear Tho. Gibson,[247] 'tis to be feared, is come a fool's errant. This

[240] Sir William Bowes of Streatlam Castle, M.P. for Durham county, who died in 1706. *Surtees.*

[241] George Baker of Crook Hall, M.P. Durham City 1713-22. *Surtees.*

[242] ? John Hunter of Medomsley.

[243] Anthony Hall. See note 156.

[244] Local tenant farmers.

[245] William Bowman had mines at Fenham. *Hughes.*

[246] A Bickerstaff family owned coal-mines at Whickham. *Hughes.* See also note 192.

[247] Thomas Gibson was a leading London financier, who financed colliery undertakings in the north-east. *Hughes.*

day or tomorrow he's to be introduced to Lord W[illiam] P[awlett]. If his designs prove abortive I shall be concern'd, for by his avertions one woud sware he was of my education. But what further regards him I reffer you to better hands and shall come to your second letter. I wish'd you joy of your black habitt, 'tis true, in hopes it might make affairs easier. I believe he was a kind husband and in affliction one's words are not to be regarded. I still hope the change will be for the better. Give me leave to desire a perticular account of Lord B[arnard] and Wheately[248] for I must be convinced that that matter is so concluded that our pupill can find no fault therewith. He, you know, has a notion that he was trickt of that lease by my neighbour. Therefore we must [be] cautious. As to the silver spoons I can't be poss[itive], but I am to the tankard and in the servatore in the parlour lay the account of the plate and the weigh writ by D[avid] D[ixon] or his order. Lett Hall shew you that for he shall not cheat my girls of their tankard.

As for your bachelor friend I think he's not return'd, but, however, I shall speak to my sister to prevent any accident. And as for the second, as I remember from what I've heard on the like occasion, there's nothing to be done; but in case I make a mistake the father has putt it in the best method, for if ever any of those things [beare?] they are given as marks of favour to Members of Parliament; but if this happens as you wish, if my speaking of the person you think will be service, in obedience to your request I will not faill to doe it.

Your last is in favour of Mr. Nelson, our pupill's master, for a living in Northamptonshire, which is not yet vacant. I'm sorry his friends have putt him upon so foolish a project. No livings in Lord Chan[cellor's] gift are ever promis'd before the death of the incumbent, and, further, those in that part of great Brittain have generally three, four or five several people about them, so are nab'd as soon as the deceas'd can be cold. If in the north anything fell in his gift, by timely notice and your recomendation I doubt not but he might succeed, for I will answer that not being in favour with the Cathedrall of Durham shall [not] be any hindrance. What remains more is to tell I suppose the rejoycing putt out all thoughts of mony with the Governour for we've had none from him. I hope you'd a merry meeting of Tuesday. Had I room I'd send you no politicks,

[248] See note 157.

but wedding news. I've some which I must refer, and now conclude with assuring the Vaudois I am to himself and spouse . . .

[P.S.] Did you tell your Mama concerning my nursery? My uncle and aunt salute you. Lord of Durham is come. I'm going to ask him how he dos.

30. London. Dec. 3rd, 1709.

By this time I hope your Durham visitant is returnd to consult with her spouse about a proper answer to be given Sanderson, who has done as he promisst in relation to that affair. By a letter from my steward I perceive you have had a demand from Duke Lau[derdale][249] for £300 on a note of my papa's, which dos not a little surprise me. Having occasion to write to my lady this post I have took notice thereof in the following manner: that if 'tis a book debt to Mrs. Malabar,[250] I can give a good prove [proof] for the clearing all when he left her shop; if to old Sir James,[251] he woud not lett him run in arrear; and if to Sir Jo[hn],[252] which I could not comprehend, I thought as all debts had been paid a more early demand might have been made of this. That I was now my bro[ther's] guardian and coud allow my Trustees to pay no further than the Court woud indemifye us in, for men who acted with so much justice, honour, and honesty ought to be preserved from after calumnys. The law was pretty strickt in our case and by it we are governd. All debt were required to be askt in a limited time. That I was sorry to find things of so long a date revived for the consequence of it (tho' not dangerous) might be troublesome to us all. Have I done right or no? Tell me and upon what grounds this thing is trump[ed] up. It may be thought impertinent in me to take notice thereof, but I will speak 300 words before I part with that summ. Last night I'd J[ohn] J[ohnson's] letter. Nothing of great consequence, tho' 'tis a confirmation of the goodness of the magis[trates]. But as matters are order'd the doing this contrary to the proclamation can't be punisht. It was not made treason (tho' the Custom House officers might for not doing their dutys), which I know will frett the Vaudois. I hear you're about taking my aunt Newton's part of the colliery. I

[249] John Maitland, 5th Duke of Lauderdale, died August 1710.
[250] John Clavering, 3rd bart., married into the Mallabar family in 1702.
[251] Sir James Clavering, 1st bart.
[252] Sir John Clavering, 3rd bart.

wish we were quit of her. I've never seen Madam Ward but once, tho' often att one another's doors. When you see my steward, my service, and lett him know I gott the bill, and in a few post shall answer his. My neighbour[253] told me he'd some thoughts of a tour to Raby. I am sure if my Lord says as many fine things to himself as to his papa, upon his account, he can make no justifiable excuse for staying away. You won't accompagny him I dare say.

In my last I said I had not time to give account of the fine weddings, and, as I believe in your next you will demand it, I've sett pen to paper this day to satisfye your curiosity in relation to that affair. The first bride was Mrs. Ann Savile in Golden Square, aunt to Sir G[eorge] S[avile].[254] She's now in her sixty-nine year, is married to Sir Ro[bert] Forbes,[255] a Scotch man [with] five children and a pension as maintenance. He's fifty. He went for a great estate and two girls and said he hoped for a heir from her. She went for twelve thousand pound and has not two. This lady had the courage and resolution to deny the dying lover three times and, had he not supported himself att the paills of the door, he must have expired with that, the last nay say. She, seing that, had compassion, and resolved to ease his grief. The marriage was a little retarded about the settlements on [the] younger children, but that being concluded the happy day was fixt. When he and she, with numbers as much as fill'd five coaches, went to Paul's and were there joyn'd, she [was] so out of countenance to mumble a few words before the parson (that she winkt when she was given and sayd she can't tell who was her father) had she not some reason when she reflected it was the first of her saying obey att 69 when she was only fitt for her grave. However the paint of her face crackt so that her real skinn was seen. The next day she see compagny in a great gown and, because found fault with by some friends, she bought a grave manto of cherry colour, which she now weres. She's breeding, but I'm of opinion [she] won't go to her full time. They are a loving couple and she declares she woud not be 15, to live so long unmarried, for the world. Thus much for them. I come in the second place to the great fortune, Mrs. Reeves.[256] She's long

[253] Sir Henry Liddell; but on this occasion is she referring to his son, Henry?
[254] Sir George Savile, 7th bart., c. 1681-1743, later M.P. Yorkshire. *Foster*.
[255] Sir Robert Forbes of Learnie, Scottish advocate, merchant and former M.P.
[256] ? Daughter of Sir Richard Reeve. *Luttrell* iii, 19.

had a ruma[tism] and Garth[257] for physician, who, for her illness, adviced her to marry. She askt if he was in earnest. He vow'd yes. She told him she'd follow his advice, upon which he proposed young Collonell Sidney. They ware married by the Bishop of Ely[258] in his chapell. Lord Delawarr[259] gave her [away] and spectators were the two above-said, young Egerton[260] and two men more, Lady E[lizabeth] Sidney and Lady Catherine, Lady Dela[warr] and Lady Brown. The bride and bridegroom they went out of town for three or four days and then return'd to receive visitts. Of the Thanksgiving Day some compagny was there when Lady Betty was saying, "How shall I gett home for squibs this night." "O", says the bride, "you shall lye with me". "What, then," cryes Lady Betty, "will you doe with my brother?" "O", says the bride, "we'll putt him to bed to his tutor". This exasperates the young man, who now thought he'd a right to govern, so [he] told his sister she shoud goe home (which she did). He satt in the visiting room all the week, where many of these speatches were made. Of Sunday they went to church in their wedding garments. He lookt babys in her eyes all the time, and in the evening went to kiss the Queen's hand, but the lady-in-waiting turn'd them back, not being in mourning. She'd all close [clothes] to borrow before she coud dress and goe. Her fortune is better than £30,000. He [has] a place in the Guards and [is] a vast deal in debt. Lord D[orset] and Mrs. Collier retired as soon as the big belly was discover'd. When I've said all this perhaps you've had it already from better hands, but I meet in compagny with nothing more new. 'Tis late and you have reason to complain of the lenght [sic] of my letters. Therefore adieu Vaudois. Believe me . . .

[P.S.] I beg my best service to your spouse. This family salute you. Do you remember the keelmen? Xmas draws nigh. We twice spoke about them. Sister Cowper has gott your £50 bill. Jack comes to town of Thursday sevennight. I never hear from him.

[257] Samuel Garth, 1661-1719, physician and poet. Knighted in 1714. *D.N.B.*

[258] John Moore, 1646-1714, chaplain to William III and Bishop of Norwich, who was translated to Ely in 1707. *D.N.B.*

[259] John West, 6th Baron Delawarr, 1687-1723, who had been 1st gentleman of the bedchamber to Prince George of Denmark.

[260] William Egerton, 2nd son of the Earl of Bridgewater, M.P. 1706-32.

31. London. Dec. 15th, 1709.

Att my return home of Monday night (from plaguing all the houses we see lighted) my neighbour, I found, had took possession of ours under pretence that he came to deliver the Vaudois' letters, for which I now return my best thanks. In answer to which I must begin with what is most material. D[avid] D[ixon] writ to Sand[erson], a copy of which I sent the Governour last week and a copy of that, he told you he'd writ, I hear send you. Both [are] extornary [i.e. extraordinary] in there kinds. You see he disowns the thing and then owns it so farr as to imploy Sanderson. He plainly taxes me &c., with ingratitude, which is no new crime in this world. He has a large share of it. I'm sure, when I reflect, my own mama first recomended him to my papa's favour. You say he complains of being charged with the stuff and no creditt given him. 'Tis true he's to give himself the creditt and then the master is to judge what is allowable. He has sent no copy of the accounts, but shuffles and cutts att a strange rate. Well Sand[erson] writes to him this post to desire that he will proceed without delay; that as he is to be att no charge things may be done with speed and friendly. That I have consented, that what vouchers he has by him for the payment of part of the mony, if he will not send them up, when they are received and attested by you and my steward, who I offer to look over them, and the copys thereof (by you both attested) sent to me, I will then allow them. If he delays and refuses this he shall hear more of me and in another manner. I take your reproof kindly and sincerly thanks you for it, tho' att the same time I clear myself. That very thing you find fault [with] I spoke of myself and to more than one concern'd in the law and all said he was to be charg'd with that as well as the rest, or we must afterwards beging afresh. 'Tis certain we said £60 tho' you said but £50. That was the Governour's fault. He said 60 and in these cases all folks charge the bigest summs. The copy of the note from my mo[ther] I insist upon shall travell to town and he shall, when we are once clear of our mony as 'tis his request, be clear of future trouble; but whisht no noise like—till it is over.

Now as to Duke Lautherdale, if the mony is realy due I must see a copy of the note and have accounts examined before I pay, for tho' I desire we may give every one there due yet such sums are not to be paid rashly. I shall write the Dutchess[261] word so when I've

[261] Margaret, daughter of the 10th Earl of Glencairn.

time, which is not this post. Jacky comes to town this night. He was the person I ment that suspect'd my neighbour. I can't inlarge on this or any other part of your letters. My head achs to distraction and am going to look after poor Betty whose ill again. When by her I shall tell you how she is by way of postscript. So adieu good Vaudois. Give my best service to your spouse. This family are your servants but none more sincerly so than . . .

32. London. Dec. 20th, 1709.

By mine to the Governour last post, which I doubt not he has communicated, you will then find me under no small difficultys, which did visibly increase as you will find. Of Saturday night Betty did not rest, her vomitting &c., continued. She was so ill that of Sunday morning the Apo[thecary] came to me [and] told me some spotts were come out and desired she might be removed with speed. So I that moment took her a bed in the same house with Peggy. In the meantime the Doctor came and when he went away told me he did not know what it woud prove, but if the small pox it woud be a very ill sort. So we lapt her in blanketts, putt her in a chair, and brought her to her new lodging and putt her in bed. Still her vo[mitting] [and] loosness continued. She complained of a violent pain in her head, a sore throat, her shortness of breath, sickness att her stomach, and extreamly cold. Tho' her spotts kept out yet no more appear'd, but were thick thick [sic] in the flesh. By these circumstances you may judge nothing had an effect so the Doctor in the evening gave us new prescriptions, but told me her case was deplorable. He woud do what he coud to serve her, but——. So he left us. The Apo[thecary] said if it proves the meazells she will be happy; if the small pox she must die. I stay'd till ten att night by her. She was no better. My servant and her nurse-keeper sett up. It pleased God what was last orderd had the desired effect. She slept well. Her malady's seased, but till Monday night the Doctor woud not poss[ibly] say what it was. Then he said 'twas the meazell, but that her evacuations and her blister (which I mention'd in my steward's letter) prevent'd there coming out so well as Miss Peggy's. She now dayly mends and I hope will doe well. Her complaints are a cough and shortness of breath. Meggy is very hearty and well, and of Sunday had a miraculous escape. Of Saturday we were in distress of a nurse. Att last one come which coud serve us att night but not days. Betty att that time was pretty hearty [so] we agreed to relieve one another in the day; but finding Betty grow worse providence brought us a laxfull woman and her we resolved on, to attend night and day [and] to beging Sunday, being she coud not come sooner. The former by the devill gott intelligence that we had one in reserve and in the morning she went quite away [and] left the poor child asleep. She waked, call'd, and having no answer fell asleep, wakes again and calls. Nobody answers so then the child riss out of bed, walkt round the room, opens the chamber door, calls and [it] was some time before she make the house hear. I bless myself she was not kill'd by it. Thank God itt only renew'd her cough. Her meazells by care came very well out. She was up to-night. But now to myself my part was as deplorable, these children ill of a desease that was terrifiable to their friends. Betty was in great hazard. My neigh[bour] was to be avoided; my sister, my aunt &c., nay Mrs. Calverley, my only support, I forbid. So that had not my aunt Ward been in town I [torn] of all help, which made my affliction sitt the worse. She now by me salutes you and your spouse. So dos my girls and hear I will leave them till next post [when] I write to my steward for mony.

I thank you for yours. My neighbour brought it me to his grand-daughter's lodgings this morning and the Doctor was not angry att the visitt; he's indiff[erent]. I've received my Dun: but this post and deny the request, which was to pay the mony betwixt this and Xmas, for [the] reasons [see] the letter she will send you. So I will not repeat them. This is all I've to say, save a reproof to you in your turn for your curositty. Why may not the Gov[ernor] goe to see his mistress without you? If he want eye-water &c., as you mention, I will do so much for him as to deliver his case to Isaac Bickerstaaf and send him his sentiments thereon. What can I do more but wish him success in his amour and assure you I am to yourself and spouse . . .

[P.S.] Our pupill is forbid, but has in good nature never sent nor ask[ed], that I can hear, after his sisters. He seems yet surley in compagny. I'm my namesake's servant. I hope her bride cake had the effect expect'd.

33 London. Jan. 19th, 1709[/10.]

Had I not had so great a weakness in my eyes since my illness that I've been uncapable of anything (but playing att cards and three times a week reading the *Tatler* by stealth) I shoud not thus long have deffer'd given you thanks for your many and frequent inquirys after me. My complaints, thank God, are now very few. I've been once abroad, but as the weather is so extreamly sharp I shall move but like a snail. This is the first time of my setting pen to paper since I writ my name in a letter to you. Your of Christmas Eve now lyes before me, since which I've received a copy of the account betwixt Sir James[262] and my papa. I find seven years rent due for the Westerhaugh Close farm of £60 p. annum, ending Mic[haelmas] 1701. This I suppose to be the farm my mo[ther] gave up att Sir Ja[mes's] own request after my fa[ther's] death. The ballance of this account comes to £258. 13. 6., which my Lady Clavering[263] says is writ by old Sir James and sign'd by my father. If what I suspect of this being the same farm be just, I can't comprehend that seven years shoud be due for it and my mo[ther] after that pay the rent whilst she had it. Has Tom Lowry ever been askt concerning it, for that was his affair, or dos We[atherley][264] know of any account that passt betwixt those two, Sir J[ames] and my dada? For as the master (and not me) must be satisfyed in this I desire a perticular account concerning it, that he may have no opportunity to call either your judgements or that of the Court in question by choosing so ignorant a guard[ian]. I will say no more as to that letter. This [has] been the material point my good secretary told me he left unanswered. As to the rest I will in right to my self be silent when I consider they are subject[s] he has already touch'd upon. So [I] shall proceed to yours from Greencroft. I condole with you in your disappointment of the 4th instant. I was in great expectations to hear of your success, having had so many assurances of the sincerity of the new friendship with the Go[vernor]. Tho' att the same time I can but own I thought it impossible for men to putt of their natures. But, good Vaudois, do not frett to much. I've just been a sufferer by it myself, for fretting I am sure did me no service and perhaps helpt on my illness. Rest you satisfyed. My neighbour, honest man, comforts himself a little with the thoughts the Whigs will make a glorious campaign against Sacheverell. Perticulars I leave to him. So now I come to

262 Sir James Clavering, 1st bart., who died in 1702.
263 Jane, wife of John Clavering, 3rd bart. He succeeded his brother in 1707.
264 Edward Weatherley. See note 189.

our pupill. I must be not well now and then to try the affec[tions] of my friends. My girls cry'd and fretted so that I had Rat[clif], as if they were mad. Johny askt after me, which was more than he did to his own sisters; and of Sunday last my aunt had her first admittance into the house he was in. He came to her, ask[ed] how I did and imediatly askt his sisters' leave to come to see me. [He] was in an excellent humour and we talkt politicks till ten a clock. This you must own a favour not usuall, which incourages me to persue his affairs with more pleasure. You mistake me as to W[eatherley]. The question I askt was not to part with him. You had formerly given me some reasons for not dowing it and this was only to satisfye some little inquietudes in my mind. I long to know what D[avid] D[ixon] has said to you. No answer yet to Charles Sanderson. What is this business with widdow Acherley? I do not rightly comprehend it. As to Monsr. Poyen,[265] I will observe your commands. Your girls are very well and I believe return this night.

I've now answerd both yours. I must give you a word or two of what you seem'd so much to desire, viz. the re[lation of] Mr. Tong and Mrs. Stote. I doubt not but every perticular has reacht you 'ere this, so will not trouble you with a repitition. But when att her age, with all her charms, she was stole, and by a clergyman, I can but be amazed to think what this world will come to. If he sues her for her fortune, she will prosecute him for his life in stealing a hairess. 'Twill be a sweet tryal. I'l hear it, for it must be new to be stole with one's consent by her order. He gott the license. She kept the ring 14 days, sett the wedding day, which was on my Lord Mayor's show, [and] was married in her Christening mantle. Nay more, the Fa[ther] did not know how to perform his office and gave the rong hand. She told him so, pull'd of her other glove and gave the other. Yet was stole! 'Ent this pretty? After this she made a modest request that the wed[ding] shoud not be ownd till May and that he was not to own her till then. He sett her home that night and att the door they parted and 'twas convenient, it being a secret they coud not lodge together for my lady is her bedfellow. In fine she's affront'd and I fear 'tis att his modesty and vows never to own him. She will be tore in peices by wild horses before she will live with him and here I must leave them for my eyes beging to

[265] Daniel Poyen. See note 62.

be very sore. So can only assure you of the best wishes of this family and to assure I am to your spouse and to the Vaudois himself . . .

[P.S.] If you see your Governour [give] my service. In a post or two I shall answer his. Pardon faults for every moment one or other has come to ask me questions.

34. Lon[don]. Jan. 21st, 1709[/10.]

This morning Mr. Sanderson was with me for I grew impatient to know in what manner D[avid] D[ixon] took my civilitys, writ by the above-said party, to which he's returnd an ans[wer] as little effectual as the rest, [and] complains of illegal proceedings as he was made a party in the Bill without his consent (as you can wittness); that he thanks me for accepting the vouchers attested by you and the Go[vernor], but he comes to no resolution save of being discharged his trust, which he mention'd to you and you were against; that he will speak of it to the Governour and then tell Sanderson his sentiments thereon. I have order'd San[derson] to write to him and to tell him from me that I doe look upon all these letters as frivolous and only to gain time; that since he slights the offer by not returning an ans[wer], as he ought to do, I shall gett the master to make a report to my Lord and so take other measures. You name him not from the sessions. Nor has he named to San[derson] the business of Acherly's Widdow. But before I quit this subject tell me, did you nor the Go[vernor] even send me word that he, D[avid] D[ixon], had att last consented to the bringing in that Bill? Something of that nature runs in my head and, if anybody can make an affidavit [of what] he ever did, it will be of singular service to us. Therefore pray inquire. I also spoke to Sanderson as to Sir Ja[mes] Clavering's business. He thinks it odd (if 'tis, as I apprehend, the same farme my mo[ther] had after my father's death) that they shoud receive her rent after so long an arrear; that, as I formerly told you, our servants in those times must be examined and things lookt over to see if no account has since that time past betwixt them, and to examing the receits my mo[ther] had for the rent of that farme during the time she held it, for that will be our chief guide in that affair to make it clear to the Masters. Is this just? I now shoud thank you for yours last post. My neig[hbour], or rather my nurse, I find loves to make complaints. 'Tis true I find a little sharp air makes me cough. He woud hurry me to Kens[ington]. My physician dos not think it necessary, *which he knows*, and that sways this family, and, as 'tis Coleb[at]ch's opinion, it increases the objection. Now what woud he have me doe? He's, in truth, as bad as myself. When his Doctor woud have sent him into the air he woud not goe. In fine he will be his own governour, and by that means has lost part of that complaisance he used to have. Before I gott abroad he had the happiness he long wisht for, seing Lady Calverley, and to the eternaly—of both. One woud rather have believed they had been educated on the Illes of Or[kney] than in France. She the more affable, for upon a small pretence, away he flew. She pursued and att Sir W. Young's[266] in a quarter of an hour they both mett. This gives me some jealousy that it was a design'd thing betwixt them. But to return to myself. Doe not be concern'd att what I say nor, lett me desire you, not to mention it. I shall doe well I believe. If otherwise D[avid] D[ixon] looses a pevish adversary.

I am glad to hear my good cosen G[eorge] B[owes] still retains the old principles of the Revolution. He's an honest man [and] therefore can have but few friends in our country. As to the impeachment yours was the first news I heard. If he need assistance, and we here are servicable, you must lett us know, being we have somewhat of an aversion to a priest. This putts me in mind of great Dr. Sac[heverell]. The usher of the Black Rod took him out of the hands of the serg[ean]t to bring him to the barr of the House of Lords without delay. This hinder'd his paying his fees and tho' the famous Bromley,[267] and long glory Lawson[268] had promist to see the serg[ean]t paid, and now he's out of custody no mony can be gott from them, to the eternaly glory of the High Church. I like this matter of Buttler's[269] if it can be made out. Now I must tell you our high birds are almost madd. Robin[270] made a noble root in the House of Commons yesterday, and, to show you how much

[266] Sir Walter Young or Yonge, Whig M.P. for Honiton 1690-1711.

[267] William Bromley of Baginton, M.P. 1690-1732, the leading high-church Tory in the House of Commons. Speaker of the Commons 1710-13 and Secretary of State 1713-14. *D.N.B.*

[268] Wilfrid Lawson, M.P. Cumberland 1701-34. *Hughes.*

[269] James Butler, M.P. and wealthy Sussex landowner.

[270] Robert Harley, M.P. 1689-1711, who ousted the Godolphin ministry in 1710 and became Earl of Oxford and Lord Treasurer in 1711.

cause there is for it, Coll[onel] Hill[271] has gott Lord Essex's regiment of dragoons, which has disgruntel'd his Grace. Now the government of the Tower should be given to Collonell Ma[sha]m.[272] I gave you an account of Mr. Tong's match. The lady tells a different storry and vows to hang him for stealing an heiress. However he's had a sitation out of D[octo]rs Commons against her, so the work is begun. I am call'd of. Adieu. I'm Vaudois' . . .

[P.S.] This family salute you as I do your spouse. Observe what I said in my first letter to the Go[vernor] for I want it extreamly, least we be suspected.

35. Jan. 31st, 1709/10.

These shoud have been with you last post, but whilst I was writing my aunt came and talkt, putt me quite out, and made me write nonsence. 'Twas then ten a clock so I was forc'd to differ [defer] it to this post. Mr. Poyen write to Mr. Wilk[inson][273] of Saturday and bid him shew it [to] Fen[wick] and desired I woud do the same in one to you, which is the occasion of the cover. I was forc'd, when the matter was argued, to be in a passion to keep me from laughing. All will doe well I hope, for here they have took the alarm and I've promist to be as impertinent as Mrs. M[asham] and expect to have my follies as calmly bore with. I can't, nor will I, hear of any more civill proceedings to D[avid] D[ixon]. My patience is flown. The master must make his report. San[derson] has heard nothing of Acherly's widdow. All this exasperates me and make[s] me a more viol[en]t adversarry. Lett W[ilkinson] pretend what ignorance he will, those receits for the rent of that farm I must have produced. So tell him, for I will take no excuses nor pretences. And as for H[all], what are you doing with him? You've hurried me to death to give you a handle to turn him of, and yet you complain of his neglect. When you see him next,

[271] John Hill, brother of Abigail Masham, the royal favourite. Mrs. Masham tried to assist his military career to the annoyance of Marlborough. Under the Tories he commanded the troops in the Quebec expedition of 1711 and the garrison of Dunkirk. *D.N.B.*

[272] Samuel Masham, husband of Abigail, colonel of horse and cofferer of the household 1707-11. An M.P. 1710-12, he was created a baron in 1712. *D.N.B.*

[273] ? John Wilkinson, agent for Sir William Blackett and mine-owner of Kenton, Gateside and Hedworth (*Hughes*) or Thomas Wilkinson, barrister of Durham city, 1667-1733. *Surtees.*

ask him from me if I did not declare to him that whichever of Jacky's servants pretended to refuse to obey your or the Go[vernor's] orders att all times, and upon all accounts, I would discharge. I'm generally a person of my word. Lett him persist and try. For out he must goe. An example must be made, that's plain. My nurse, I find by both yours, continues to make complaints. Sure he's the troublesomest man alive. He tells you storrys, mis[represen]ts things and woud have me worry myself into the country when I am as fatt as ever on my face and have a fair clear complexion like a lady. This I affirm for three days agoe I was told that in a room full of com[pany]. It was said that if ever Mrs. Clavering was handsome 'twas since she'd the meazells, which has given me so great an opinion of myself, that I dare not goe into the Citty least I be forc'd into [St.] Paul's for my beauty, as Mrs. Tong was for her mony. The orders of the Eccles[iastical] Court has been twice posted on her door. If she gos not home to him before tomorrow night he'll have my Lord C[hief] Justice's warrant to fetch her. Poor wretch, what will then become of her when she now vows the sight of him will kill her? Nay, were they to continue separate she shoud doubtless dye the moment she hears he has seized on the estate. My neighbour is just come in so adieu. I'm . . .

[P.S.] You see my neig[hbour] sent me not gilt paper tho' I was to write to an alderman or for him to see. This family salutes you. You find in the cover I desire this to be deliver'd to your spouse to prevent the suspition Fen[wick] may have by the [illegible] mark when you shew it, which you must doe.

36. London. Feb. 22th, 1709[/10.]

When I'd gott a frank last post and putt myself in a writing posture and all materials ready, Sister Cowper sent that moment for me and kept me till 11 att night, which prevented my thanking the good Vaudois for the favour of his letter and telling him that I rejoyce att his being so well recoverd as to be able to gett a hunting. As you make no complaints I judge you gott no harm, tho' I by my last night's visitt have gott so great a cold in my head I can scarce see. I find by woefull experiance I'm fitt for nothing but a wanded chair in the chimney corner.

I am sorry our affairs give you so much trouble. I desire you make take what assistance you think necessary on this occasion. I fear we must strugle with many difficultys before we shall come to be tolerable easie. To be perfectly quiet I'm convinced is beyond the reach of a collier. The devill has possessed our men I believe. I wish when you see Lowry next you'd ask from me the reason of this change, that as soon as his master was dead he shoud loose his honesty, for being fully convinced of the truth of this, by conceal'd mismanagements, I fully resolve nobody, that has a horse in our waggon way, shall take the way off us. So lett them be att rest. I'd, if I coud, have every servant of ours born with a mortal aversion to each other. That's the only thing can secure one from being great sufferers. I doubt not but the good caracter Hall has given me has increased this peartness in them. Therefore this, with the other misdemeanours, I'm resolved he shall change hands and I desire you will advice Mr. Barnes, who is an honest gen[tlemen], to recomend that fellow no more. I send you the inclosed open, for you and the Gover[nor] to read, that Hall may father no more lyes on me. I heartily pitty you in this juncture when I look upon you as loosing your Guide and Go[vernor]. The resolution my neighbour has took, to have my steward up, who has so long laid dormant on the account of his indisposition, I hope will be seconded by you, who must be an eye-wittness of his sufferings. Perpahs [perhaps] as our affairs now stand you coud be pleas'd with his stay. Yet you are to consider to what a height his illness is grown, and, by longer neglect, we may loose him for good and all. What then woud the Trustee and Madam Guardian do in relation to Johny's affairs. Therefore press him to leave you that he may putt himself under his doctor's care, whose [who] has hopes, when under his eye, to relieve him. I look upon him as in a deplorable way wherefore he ought to shorten his present stay amongst you. I see my neighbour this day. He looks better than I've seen him this month.

I'm forced to writ this over night that I mayn't be prevent'd again. I've not yet seen Sanderson tho' I've writ to him, and my neighbour went and left word att his house that I want'd him and all this won't doe. I beging to fear I'm as farr versed in Chancery proceeding as I shall ever arrive att. This evening I passt att Cosen W[ard's] [or Waites'], where I spoke of J. Do[uglas'?] civill return to those who had gott his son that place. He condems I hear, *said I*, those who stopt the proceedings in Councill, which I take to be aim'd att my bro[ther], by the application made to him after;

or me, perhaps, he suspects to have given notice. When the son, *by you*, spoke to me, I gave my advice as a friend, from which they mett with no ill success. This then deserved a more gratefull return. My Lord is beyond his reach, and will, as long as possible, keep out of his clutches, having made this resolution, that I never will submitt to anything within the walls of Newc[astle], but when necessity obliges me. If the thing has been rong represented to me, I've took care to do it to my Lord, for when I make any request to him for others I always tell how 'tis received. This I hope will bring a confession, which, if a true guess, you shall know. I suspect you to be concern'd.

I come in the next place to the affairs of the Portuguese Am[bassador's][274] Ball. Nothing was ever seen so sumptuous and fine; 39 ladys he invited to supper and the gen[tlemen] came after att 11 and the maskers att one. There was all sorts of dresses amongst those people, even to a Dr. Sacheverell, who was half our parson and half Spanish friar, which some of his compagny obliged so farr as to desire an unmaskt lady to take the Doctor out to dance. The supper was magnificent and in wast [vast] order, all sorts of fruits as melons, grapes, &c., so naturally done in ice that nobody coud tell them from real. But, what was to me the worst part of the cerimony, he'd gott the gout, which had put of this intertainment a week, but that he might no longer disappoint the ladys he ordere[d] his physicians to strike his disease out of his limbs into his head or stomach [for] he valued not death after that night. And the next day when he, in the morning, sent his body squire after the ladys invited to supper, and in the afternoon went himself. 'Tis late. Adieu. I am . . .

[P.S.] I beg my service to your spouse. This family salute you. Feb. 23. San[derson] has been here and brought me a letter D[avid] D[ixon] has honor'd me with, and the things relating to Acherly's widdow. Next week we are to look over all the accounts, for D[ixon] now makes himself debtor only £392; a good deduckment. Did he ever pay for Jacky's board when att Howton? I hear this moment the boy's not well att Eaton, but my sister said nothing of it this morning, tho' she'd a letter. Worthley,[275] this night, burries his

[274] Dom Luis da Cunha.
[275] ? Sidney Wortley, coal-owner and later M.P. *Hughes*.

eldest daughter, who died of grief for the follys and imprudences of the younger sister. Adieu.

37. London. March 18th, 1709/10.

Since this tryal[276] I've been so ingaged that I've not had one moment to spare betwixt Westminster Hall and my bed. However, as great as my fatigue was, by rising att four a clock in the morning [I am able to write this]. Had I not known the Vaudois had an account from better hands, I woud not have grudged sitting up an hour later att night to have inform'd him of our proceedings, [of] which I fancy he dos not disapprove. To me the Commons made out their articles in a very plain way and by undeniable truths. Some of the Managers spoke like angels, others might as well have been silent, but that's no matter. The criminal, when he'd lost Sir Simon,[277] shoud have yield[ed] the cause, tho' the non-resisting ladys say his own defence was moving enough to draw tears. The Dutchess of Graf[ton],[278] Shrewsberry[279] and Lady Greenville,[280] &c., wept so much that, had they that moment become widdow, they coud not have acted a more hipocriticall part. But the Lords, that since have clear'd themselves of having had any share in the revolutions, kept them in countenance, which were Ro[chester],[281] Nott[ingham],[282] Guern[sey],[283] &c. This speech, or whatever we are to call it, of the Doctor's had the contrary effect upon me. A parson I never loved, but now I've so great an abhorence to them that, were itt not for a few bishops, I shoud think the imps of Lucifer had putt on that habit to distroy us. The modest assurance of the party, to support what they call the word of God, is not to be exprest. No bear garden was ever more noisy than the Lords have been upon their debates. When, of Tuesday, the Torrys had a mind to adjourn, and the Whiggs woud not, but upon the division

[276] For this trial see *The Tryal of Dr. Henry Sacheverell*, London, 1710.

[277] Sir Simon Harcourt, 1661-1727. M.P. 1690-1711, he was formerly Solicitor-General and Attorney-General. Appointed Lord Chancellor later in 1710. *D.N.B.*

[278] Isabella, widow of the 1st Duke and mother of the second Duke of Grafton, married Sir Thomas Hanmer in 1698.

[279] Adelaide Paleotti, an Italian widow, whom Shrewsbury had recently married.

[280] Rebecca, wife of John, Lord Granville.

[281] Lawrence Hyde, Earl of Rochester, 1682-1711, was a leading Tory peer. *D.N.B.*

[282] See note 35. Nottingham was a leading Tory peer.

[283] Heneage Finch, Lord Guernsey, later Earl of Aylesford, 1649-1719. He was brother of the Earl of Nottingham and a prominent Tory.

carried it by five, Lord Nott[ingham] said he'd intertain the House for an hour and half, but, alass, when he'd spoke one half hour, and not one word to the purpose, the Queen riss and left him, which blew'd the good Lord. Wednesday you know was the fast and Maningham, Bishop of Chichester,[284] preacht before the Lords. The subject he chose was the same of Dr. Smith's,[285] the dignitys of the clergy and how formerly they were respect'd and advanced to the highest post of honours, but now 'twas the reverse. In fine [he] told them, [that] no way was more effectuall to show how much now they were in esteem than by restoring the abby lands to the Church. This good sermon will be burried in oblivion. The Lords, as I hear, won't thank him. But now's the jest. Who shoud reprove him for this of Thursday but the honest D[uke] of Argyle, and whilst he was raiting him the bishop turns to my Lord of Sarum. "Who", says he, "dos the Duke mean?" Which made the undanted Church of Eng[land] Bishop give him a patt cross the forhead with these words, "Who shoud it be, but thou child". The House that night satt till past eleven. The Queen staid till near ten. When Lord Guernsey was clearing himself of the Revolution, she riss and left them, which so confounded him that he'd much ado to proceed. The D[uke] of Som[erset][286] woud have attend'd [the Queen], but she told him no, not without he brought a lord of the other party [with him], for she woud not have a vote lost on any score. She'd the pleasure that day to hear the Bishop of Oxford[287] make for us one of the finest discourses was ever heard. The Whigs that night carried the point and yesterday I made my appearance. The House open'd with the desire of Lord North [and Grey][288] to have the messenger come with the original papers of Green[shield's][289] business, brought from Scot[land], which he delivered

[284] Thomas Manningham, 1651-1722, was a former chaplain to William III. Bishop of Chichester in 1709. As a Whig he probably meant to exaggerate Dr. Sacheverell's case in order to make it appear more ludicrous. *D.N.B.*

[285] Dr. John Smith, a learned antiquary, was domestic chaplain to the Bishop of Durham and rector of Bishop Wearmouth. Died 1715. *D.N.B.*

[286] Charles Seymour, 6th Duke of Somerset, 1662-1748. A moderate Whig, he was Master of the Horse 1702-12 and 1714-15. *D.N.B.*

[287] William Talbot, 1659-1730, Bishop in turn of Oxford, Salisbury and Durham. *D.N.B.*

[288] William North, 1678-1734, who lost a hand at Blenheim and was later, in 1722, arrested as a Jacobite. *D.N.B.* and *G.E.C.*

[289] The Rev. James Greenshields was prosecuted for reading the English liturgy in Edinburgh, but he appealed to the House of Lords. His case was considered in March 1711. See G. M. Trevelyan, *Queen Anne,* vol. iii.

in at the barr. For you now much [?must] know, that finding Sache[verell] lost, they woud stirr up this, in order to raise a Re[bellion] in Scot[land]. But take no notice of this I desire. Then the good Bishops of Lincoln[290] and Norwich[291] spoke to the second articles like two apostles. Had we ever heard of two St. Pauls I shoud have believed they had now been with us. And in conclusion both said that the Comons had made out that article. Who shoud oppose them but our Lord Lieutenant?[292] But having no second, the contents carried it. The 3d [article] was also imediatly given up. The 4th caused some warm words. The Torrys do not say but some refle[ction] may be upon the ministry, but that that dos not touch the Queen. The others say it dos. The D[uke] Hamil[ton][293] and Lord Mohun[294] were very sharp, but the latter had the best end of the staff. Lord Ro[chester] said that, as he had the honour of being so near a relation, he shoud be as capable of disserning any reflection thrown upon the Queen as any other. The D[uke] of Leeds[295] is so sick, I suppose, of the arbitary proceedings of the Whigs, and has so much concern for the welfare of our sovereign, that he coud not attend yesterday to enter in his protest, as I perceive the most of that worthy party design. When all the Articles were yielded the Torrys moved to adjourn, for today, that they might have time to debate whether, or no, the 4 Articles amount'd to high crimes and misdemeanours. I shoud have been there, but sister Cowper sent me word [that] my Lord told her it woud not be worth hearing. Lord Whar[ton][296] was for the adjournment, but did not comprehend the slow way of proceeding. He agreed with the opposite party that the Lords had tryed their healths as well as the Doctor, but he was but one and, "No matter", says he, "what becomes of me, for I'm resolved to attend the worthy Lords and

[290] William Wake, 1657-1737, Bishop of Lincoln 1705-16 and then Archbishop of Canterbury. *D.N.B.*

[291] Dr. Charles Trimnel, 1663-1723, Bishop of Norwich 1708 and later translated to Winchester. *D.N.B.*

[292] Lord Scarborough. See note 57.

[293] See note 14.

[294] Charles Mohun, 4th Baron. 1677-1712. He and the Duke of Hamilton were involved in a long drawn-out law-suit and they killed each other in a duel on 15 November 1712. See my article on this duel in *Durham University Journal,* June 1965.

[295] Thomas Osborne, formerly Earl of Danby and now Duke of Leeds, 1632-1712.

[296] Thomas, Marquess of Wharton, 1648-1715, was a member of the Whig Junto and was at this time Lord Lieutenant of Ireland. *D.N.B.*

chuse rather to dye on the spot than disert them". Another notorious Whig was for debating as long as the Torry Lords has one word left amongst them to speak, did they spin the time out never so long. Lord Islay[297] spoke twice for us very handsomely, and Lord Halifax,[298] in his speech, said this must become a president, for they had none, except that impeachment in which he had the honour to be joyn'd to two worthy Lords there present. Lord Ossulston,[299] Lord Winchelsea[300] and the D[uke] of Bedf[ord][301] are with us. Lord Rivers,[302] I hear, gos rong. Sure I've, by this narrative of my 3 weeks work, made an attonement for my silence. Especially if I tell you for 5 days in Westminster Hall I had like to have fought for Lord Sarum[303] and other good Whigs. It was so near. I used to raise the people quite round me.

As soon as censure is past I will sett to my word and look into our affairs, but as yet I can't settle my head. I shall obey your orders as well as I can in regard to your Go[vernor] and, from time to time, you may expect to hear of his menagement. My neigh[bour] looks well today and was no Presbyterian. A saying I must explain. This dam'd priest has made all people declare themselves of some party. I, proclaiming myself an ennemy to the Doctor and an intire friend to this [House of] Comons, gave offence to some Torrys, who pretend a great esteem for me, and, which drew from them the following declaration. "No wonder", says they, "Lady Ann is so low in her principles, for I now find they are corrupted". ("By whom", says my aunt, to whom this was said.). "Oh I know, I've had it affirm'd to me in the Citty, that Sir H[enry] L[iddell] is a Presby[terian] and doubtless conversing with him has corrupted her principles". Which makes us very merry, and when he's gott the vapours we call him Pres[byterian].

Jacky, poor boy, has been ill of a rash and, I fear, occassion'd by fretting. His master Bragg complains of him, he of the master, that the house is not so good as it was, that they gett him whips for faults

[297] Archibald Campbell, Lord Islay, was the brother of the 2nd Duke of Argyle, whom he succeeded in 1743. *D.N.B.*

[298] See note 7.

[299] Charles Bennet, Lord Ossulton, 1674-1722.

[300] Charles Finch, 4th Earl of Winchelsea, 1672-1712.

[301] Wriothesley Russell, 2nd Duke of Bedford.

[302] Richard Savage, Earl Rivers, 1654-1712. An army officer, he was won over by the Tories and appointed envoy to Hanover 1710-11.

[303] i.e. Gilbert Burnet, Bishop of Salisbury. See note 103.

he dos not comitt, that the Mrs. won't lett him lye in his own sheets or use his silver porringer, &c., which usage has occasion'd the illness. I fear we must remove him. But more in my next. Adieu. I salute your spouse and am to the Vaudois a most faithfull servant.

38. London. March 23, 1709/10.

This is to condole with the good Vaudois the loss we've so lately sustain'd. A thing so surprising that the whole universe must have us in horror for it, were it not for the mony with which we supply our own troops and those we hier. Of Monday to have a majority of 17 votes and of Tuesday loose the small punishment design'd but by one, and that voice that——. I will say nothing but [he was] the absented Lord the day before. The D[uke] of Somersett, one whom the Queen of the Friday had, in civill terms, askt a vote, and yet drunk waters the Monday and cast us of Tuesday. You know I'm Truth, as is said in the play. I never goe to a Court and therefore understand not Court politicks. Lord Pres[iden]t[304] was not well of Tuesday. No b[isho]p appear'd that day but Salis[bury] (except Oxford, but of that I'm not certain). The punishment desired, by the Lords we esteem, was this, a silence for five years and during that time to be incapable of any benefice. And had they askt but one year, it had been denied. The silence is now 3 years; the sermont burnt att the Royal Exc[hange], the Lord mayor and sheriffs being present; the text cutt of, because that's scripture. Well Vaudois, happy are those who were [wear] a black robe, when the doctrine they preach is to be disavow'd and yet not sufferd to be punisht. I shoud advice all house breakers, &c., to were that habitt. Now I'm convinced 'tis the sanctuary of all villainy. Be not surprised att the rejoycings made on this occasion, when here we'd bonfires, eluminations, &c., of Tuesday. The Min[istry], thus insulted, is insupportable and to be overlookt. 'Tis true the English never know when they are well. A Church Ministry we now want and shall have, as soon as Johny[305] can decently be thrown aside, I doubt not.[306] May those who love to be priest-govern'd have enough and obey passively there superiors. I abhor that doctrine and am

[304] i.e. Lord Somers. See note 99.

[305] i.e. John Churchill, Duke of Marlborough. See note 86.

[306] In fact the Godolphin ministry collapsed throughout the summer of 1710 and was replaced by Harley's Tory ministry.

resolve[d] to espouse that of resistance, when 'tis lawfull, but in that I'll be my own judge. Keep up your heart. I warrant you God is above the devill. We have not seen the end of this yet, and, for my part, I wish we may not feel a heavier blow. In the meantime learn to bully your adversarys, as they do us. After all this I must tell you I've some favourites amongst the clergy and none more so than the Dean of Windsor,[307] who has been sent for to St. James. I know not what for, but he told a lady I see last night, "Madam the doc[tri]ne of passive obe[dience] is so farr from being the doc[tri]ne of Our Saviour, that 't has been putt into men's heads by the devill".

To cheer your drowping spirits I must conclude with a story of the D[uke] of Rich[mond][308] and a mis-coted text of Harry Mordaunt[309] to the Comons yesterday. The 1st was this. The D[uche]ss of Clevel[an]d[310] told her Duke he was to vote for the Doctor and speak as his bro[ther] Northu[mberland][311] did. To which end, of Monday, she lock[ed] him up and bid the servants tell the Du[ke] of Ric[hmond], he was gone out. (Fearing him), the Duke comes. The servants obey the Dutchess's commands. His Grace, not satisfied, lights out of his coach, run over the house, meets with one room lockt, calls and was answer'd, "I'm here, but can't gett out. My wife's lockt me up". To which the Duke R[ichmond] says, "I'll release you". Away he runs, fetchs a ladder, sett it to the window, take[s] the Duke out, and putt him in his coach and bids him say in the House as he did, for he'd speak loud, which, I can wittness, was observed. The former part I don't aver. However 'tis a good storry; and in that of H[arry] M[ordaunt] I shall be short. He, yesterday, banter'd the Lords on the punishment, by representing how dear this had made that insignificant creature to his party, and beg'd leave to conclude with a miss-conster'd [mis-construed] text of scripture as the reverend divine had sett the

[307] In November 1709 Dr. John Robinson was appointed Dean of Windsor. Later he was appointed Bishop of Bristol and then Bishop of London, and he was a plenipotentiary at the Utrecht peace negotiations. *D.N.B.*

[308] Charles Lennox, Duke of Richmond, 1672-1723, illegitimate son of Charles II.

[309] Lieut.-Gen. Henry Mordaunt, brother of Lord Peterborough and Whig M.P. 1691-1719. He was one of the Commons' managers of the impeachment.

[310] Anne, daughter of Sir William Pulteney and wife of Charles Fitzroy, Duke of Cleveland.

[311] George Fitzroy, Duke of Northumberland. He and his brother were sons of Charles II and Barbara Villiers. See note 118.

example. His words, H[arry] M[ordaunt's], were these. "'Tis the Lords doings, but not mervalous in our eyes". God send this well over. I like it not. But adieu. I'm for the opera, it being the first time I've been a play-house these 13 months. I salute your spouse and am . . .

39. Lond[on]. April 1st, 1710.

Thanks to the Vaudois for his 2 last letters, which I read with concern, to see so zealous a Whig have so little power to defend himself from the insults of such a turbulent faction. 'Tis what has been allow'd here, and so rest content. Be satisfyed the sermon is burnt, the doctrine censured, the Oxford Decree burnt, tho' the rights of the Christian Church went along with them. Praise the clemency of the Whig ministry, otherwise call'd by the Torrys the Comon-wealth ministry. 'Tis that is aimd att, and not the succession. Dr Sac[hevere]ll was a true Churchman, a pious soul, an angell sent from God to exort us to follow the right way. How then can you be angry att rejoycings when no guile was found in this man? Sure you interpret his words in a rong sence and fancy he talks against the dissenters, and favours papist. Good creature, he meant no such thing. He was only doing his duty and preserving the rights of the Church. This is mostly the cant of that sett of people you hate. The mobb was also Presby[terian] who were *doubtless* weary of the Toleration. Tho' the parsons are not of thundring out there eccles[iastical] anathemas for a young Oxonian last Sunday att the Temple say'd, no Prince on earth had power to call God's vicegerents (for so he stiled the parsons) to account on any score. Their power was from a more supream being &c. So went on. Att last says this Moses for meekness, the primitive moderation was allowable, but for this modern moderation, if I understand my business, 'tis a damnable sin. I've this consolation yet from this doctrine that now they've rope enough they'll hang themselves. I suppose you've heard how our neighbour of Hedley-fell has carried himself. The Duke of Rich[mond], I hear, plays him a good trick. He's to sumonce the Kitt-Katt[312] to meet, to make inquiry after one of the society who has made an elopement with Robin the Trickster.[313] A very good whim I think. 'Tis of a giddy person. Now I must tell you

[312] The Kit-Cat Club, haunt of most leading Whigs.
[313] Robert Harley. See note 270.

I was lately myself insulted. On this occasion I went to make a visitt where the picture of the perjured priest was, which putt Lady Ann into a raving fitt. I left nothing unsaid that coud, I thought provoke. Att last I was told in derision, "If you are so warm and firery you'll never gett a husband". "O Madam", says I, "you mistake that matter. I despise all Torrys, were their estates never so large, and yet don't dispair for I am sure the Whigs like me better for being true to my party". And so we parted. The perjured priest read prayers att his own church, of Sunday morning, where there were such members of the mobb, that those near him kisst his hand. Others touch'd his garments and were blest. Yet I do not hear that all this has produced thanks to the Glocester Address.[314] Dare you venture to give my service to the minister of Gateshead and tell him I am sorry he has so publickly distinguish'd himself on this occasion? I fear he [will] neither gett by it in the time of this Bishop nor in any other, betwixt you and I. But here I must quitt the parsons. I am weary of them.

I thought I shoud have had some business to have sent you, but the Go[vernor], I believe, told you all last post, which was that we had orderd a view to be took of Hedley-fell for to try what we coud do there. So can sett no wag[on]-way till some end is made of this project. Your Gover[nor] has been a house-keeper ever since he came to town and till today has, I assure you, given his doctor great uneasiness, he being much worse than his own accounts represented him, which made the other give little or no hopes of his duration here. I see his doctor this day, and he says his legs are better, and, if they continue, he shall hope well for him. However it be, sure he's now in a deplorable condition. Patience is counted a vertue but in him 't has been a fault to an unpardonable degree. Adieu. This family salute you. So do I your good spouse and am to the Vaudois . . .

40. Lon[don] April the 20th, 1710.

I should sooner have congratulated the Vaudois on the late piece of good fortune, that befell him by the exit his kind aunt has made, had you not in your last told me that you were for diverting yourself on the moors a week. I won't say I envied your pleasure when of

314 Many royal addresses were presented to the Queen in 1710. One of the first presented was a high-church address from Gloucester.

this day 7 night we had the agreable news that our army had made themselves masters of the French lines by their practicing our H[igh] Church doctrine of non-resistance. But this news was soon allay'd by a new Lord Chamberlain,[315] who has crept into the cabinett, a province not belonging to his office. That was a surprise on the world and what no Whigg can disgest. More changes were imediatly spoke of and nothing but a thorrow reformation in both church and state was to be lookt for. Then I wisht my self out of the hearing of everything and coud but think you happy in a place not troubled with politick designs. This neighbourhood of Saturday were so pevish on this subject that I, who had appointed Mr. Sanderson to come to me to look over D[avid] D[ixon's] affairs, (and by that means forced to look amongst the vouchers), was so madell'd that all my papers I thought were sign'd by Sheus . . . [?Shrewsbury.] However we sett ourselves right and Sande[rson] was to write last post to desire him to pay us in his balance to the account speedily, by which means he might hope for better usage in the objections we make to the accounts. As soon as my brains are settled I will look in the vou[chers] for that mony you mention'd that Hall (has rong bookt) paid Mr. Silvertop[316] and that of the fitters, but the journalls of every year are in my master's hands. But I must return again to our new officer the defence of the Church——. His having but one eyes[317] [sic] speaks his praise as much as his meek and gentle carriage did att the tryal. He has alloted the management of the Playhouse to her Grace, which made her of Monday night so farr forgett herself as to undertake the shouldring out of the lady in waiting and playcing herself there, which gave her athority to marshall all the ladys as she pleased and to entertain the Queen with the news of my Lord Mayor of York's going to travell, which made all people laught. She'll soon, I believe, aquire the title of the Queen Church Warden. This has putt the Torys into an airy temper, insomuch that our Bishop, who I dined with of Monday, coud not contain himself but chatter'd like a mag-pye. He then was in hopes of delivering, or introducing, the Durham address, but as the Queen will here no more of those papers read of, no side,

[315] Charles Talbot, 1st Duke of Shrewsbury, 1660-1718, appointed Lord Chamberlain in 1710. As he was at this time working with Robert Harley his appointment was a blow to the Whigs.

[316] Albert Silvertop of Stella, 1667-1739. *Surtees.*

[317] The Duke of Shrewsbury had lost an eye.

his honour gos away with a flea in his ear, which dos a little divert me. You will by this post have a letter from Red Lyon Street so I will say nothing of them. The Go[vernor] can give the best account of himself and of the world. So [I] referr you to him and shall conclude when I've assured you the news att Whitehouse relating to sister Cowper was not false. I salute my cosen and am to the Vaudois . . .

[P.S.] Betty has gott her cough again for which I've order'd her some linseed oyl. I durst not omitt this post writing least you shoud say I was grown great and lazy and imploy'd a secretary.

41. London. April 27th, 1710.

I perceive by accounts I meet with, that Mr. Cotesworth has took a view of our waggon-way, which he's found in a most miserable condition and the stock of rails of 12000 yards last and the worst was ever seen, tho' I'm sure we've paid the best price for them. This therefore to beg of you to lett all the people concern'd in the way know, 'tis my express comands they be observing of his orders, for I impower him to overlook it, and whomsoever I find refractory shall without delay follow G. Hall and Coulson.[318] I've no respect to persons and in a particular manner I desire Lowry may be acquainted with it, for his injustice to us is come to equall W[ilkinson?] if not outdo him. In doing this you will infinitly oblige . . .

42. London. April 29th, 1710.

I am at present secretary to my steward, a thing I own not usual, but as he has many letters to write you must pardon him att this time and be content with an answer from Madam Guardain. In yours of the 18th you seem to approve perfectly with Mr. Ber[nard?][319] being concern'd. The trouble you must have had woud a been much worse than that you are like to have yet for 9 years; and 'tis already so much that I fear my pupill will never be thorowly sencible of the obligations he has to you. I went into Lincolns Inn Fields yesterday on purpose to ask my Lord's opinion and consent in what the Go[vernor] formerly writ to you about. He

318 ? Alderman Stephen Coulson of Wolsingham, who was a freeman and common councillor of Durham.

319 ? Alderman Bernard (*Hughes*) or Mr. Bernardean (see letter 65).

desire[s] that you'll be pleased, in the contingent charges, to putt under general heads what sum you think convenient for the time by-past, as 'tis not reasonable that with all the trouble we give you, [to] putt you to extraordinary expence. 'Tis what are allow'd all Trustees under this method but not in a fixt sum. My sister also beg'd of me to tell you, in case your aunt Ro[gers][320] shoud oblige you to quit Lamesley, she hopes you will except of a habitation at Chopwell, which, in the name of us all, is sincerly att your comand. You are desired to keep Sir John[321] and his lady from the artifice of Ald[erman] Proctor[322] in the business of Tanfield. Sure the Go[vernor's] good advice to them will not be lost. He writes Mr Cotes[worth] this post upon this very subject so I need say no more of it. I see in your last you recomend to my care the putting out of the commission of peace some black coats &c., and ading the Capt[ain].[323] To the first I can do nothing without good proofe that they deserve it. Ant[hony] Hall[324] is the person I see the most likely to scratch out. If he's no free-holder and no land it may be a means to make his name to be blotted out. That, I now leave to you. The Capt[ain] shall be aded if my neigh[bour][325] gives leave. Next post J[ohn] J[ohnson][326] shall have a letter to second your just demand of her conforming to the rules of the office. As to H[arry] H[ayhurst] and R[alph] Richardson[327] I will not agree to that demand of theirs. They have enjoy'd many libertys and privileges, under pretence it came first by my mo[ther],[328] which I approve not of. So must be more fully inform'd in this particular 'ere I acquiesce. Dick Allen[329] shall be remember'd for I think he justly deserves it. I've now nothing more to recomend to you, but look

[320] Elizabeth Ellison, sister of this James Clavering's mother, married John Rogers.

[321] Sir John Clavering, 3rd bart., or possibly Sir John Eden.

[322] See note 123.

[323] George Liddell, younger brother of Henry Liddell (the "Governor"). See note 218.

[324] See note 156.

[325] i.e. Sir Henry Liddell, the father of George Liddell.

[326] See note 128.

[327] Clavering tenants. See the two following letters.

[328] Anne, daughter of Sir Henry Thompson of Escrick, Yorkshire. After her death John Clavering remarried. His second wife, Elizabeth Hardwick, was the mother of Jacky Clavering, and Betty, Peggy and Milly, who appear regularly in this correspondence. *Surtees.*

[329] ? Richard Allen of Newcastle, brother-in-law of Charles Sanderson, the attorney. *Hodgson.*

for our lease of the staith, that I may be satisfied what term we have. The Go[vernor] salute you and your family. So do . . .

[P.S.] The Go[vernor] has sent you the Worcester Address to please you. Adieu.

43. Lond[on]. May 13th, 1710.

My steward became my secretary and answer'd yours of the 2d in every perticular, and I desired to know your final resolution about Mr. Craster,[330] but, as you second that demand in yours to my steward, I will venture to tell you your request will be grant'd, tho' the party is a Torry. I am in your Gov[erno]r's name to thank you for the letter you writ him. As lazyness always effects one of us you need expect no return of it fr[om] him this post. Sir J[ohn] De[laval][331] will be added for Bedl[ington]shire and, if we can but find ways and means, I may venture to say a good inclination is in our friends to putt in some other for Newcastle. As also from the same hand to tell they are concern'd to hear of your wife's usage to you, but as 'tis easy to remove the cause they desire her comissions may be return'd up, and tho' the fleet is not yet arrived yet will take care to supply your demands &c., and make your life free from strife; and himself for ever pulling his brain about other people['s] affairs for the sake of Duke Lotherdale's Dutchess.[332] So much for him. Now to our joynt concern. I thank you for your care in building the pew att Medemsly. I love to keep my pretentions in the Church and to anything that can intitle me to a word with the parson. I hope we've no incroachers on us att Ryton. I congratulate you on your late success with J[ohn] J[ohnson]. The Go[vernor] write to him, Tuesday was 7 night, and no answer. I writ last Tuesday and Thursday, by a complaint that came express from the Gate of his obstinacy, and desired a speedy answer. I wish I was as terrible to him as you observe I am to H[arry] Waters.[333] What dos G[eorge] Hall[334] mean not to have his accounts ready? But remember me about his £60. As to his cosen's £70, since the Gov[ernor] has often

[330] ? A member of the Craster family, of Craster, Northumberland.

[331] Sir John Delaval, 3rd bart., Whig M.P. Morpeth 1701-5 and Northumberland 1705-8.

[332] See note 261.

[333] See note 196.

[334] See note 156.

warnd him to pay the mony, or expect to have us make use of the law, I shall no longer forbear, but imediatly order C[harles] Sanderson to proceed against him. Be pleased to intimate as much. As to Hayhurst and Rich[ardson] I doe allow some coals ought to be given, as you mark, for the advantage of the house, but I must be convinced that those coals are burnt in our own rooms. When dos Hayhurst quit our farm? We shall have no loss of him. By the Mayor of Gateshead's silence last post I fear his spouse is ill. How succeed we in the way? I can say but little in regard to my steward. He's in great pain from his, but suppose[d], illness. His doctor is att present out of Town, but when he returns I will way-lay him and send you his opinion of his patient. Adieu. I salute your spouse and am ever . . .

[P.S.] This family salute you. I've not time to read this over.

44. London. May 27th, 1710.

You will say that you made but a seasonable complaint of Harry's manner of leaving his farm when I tell you my sister Cowper, who returnd from Hertfordshire last night, this days has made me a load of complaints on this account, viz., that the old back parlour was the tipling room; that the best of the guests were intertain'd in our room above stairs; that Harry laid his corn in the best parlour till the floor is mildued; the butter firkens were in the little parlour and the brian that run out of them had spoilt the boards; that he has took away the great pott in the furnace att the end of the kitchen-grate and says his m[ist]r[es]s gave it him. He lyes. It was sold when the kantin was att Chopwell, but not to him. He's also gott one of the barrs in the kitchin-grate away. That one of the dressers in the kit[chen] was allways 3 dressers, and the pan out of the stove there is gone likewise. Out of the garden house is gone all the shelves, the glass of all the windows, and what glass frames there was for the cocomber beds. The windows of the house are all out of repair. The fires made so seldom that the sealing [ceiling] of the rooms is droping. That that of the porch wants mending. That Ralph and he quarrell'd about this affair, but his answer was, he was putt in trust of the house by his late m[ist]r[es]s and he shoud do as seem'd him best. What is worse he has not laid any manner on the ground, but carry'd it of with him. This has made a great cry in Lin[coln's] Inn Fields and what you must see redress[ed]. He must either restore or pay for what he's took away. 'Tis not being Weatherly's friend shall make me favour him. Well Vaudois, what say you? Is it necessary by this representation to allow 40 fother of coals for fires when there was none made? No, no, that trick will not pass on chancery folks. Nay, Ralph [is] not clear. There's a great crack in the wall betwixt the pantry and the stable, which are his apartments. That the buttery, the two rooms that were nursery's were for Ralph. The new painted room as 'twas call'd, the kitchin, still-house, and the old parlour, where Duke Lauderdale used to lye, were for Harry. The rest of the house reserved, only the hall on Christening days. Pray look and see how the brewing vessells are in the brew-house and if the blew and gold leather is in one of [the] room[s] above stairs.

The Gov[erno]r bid me to tell you he's gott your knifes and forks, but Lord W[illiam] Pawlett, and Sir Harry [Liddell] have agreed that the sett coud not be compleat without spoons; that the blame is to lye on them and so the Gov[ernor] and Segnior, att a venture, have bespoke them. Your cradle and baskett I goe about of Monday and 't shall be sent with speed. As to other materials of your letter I refer them to another post when I can have more leisure to treat of them. Only before I conclude must advice you not to fear Dyer's[335] threats. The Ministry, att this bout, won't be alterd. A stop is putt att present to that schem. Adieu. I am to the Vaudois . . .

[P.S.] This family salute you. So doe I my cosen. I'd forgott to tell you Dr. Coleb[atc]h has great hopes of your Gov[erno]r, tho' he's often uneasy.

45. June 13th, 1710.

By searching my pocketts I fear I find two of the Vaudois' letters unanswred. The one of a long date and what I ought to make a long apology for had it not been caused by a mistake of your Gov[erno]r's, who, when he writ to you, was to have inserted that we agree with you in letting that part of Chopwell you mention. Fires doubtless will be of great service, yet was pleased to make a forgett thereof. Suppose, as the pott in the kitching belong'd to the girls, I take a fitt to make Mr. Hayhurst return it me and sett it in the right place. I shoud but serve him as he deserves. I am glad our coals prove so good, thought [sic] we have no vendor.

[335] See note 197.

I shall now proceed to the most materiall part of your last, which ought to have been answered last post, durst I have ventured to have given of my own head. The same I must now return you, which is, that att this time, you can have no opportunitty to proceed against your prelate. The proragations are to short.

The uproar amongst you are surprising. What are we to do? Vindicate ourselves before the Councill, and what then? I rejoyce poor Dan [Poyen][336] has escaped their furry. I hope to see a revenge, but this subject has given me the spleen so much I dare not inlarge, least I convince you of it. Therefore adieu. Believe me . . .

[P.S.] I salute my cosen, whose cradle will be ready in few days.

46. London. June 17th [1710].

'Tis well for you I was not in a writing mood last post or you had had a double trouble, for my spleen and resentment went then so high I must have comunicated some of it to you. The turning out of glorious Lord Sunderland[337] gave me some uneasiness [that] affairs had an ill prospect and I almost apprehend that might add to the necessity of my loosing some of my giddy blood this morning, for a pain in my side; but those fears are a little vanisht since the Whiggs have been so brave and daring, all to lett know that no mony was to be had, for they could not advance for the army when a Torry Ministry was to succeed, for all securitys then were nought, which alarm'd all and, by the help of present Councilours, the head Whiggs of the Citty sent for, and assurance given from the Queen's own mouth of no further change. This did not sufice, for yesterday all foreign ministers were sent to, the like assurance given them and, as I hear, a promiss not to disolve the Parliament. So they are now [beaten?] and a stopp putt to there present insolence.

The next thing in view is our girls, who the Gov[erno]r has writ about to you some time ago and proposed their coming up with his widdow, who by a letter to him, I perceive, is willing to undertake the trouble on the road, but [she is] sending to Mrs. Mitford's in your absence to lett them know when she shoud be begining the

[336] See note 62.

[337] Charles Spencer, 4rd Earl of Sunderland, 1674-1722. A Junto Whig, he had just been dismissed as Secretary of State and replaced by the Tory, Lord Dartmouth. *D.N.B.*

journey. By the message return'd it seem'd as if 'twas a surprise the children were to be removed. As she is willing to take the trouble I think, with submission to the Vaudois, we ought not to slip this opportunitty. If Milly's weakness requires the cold bath she shall goe in with me. And as to any other pretence of not having close [clothes] &c., for the journey 'twill be better to provide here. These girls were made so little and streight that they were almost useless, but to your directions I leave them. Their sisters are impat[ien]t till they see them, and, by former assurances from you, I give them hopes 'twill not be long 'ere they meet. Sure your kind indulgence to their aunt, in granting them so long a stay with her, dos not make her mistake your kindness and look on them as inheritance. They are now old enough to receive education. Jacky was never so good as this time in town. In his days [he] received praise and thanks of his friends for his courteous behaviour. I shoud inlarge, but my hand you know is tyed up so must conclude when I've assured you, I am to the Vaudois and his spouse . . .

47. London. June 27th, 1710.

I am concerned for the Vaudois, who has of late had so many afflicting peices of news sent him and perphas [perhaps] may not guess amiss, a new parliament if I say I believe my neighbour's letter last post containd as disagreable news as any. I hope I may now venture to tell you my steward is upon the recovery, having had a pretty good night last night; that before was terrible. His paper riss and satt by him for 3 hours in his nightgown. He was so ill they bled him and that operation, with a prescription of his Doctor's yesterday morning, has not only took away the pain in his side, but given great hopes of his getting a-foot again in a short time. I sent him yours yesterday with the inclosed paper and, from him, am orderd to desire you to send up the exact length of the natch of your fore and hind wheeles. He says you'd directions from my neighbour of Saturday concerning our affairs. I shall be glad to hear you came safe of from your Newc[astle] exploit and, when I know how the fitters received you, I shall presume to give an answer to J[ohn] J[ohnson's] two letters I long ago r[eceive]d and since under his own hand perceive his innocency in this riot. Since you petition so charitably for G[eorge] Hall I allow you the 14 days, or 3 weeks, he askt for; but in case of failure then, as he's often done, I expect you shoud give Mr. Barnes orders to proceed against his as the law allows, for I no longer will run these hazards, especially by those, who think themselves not obliged by the two mild and kind usage they have ever had; and had he at 1st when he entered our service, followd my advice, he might have continued in his office till his master was of age. The expence Mr. Gowland[338] putts us to is so necessary that I shall never grudge it. When I see the note you speak of, I can tell you who those things belong to. (You found them in the little cabinett I suppose.) The paper direct'd by my mother's hand, I can tell you, is a peice or 2 of gold for Mr. Bourchier,[339] left him by his grandmother and which, I think, he ought to have. I've now answerd every paragraph of yours, save the girls, which I writt about 2 post agoe. Therefore shall only add that my steward thinks the sooner remov'd the better, and as for Mrs. Bla[ckett?], I know she'd think it below her, or if condesended too, so great an obligation, it could never be return'd. 'Tis Park time. I'm call'd of. Adieu. I salute my cosen and am to you both . . .

[P.S.] Was Mr. Cotesworth ill? The Gov[erno]r had no letter from him last post. You had larger paper had I had any, but this is the last sheet of any sort I'd left. Lord Chan[cellor] is gott again to Westminster, but is farr from well.

48. London. July 1st, 1710.

As the first part of the Vaudois' requires a speedy answer I won't omitt a post, in hopes this may meet you att your return home. Our girls are now the matter in debate. I have already given you the trouble of three letters about them. This I hope may conclude the affair. Had not their friends [here?] desired they shoud have a careful eye over them upon the road, that proposal woud scarce have been made to the widdow. I doubt not of Mrs. Mitford's care and shall ever acquiese in whatever you think necessary for them; but if you keep them according to her request till after the assizes you must not think of sending them up this year. Sister Cowper will be in Hertfordshire, your Governour gone, and this family taking the fresh air somewhere, so that there will be none to whom Mrs. Mitford can deliver her charge as she desires. Before any of us return the roads will be bad and consequently the season to farr spent for child-

338 See note 124.
339 See note 76.

ren to travel. As the case is, I hope I may be allow'd to petition for an early removal, that my steward may see them settled with their sisters, before he takes his summer's progress.

My paper will not allow me to trouble you with politicks. Dyer, I fear, is not the author of a false report as to the Parliament. All things seem to tend for the advantage of the High C[hurch]. Every action confirms their power. Adieu. I salute my cosen and am to the Vaudois . . .

[P.S.] I expect our friends to return from Hertfordshire this night much better. I will answer for the country air.

London. July 11th, 1710.

49. Yours of the 4th of July came safe and, as the world goes, I comend you for your prudence. Sure the moors are the happiest abode now in Great Britain, where one is free from the busell and madness of the world. I see nothing but confusion can attend if a new Parl[iamen]t follow the changes we speak of, viz. Mr. Boyle,[340] Mr. Smith,[341] Mr. Walpole,[342] and Sir J[ohn] Holland.[343] God deliver us and send us settled in mind.

In yours I perceive I am by Hall charged of finding faults with the tenants' repairs of their houses. 'Tis false. I found indeed fault that the repairs were not sooner lookt into, for it were better for landlord and tenant; but not to repair is what I never once thought of, but this request that our materials may be gott as cheap as we can.

My steward by last post had an impertinent letter from Tom Hall[344] about giving security for our seventy pounds in case he coud not in some time pay it in, but names no time. Wherefore I beg of you to take no notice of it, but make Mr. Hargrave[345] continue the former orders he's had about him. What is G[eorge] H[all] adoing?

340 Henry Boyle, M.P. 1689-1710, who was Chancellor of the Exchequer 1701-8 and Secretary of State 1708-10. In 1714 he was created Baron Carleton.

341 John Smith, M.P. 1679-1723, Chancellor of the Exchequer 1699-1701 and 1708-10, and Speaker of the Commons 1705-8. *D.N.B.*

342 Robert Walpole, 1676-1745, who was at this time Secretary at War and Treasurer of the Navy.

343 Sir John Holland, M.P. 1701-10 and Comptroller of the Household 1709-10.

344 ? Son of John Hall, alderman and draper of Durham.

345 ? Nathaniel Hargraves, attorney to the Merchant Adventurers Company of Newcastle. *S.S.* xciii.

Pray inform me. The treachery that's in the world makes me weary of living. We were to have a motion in Chancery today. Sand[erson] has almost (by his delitary way of proceeding) made me mad. He must be changed, I believe. The opportunittys he's lost us we shall be sencible of, when there's another Keeper on the Bench. He gos northwards this sumer and then do you roast him. My neig[hbour], my steward, and self have done it sufficiently within these two days. Compagny is come in [and] forces me to cutt short. Adieu. I salute my cosen. The cradle the Gov[erno]r tells me went by one Procter, but whether he's of Newcastle or Shields, I've forgott. 'Tis direct to Mr. Mitford. I am the Vaudois' . . .

[P.S.] You and three or four more justices will prove a surprise on my Lord of Durham.

50.

Lond[on]. Aug. 8th, 1710.

By yesterday's post I r[eceive]d your kind reproof for my silence. I own 'twas the second letter I was indebted to you, but had you not two of mine before I r[eceive]d yours of the 22d of July, which I shall first return thanks for and beg of you to make my compliments to my cosen for the favour of hers, which came inclosed in it. By the account you give you've had glorious doings since the Holy Prelate came amongst you. How many more knaves and fools are there in the county than I thought of. But upon reflecting sure they have been the worst enemys that ever the B[isho]p [of Durham] had, that putt him upon this publick entry. Can this have been the best of his actions for many years, that she shoud thus be applauded? He spoke not for the Doctor, which his Br[other] of Bath and Wells[346] did. I heard indeed of one good effect, which was that his Lordship now knows what party he woud be of. For 76 years consideration he professt himself a Tory, a thing suitable to his genius, for all F[ools] and K[naves] are of that faction. But I will quit him to tell you of a glorious young rogue, Lord Ashburnham,[347] who, by the E[ar]l of Paulet,[348] was as good as closetted, to endeavour to perswade him he

[346] George Hooper, 1640-1727, who, as a high-churchman, was made Bishop of Bath and Wells in 1703. *D.N.B.*

[347] John Ashburnham, 3rd baron, who succeeded his brother William and his father John, both of whom died in 1710.

[348] John, Earl Poulett, 1668-1743, who was a Tory accomplice of Robert Harley and became first Lord of the Treasury 1710-11. *D.N.B.*

ought to resent Lord Portl[an]d's[349] being preferd to Lord Albem[arle's][350] Troop of Guards before him, who was major in the Troop; a man of quality and fortune, who might comand an interest wherever he came; and that he hoped his Lordship woud not enter into the schemes of some men, but woud always be a zealous server of his country and joyn with the Queen and her Party. The youth, with patience, heard him a full hour, then told him, "My Lord, I am not sencible of any injury done me in my Lord Portl[an]d's prefferment. Methinks 'tis an honour done the nation to have the Guards comanded by one of his quality &c., and I think it an honour to serve under him, for which reason I will keep my comission. Indeed had that empty-headed, ridiculous &c., D[uke] of Beauf[or]d[351] been preferd I should have took it for an affront and have thrown up the next day. As to the other part of your discourse [that] it tends to a vote, I will deal with you as an honest man. I design you none and, to prove myself sincere, may my estate sink under ground, my tenants be ruin'd, my family perish, and myself d[a]mn'd if ever I give you a vote". Is not this a tight Whig? Thank God his brother made room for him. Lord Albe[marle] did as well. He writ word he heard the Duke of Mon[ta]gue[352] or Lord P[ortland] had a mind to his Troop. If so, they shoud have it att their own terms, but if the D[uke] of B[eaufort] or his Party, he woud not sell. They might take it from him, but he woud't part, in that manner, from a present of his masters. This is all the news I've for you so shall proceed to yours by the last post. I am sorry to hear poor Milly is ill and of so ugly a distemper, for 'tis a devilish corrupter of the blood. I know by experience, you cast not the ill effects of that disease of some years. I am glad she was amongst you. This putt me in mind of asking your pardon if, in a letter, I some time ago writ to you, about their coming up, I said anything you coud take amiss. I designd not to give you any uneasiness. You know you last year told me they shoud come up att my sumonce and I thought no time coud be more proper than when my steward was in town, whose actions are justly approved by all. Though this, perhaps, may meet with a little sencure being a request of Lady Ann's who sure

[349] William Henry Bentinck, 2nd Earl and later Duke of Portland, who had been a Whig M.P. 1705-9.

[350] Arnold Joost van Keppel, 1st Earl of Albermarle, 1670-1718. Colonel of the Horse Guards until 1710, he fought at Ramillies and Oudenarde.

[351] Henry Somerset, 2nd Duke of Beaufort, 1684-1712.

[352] John, 2nd Duke of Montague, 1690-1749, who had served in Flanders.

never merited a good word from any northern body, having never had any. Nor can she say she is ambitious of it from any inhabitant save the Vaudois, who has proved himself so sincere a friend to the family. From all hands I hear Madam Gov[ernor] &c., makes loud complaints of the remove. I expect'd it, and, as I always fear'd a brush on this occassion, the sooner 'tis over the longer time we shall all have to forgett it; and I can but say, I hope 'tis not in the power of any to make a difference betwixt 2, who are using their utmost efforts to preserve a poor family from ruin. Adieu. I salute my cosen and am to the Vaudois . . .

[P.S.] You are desired to give an account of what happens to Mr. Baker att the Assizes.

[Enclosed.]

Kind Friend,

I think Lady Ann has given you suffic[ien]t measure and may serve for answer to two (you say) she was in your debt. However here is room enough left for the invalid to lett you know, that he rec[eive]d yours of the 28th ultim:, as well as that of the 4th, for which his thanks are due. By the first, you discover an anxiety more than ordinary ab[ou]t the menagement of publick affairs, which perhaps may in a great measure deserve itt, but you have painted to yourself a cloud much blacker than I hope itt is in reallity, which is of no other use than to plague yourself and dispiritt the well-wishers. I remember when in the utmost extremity of my illness my Dr. allways gave me hopes, tho' perhaps he had but small himself. Yet itt had a good effect. Itt raised my drooping and sunk spirits. You, in another capacity, are the Dr. You are one of the chief supports of our cause, and, when the capt[ain] hangs down his head, very well may the comon souldier, that fights under his banner, dispair of success. The fate of the Parl[iamen]t is not yet determin'd, so everybody hopes as he wishes. Neither your to Lady Ann, nor self, mentions a word of Lord B[arnard]'s resolution, which was to be deliv[ere]d you att your assizes by Mr. Forth,[353] but I guess itt, having seen a letter under his own hand 2 posts ago, wherin he discovers his inclination to the fashionable doctrine of passive obedience, by this expres-

[353] Possibly Henry Forth of Darlington who married Albinia Vane, or his son of the same names.

sion, *'tis folly att this time of day to strive against the stream.* No news fr[om] abroad, but Johny Mann's intelligence says Bethune will be in our hands by the 12 inst. att furthest. Mrs. Clav[ering's] comission to Mr. Richardson shall be executed tomorrow without fail. My man shall take his reciet. I heartily thank you for your congratulation. [I] design for the Bath middle next week. My dadd will be with you almost as soon as this. Sign[eu]r[354] salutes you, and we are both much concern'd att the irreparable misfortune befallen your table. The man shall not want a severe reproof, but that is no satisfaction to you. Certainly the breach must have bin made on ship board. My devoirs to your dowey. I am in reallity honest Jemy, thy faithfull friend.

Gove[rnor].

51. Lon[don]. Augt. 22d, 1710.

After having thankt the Vaudois for his two obliging letters I must return to my old custom of answering them as they bear date. I am glad to hear my Godson gott safe amongst you and am not a little rejoyced to hear he, by his good looks, disappointed his monkeys and went with them to church so devoutly. Pray, what remark did he make that putt a stop to the new keeper's health, who, if I am justly informd, will not att this bout have his horns exalted above those of his fellows? I writ to Doll about what you mention of the Duke before I gott yours, if 'twill have any effect.

The girls are by me and charge me with dutys to you. They goe of Saturday to Richmond for 3 or 4 days. I am sorry for the account you and Dr. Brady give of poor Milly. Pray, what dos he call her illness? For by the description, I take it to be either consumption or green sickness.

You seem pretty sanguine on the coal trade by what the judges heard, which I am glad of, though S. Swinburne,[355] I think, makes it otherwise. That is, I suppose, as his clod pate woud have it or he'd never given any account had he thought the news coud have been agreable.

I come now to yours of yesterday's post, relating to G[eorge] Hall. I wish it had been a post sooner, for my steward left us but yesterday.

[354] Sir Henry Liddell or his eldest son, Thomas.

[355] Surtees Swinburne, a Newcastle merchant, who married Jane, daughter of Cuthbert Ellison. *Surtees.*

Seg[neu]r's indisposition kept him in town 3 days longer than he design'd. I don't know what to say to you in this affair of Hall's. 'Tis what I always feard and durst have sworn, but as he's now provoked me he shall, if he pays not the ballance, rott in gaole, as his cosen shall, till my money is paid. I will now look to my pupill for he [has] been to indulgently dealt with. As to the Master business, consult my neigh[bour]. I doe find a jugling att the gate with all sorts of people. As to aunt New[ton], I refer you to the same. But for the lead I think it may yet lye. It eats no bread. I have the two bills on Mr. Lambert.[356]

Now for politicks. Did you read the cover of my last letter, wherein I sent you the news of Lord Treas[urer] being out, and desired that, with my service, you woud tell Sir Harry [Liddell] the row wisht him success att the new election? We've no new alterations yet, but dayly expect them. The Admiralty have had 2 letters, one under the Queen's own hand, to send out a fleet, for she has information that the P[retend]er is coming; and att the same time we talk of changing the Admiralty. Lord Peterborough[357] is to be in Orford's room, and assisted by Lord Haversham,[358] Sir S[tafford] Fairborne,[359] Sir J[ames] Wisherd,[360] and Mr. Trenchard[361] in this row. All the world are mad, as we shall find. Lord Scudamore[362] has broke his next [sic] by a fall from his horse, to the great regret of the Torys. Ask Sir Harry for the papers of Querrys. There's all the news. Adieu. I am to the Vaudois and his spouse . . .

[P.S.] I forgott to tell you the Queen's compliment to Colonel Crofts,[363] after she'd given him £500 for his news, was, that what added to the satisfaction she had in hearing K[ing] Charles[364] had

356 ? John Lambert, London merchant and financier. He aided Robert Harley to put his new ministry on a sound financial footing. *Boyer,* ix, 333.

357 Charles Mordaunt, 3rd Earl of Peterborough, 1658-1735. He was in fact appointed General of Marines and Ambassador to Vienna. *D.N.B.*

358 See note 16. Died 1710.

359 Admiral Sir Stafford Fairborne, M.P. Rochester 1705-10. *D.N.B.*

360 Admiral Sir James Wishart, Tory M.P. Portsmouth 1711-15 and Lord of the Admiralty 1710-14. *D.N.B.*

361 ? George or Henry Trenchard, both M.P.s from 1713 onwards.

362 James, 3rd Viscount Scudamore 1684-1716. He was a Tory M.P. 1705-16.

363 Col. Crofts returned from Spain in August, with the news of Stanhope's defeat of Philip V. *Luttrell*, vi, 619.

364 The Archduke Charles of Austria, who, as "Charles III", claimed the Spanish throne. In 1712 he became Emperor Charles VI of Austria.

beat the D[uke] of Anjou,[365] was that Stanhope[366] was the general, who she always thought an honest man.

52. London. Sept 2d, 1710.

I was of Thursday obliged to go wish joy to Sir J[ohn] Franklin's[367] daughter, who this week was married to young Mr. Worstley of Ovingham, or you then, as you expect, had your chide. Be not displeased, good Vaudois, att a few reasons I give for not joyning in your late proposal. You first say the disburstments from Christmas to May-day out-strip the rec[eip]ts and brings the ballance to six hundred and odd p[oun]ds, for which you take a morgage of 30 p. ann. att 5 p. cent., with the son's and son's son bond and judgement, and give your receipt for so much ready cash. My own sentiments on this is that you cannot doe it. You are not safe. There may be a prior morgage. If not, consider we are in Chancery and, without leave, this can't be done. But as my lawyer will be this night in town, I will inform myself and send you word next post. Next, consider, if we accept here of this security, we shall be obliged to doe the same to D[avid] D[ixon], where I must have ready mony; and that, if you ingage alone in this affair, you putt it out of my power to serve you for the future in getting the court to discharge that trustee, by desiring the mony rec[eive]d and disburst may be yours and my steward's joynt order. Consider with your neighbour, if you see him, of this till you hear again fr[om] me. And had he used us as he ought this must have putt a stop thereto, but as he has dayly repeated his insolences and I've so just a reason to resent it, don't, good Vaudois, involve yourself, for that villain. Confinement has a little terrifyed the cosen and may doe the same by this. Are we to suffer him to sell land and turn the mony to another use than paying our debt and then take what securitty he will give? No! No! Then we must doe the same by all other abusive servants. Say what you will to him till next post, but my own thoughts are rigour. And, after the letter I writ him, to think himself above writing and acknowledging his faults! It shall make him sencible the law is in my hand and that, from a friend, I can become an enemy. For may I never find mercy, nor justice, from

[365] Philip, Duke of Anjou, grandson of Louis XIV. He secured the Spanish throne as Philip V.

[366] James Stanhope, who commanded the English troops in the victories at Almenara and Saragossa, but was later captured at Brihuega in December 1710. He was a Whig M.P. and was to become a great statesman under George I. *D.N.B.*

[367] Sir John Franklin, Master in Chancery, died in 1707. *Luttrell.* vi, 200 and 205.

mankind if I bate that £600 or one farthing. Your kindness in this *as well as other affairs* my pupill and self must ever acknowledge. Our gawdy Chancery days are att end. We must walk wearily and tread sure. I wish my aunt New[ton] woud keep her promise. She's much in arrear.

I am sorry that Mill's illness increased. Her sisters are by me and very well. [They] are all your servants. They have been 4 days att Richm[on]d this week, which they are all delighted with. They send you their dutys.

No[w] for the old subject; the account of the Durham exployt in intertaining the Beaus. E[den][368] and Dav[ison][369] are valiant men. Coud they so couragiously take a boy of 9 years old prisoner, what woud they doe in a field of battle? Had I such sons, they shoud not stay att home now the comon enemy threatens us. I hope the Querrys, that I hear are dispersed over the nation, have reatch you. They are very shrewd. I see one of each and hear Mr. H[arley] and the D[uke] of Sh[rewsbury] had sent them. You don't, I hope, dispair of your namesake's election. His mama, I hear, will spend freely. God send him success. You, by my g[od]son's letter, woud hear of a lady under examination. I can, on that head, only add she is discharged, and the writs for a new parliament, I hear, will bear date the 20th instant; that Lord P[eterborough] is to be Lord H[igh] Ad[miral], Lord Ro[chester] president [of the council] and some seem to think Lord Carm[arthen][370] will comand your fleet. Sir J[ohn] Jenings,[371] they say, will keep in. Both partys love him so, that they joyn in chusing him att his borrough, and yet both own him a tite Whig. If I hear more in the evening, [I] shall add a P.S. In the meantime will only desire you to inform me if Sir J[ohn] Delaval is in the country and how his letters are direct'd. Ask no question to me. I must own business must not be neglect'd, and the thing has long depended. Adieu. I salute your spouse. When lyes she in? This family are your servants and so am I to your mama[372] and sister Alice,[373] but more perticularly the Vaudois' . . .

[368] See note 72.

[369] See note 47.

[370] Peregrine Osborne, son and heir of the Duke of Leeds, 1659-1729. Known as the Marquis of Carmarthen 1694-1712, when he succeeded his father. He had been a vice-admiral.

[371] Admiral Sir John Jennings, Whig M.P. 1705-11 and 1715-22. He was second in command at the capture of Gibraltar. *D.N.B.*

[372] Jane Clavering, daughter of Benjamin Ellison. *Surtees.*

[373] Alice Clavering. *Surtees.*

[P.S.] Cosen Smithson[374] writ to me to desire her spouse might be employ[ed] in our affairs, had we any. What say you?

53. London. Sept. 5, 1710.

As the contents of your last required consideration, so 'tis travel'd into Hertfordshire and you must wate its return for an answer. As this has happen'd I once hoped I might have given the Vaudois a letter of only congratulation on the birth of his son, which I sincerely wish him, and the mama, joy of; as also her a good and speedy recovery; but my well design'd compliment was spoild by two visiters I had this morning, viz. Mr. Oldner and Ja[cob] Linskell,[375] with a loud complaint of our coals, which are so bad and small that they won't goe of. Ja[cob] told me as he'd loaded att Stella always he wisht to continue it, but now the coal-burn mixture was so great, and the coals withall wrought so small, that they woud not goe of here; that besides they were mixt with a few of Bensham or Team, if not Wm. Cotesworth's, what he had often complaind, but in vain; that he, the next voyage, woud up to Lowry, and, if the coals proved no better, he and several customers must leave us, but 'ere they went of he'd tell me and beg I'd use my authority with the servants, for Johnson's answer was, he was by you comanded to obey Cotesworth's orders and that was the thing. I told him I was heartily sorry to hear this compl[ain]t. That the coals this voyage all over might be worse, I doubted not, for the coals we had been forced to work during the time they play'd the fool and laid idle in town, must be sold and they must blame themselves for that. That we were forced to work to keep the pittmen free of the keelmen, they had spirited up to rebellion, and the fitters [with] them.[376] I know all your tricks tho' I come not to the Gate.[377] I will assure you I will use my endeavours to have you pleased next voyage, but I can't promise. Tho' I'm the comander of the Master's affairs, every servant thinks himself above observing my orders, and no body more so than your friend J[ohn] J[ohnson], who has never, like other fitters, given me a line since the rebellion, tho' he may justly believe I know it. But when he was wanted was always gone to his country house. I observe this the more, because

[374] Mary Clavering of Callaly, born 1692. *Surtees*. She married Charles Smithson, the Newcastle attorney in 1707.

[375] Newcastle hostmen. See *S.S.* cv.

[376] See *Letters of Daniel Defoe*, ed. G. H. Healey, pp. 332 and 369.

[377] For the "Gate" see the chapter on the coal trade in *Hughes*.

formerly I knew of him how things went. But the last letter I writ att Mr. Oldner's request was answer[ed] as to a servant, which I took not myself to be. That, as to Cotesworth, I had appointed him over the servants that I might have some intelligence and know how things were; that Johnson and he were so great enemys I was sure he woud sell none of his coals, and if we mixt with Ben[sham] or Team I wonder'd they sold not better. That I feard J[ohn] J[ohnson] mixt elsewhere or he'd give an account, as other servants did, of what ships loaded and with what coals, which he would not comply to. That H[arry] W[aters'] masters, I supposed, cry'd out too, but he coud mixt with his own. "And so", sayd I, "My friend, if thou coudst but tell what a life I've amongst them, you'd pitty me, but your cry is loud now you have no gift and the fitters a constant salary". "I", said Mr. Old[ner], "Madam you realy have hitt the thing, but I must joyn with my friend. Your coals were never so bad since I knew them". "Mrs. Anne", says Ja[cob], "Thou must govern or the squire is ruin'd". "I play", says I, "The devil att this distance and you see it won't do. I think, I must come play it amongst them. However, I will do what I can for you now". Good Vaudois, as this is like to be the last voyage this year, I beg we may goe of with what credit we can, in hopes next year of success. Recomend it to Mr. Cotesworth from . . .

[P.S.] I salute your family.

54. Lond[on]. Sept. 12th, 1710.

Of Sunday I went to inquire after the method we were to follow in relation to G[eorge] H[all] and my lawyer told me, 'twas the master must consent or reject and not us, which woud indemnifye us whatever happend. That in those cases nothing is to be agreed to but [torn] the master, for that was the end and purpose of an infant's coming into that court. So that as Sanderson is abs[en]t, I must, in person, be forcd to attend him, if in town. I'm heartily concernd that the imploying of such a villain shoud run you to so great a pinch to accept of such security in so short a time, before that you coud receive any direction, tho' you may depend I will do all that lyes in my power to serve you in this *or any other* affair. But what I most dread is the consequence from D[avid] D[ixon].

I was this morning by appointment with Mr. Lambert, but he was gone to the Treasury, and so I've to trapes tomorrow to him again.

I've no news to send you. We [have] no alterations nor dissolutions yet. I wish my cosen a speedy recovery and am the Vaudois' . . .

[P.S.] The Go[vernor] seem inclinable to have a letter writ from the north to Capt[ain] Oldner, that the masters complains of neglect and discouragement att the Gate.

55. Sept. 19, 1710.

Thanks to the Vaudois for his of the 9th with the inclosed bill, which I leave with your acquaintance Alexander to re[mit] when due. I thank you for your kind invitation northwards. Had I been in earnest with J[acob Linskill or Johnson] I assure you I should have proposed no pleasure by the journey, but the seing of the Vaudois. We're att so great a distance and you so good and kind a manager, that I dare trust you with the administration of our affairs and am thankfull we are in such hands. Mine to you of Tuesday woud acquaint you with our lawyer's opinion. As things have fallen out I can't now waite on my master. Must refer it till Oct[ober]. (That Mr. Lambert's other bill becomes due when I must return to town. He remitts mony for the new Treasury so I will not putt to much confidence in a Tory. I've a bank bill in exchange for the first). I doubt not but we shall all agree, but I'll goe myself and not trust Sanderson so much with my Beau Master, nor so often.

In my last I believe I told you my steward was for a sharp letter to Capt[ain] Oldner upon complaint of our fitters, but they, I fear, give the cause, since our best efforts don't aswayge their complaints. I'm pleasd to see a bill of Harry W[ater's]. 'Tis the first I ever had the honour to look upon. I'm glad aunt Newton has performd. If I can I'll send you the girls' mony, r[eceive]d when in the country. If I'm mightly hurried then you must waite till I return to town. My steward has my rec[eip]ts for the sums he's lately given us a supply. When we've anything more to doe lett Matt. Husband have a little to try him; but he's a confounded Tory. I'm glad your spouse is in so hopefull a way. I salute her. She's not so hasty as our madam,[378] who left Lond[on] of Monday evening and Tuesday was brought to bed of a girl, before any body coud gett to her from Hertford. So she'd no midwife nor friend. We goe of Saturday, so direct as usual. Yours will come safe. If I've omitted anything, I'll make amends when in

[378] Mary, Lady Cowper.

the country. I've no news to send you. You receive no packetts; hoping my god-son gives his friends a part of his sweet-meats. Duke Laud[erda]le has obliged me for I desired and wisht his fools might see his letters. Lett him beware of H[igh] Sheriff next year. The Duke of Som[erset] is disobliged att the Torys. But say not one word. I'm glad Milly is better. Pursue what rules you please. I leave all to you. Adieu . . .

56. Sept. 28th, 1710.

I am uneasy not to have heard of the Vaudois for sometime. I, one time, fear the illness of his spouse prevents his writing. Att others, I fear thy letters, which are open'd, are lost. However 'tis, I take the first oportunitty of acquainting you I re[ceive]d the bill of £62-12s-3d and shall pay it to my sister for Jacky's use. Pray send no more. I'll live on creditt till I can say your letters are not open'd and you see my old seal, unbroke, come to your hands. I should be concern'd att this usage, did I not reflect it was for the improvement of the ignorant. For a free air is now amongst us, and that so often complaind of nicety of the English, laid aside, for a more familiar correspondence. Pardon this digression. (Now I've resolve[d] to submitt passively to fate and lett the Church doe what it will, but touch my lands) and tell Harry Waters, Mr. Dove[379] never had notice the bill was drawn on him, tho' he's paid it.

All here are well. Our little one will receive a name this week. I wish good news from you and as much as you please of our own affairs, but no politicks, I charge the Vaudois, whose friends here live att ease and now, I may say, enjoy themselves. The family salute you and spouse. So dos . . .

[P.S.] I wish my godson success.

I have not time to write a larger letter. The mail stays. Therefore can only thank you for yours, which I r[eceive]d since this was writ and that I wish my cosen a speedy recovery and that my service may be returnd my godson whose loss I lam[en]t.[380] This family salute you once more. I'll [torn] over Wm. Cotesworth. Yours came unopend.

[379] John Dove, c. 1684-1734. *Hodgson*. For the Dove family see W. W. Tomlinson, *Historical Notes on Cullercoats, Whitley and Monkseaton*. (1893).

[380] James Clavering lost four sons and two daughters in infancy. It was not until 1718 that Thomas, who was the first to reach maturity, was born.

57. [Endorsed: Oct. 3rd, 1710.]

I take the first opportunity of thanking the Vaudois for his letters as well as reproofs. Since I writ my last our little one is become a Christian, and my namesake, and who shoud be our gossip but the great Tory Coulson. Dos not this look like triming and yet I assure you we are as firm as rocks. I durst not write in the changes. The letters from hence I believed had the fate of others, wherefore I thought it best to be silent, which I hope may plead my excuse to you.

I am glad my cosen recovers. If wishes have any effect, she comands abundance from hence. As to our pupill I can say no more than that the messenger, which carris this [to] London, putt me a letter into the peny-post to Captain Oldner, to whom you gave me a fair opportunitty to return complaints. And what answer, you shall have. But this [?business], good Vaudois, I understand not, and 'twas not done with my consent nor approbation, which, you may intimate, is a liberty I approve not of, nor allow. If my steward has been consulted in it I'm a stranger. We're now att a great distance and I suppose he's again took occasion to [act?] ill.

I must now proceed to tell you that your last spoil'd my supper and broke my rest. Oh God! What can become of us when our friends refuse to be such. 'Twas, I own, what I apprehended from my god-son's[381] first leaving us. Give me leave to ask, is he less healthfull than he was or dos he propose benefitt by the country air this winter? This is establishing the interest of the youth for ever; and can he be so cruel to his friends, who for so many years have suffered persecution for his sake, to dissist att this juncture. Can he, after having so often prevail'd by that God, money, throw up att a time when he must be of use and when he might lay a claim for others to come in upon. When I am turnd out by force is one thing, and when I give up is another. Nay when my monkeys were divided and an honest man att one time or another, by that interest, might have prevaild, when now he renders it impossible. He had notice of the Diss[aster?] to prepare for it, tho' he believed it not. Who joyn'd with him in opinion, I know not. But, like all conceited folks, I fancy'd my intelligence good, therefore always acquainted him. I pretend not to advice, but must be concern'd att this resolution. He's a person who need no directions and, I dare be confedant, dos what

[381] Jacky Clavering.

he thinks best. Yet I wish he, att this time, had a more daring spiritt. We Cla[verings] have too much in every respect, but, whigism and my heart, I'm resolved to keep above water. When I can conquer this stroke, my god-son shall hear from me. In the meantime I beg of you to deliver a service, as also to your spouse, and Matt. and spouse, if with you. This family salute you all. 'Ere I conclude, must not omitt to tell in my last from Bath my steward markt, you woud do well to covenant with Mr. Sm[ithson][382] before we employ'd him. I suppose it relates to principles. If our girls are for coming, might they not come up with Doll Waite,[383] whose care I will answer for. Adieu.

58.

Oct. 16th, 1710.

I re[ceive]d yours when last in town, but was so hurried I had not time to thank you for it 'ere I left London. I went on Mr. Lambert's bill, which was satisfied. This is conveid by Dr. Colebatch to the post. Our Lady here has been two days so ill of the gripes that we fear'd the bursting of the guts. She's better I thank God and in a hopefull way to be sett right if she follows directions. I am concerned my poor cosen continues ill so long. I sincerly wish her a perfect recovery. As to my girls I am, with you, concernd you shoud meet with so many disappointments. I've spoke to Mrs. Caverley and desired she may inquire after some carefull person to take the charge of them up and then acquaint the Gov[erno]r for his consent and to advice you thereof, if you approve of this method.

For politicks, all things are so ill I will, if possible, never think more. My godson, I hear, sees his cause revenged, and, tell him from me, I beg, that his guardian thinks it time for him to look southwards, especially as we all suspect he will make visitts upon the road to the houses in affliction. Time, I hope, will come when your namesake's interest will be of service, tho' att present slighted. I am glad you've ended with G[eorge] H[all]. I've only time to tell you I writ from hence to the Gate, but have had no answer. My steward will be in town of Saturday. So then he may look after them. My letter is call'd for. Adieu. I salute your spouse and am good Vaudois . . .

[P.S.] My old sceal must be your guide.

[382] See note 374.
[383] See note 59.

59. London. Oct. 31st, 1710.

My hurry has been so great since I went back into the country and returnd to town that I have now an opportunity of thanking you for two letters. I had writ last post had not sister Cowper sent for me to her, before she left the town. I am heartily concernd to hear your spouse is still so weak. She has my best wishes for a speedy and perfect recovery. I beging this in the morning before I can give you the sentiments of my steward in regard to our pupill's affairs, so shall beging with my own. I am sorry you coud not send me a copy of my own and I fear you will have no opportunity. It must only be handed amongst the Torys. I have, sometime agoe, raised that sett of liars southwards, as I've intimated to the lady by this post; but you are not quite in the secret I find. 'Tis Tom T[itt?] and R[obert] W[alpole?], who first sayd it was a reflection upon the prelate and lady, but as yet coud not be made out. I find the other raised. The lady and Duke have quarrel'd about the Duke's warmth, so I've thank'd her and told Sir Jo[hn Clavering] that ingratitude to my fa[ther's] memory may be worse to him than all the services that those 2 men can do for him. Lett us comfort one another, good Vaudois. Mine can't be made scandal magnatum so I keep up my whigish phylosophical resolution and the courage of Robin Walpoole, who is the person I copy after. Capt. Jumper's[384] letter, writ by Lord Orford's comand, the Post-Boy printed. If mine have the same fate, I shall take it for a great honour to succeed so great a man. Yet you and I are in better circumstances than Mr. Tong,[385] who I'm told is to be suspended for calling Sir H[enry] B[ellasyse's] lady, att the election, "w[hore]". If the priest have that liberty, sure the liberty, laity, that depend not on them, may take it. But I abhor that name and I can't tell you the Dut[chess] takes it not to herself nor so ment, and as for copys there was one att the High Sh[eriff's] sometime agoe. Inuendos and forced constructions are the only means left them; and I only desire you will give my service to my godson, whose indispositions I am sorry for and whom I desire this may not be a matter of concern. Were I not once in 4 or 5 years to do something extraordinary, I should not be remembered amongst that sett of vipers. I shoud be glad to see you, but not on the account you mentiond.

My sister come this night to town to look [for] a house. They mett

[384] Sir William Jumper, a navy captain who had served at Cadiz and Gibraltar.
[385] Rev. John Tonge. See note 233.

not with one when last in town. Lord Keeper[386] comes into theirs. Your friend, young Hetherington, is advanced to be Deputy Purse Bearer in the room of Roberts, who sometime since caned the P[ost] Boy. I can only, on that subject, add that that new lord is resolved to follow the steps the other trod. The Chancery is to be kept in the same manner. Mr. Cowper[387] is the 2d man, without the bar, calld of, which the Torys res[en]t.

Now to my pupill. The reproof you've given Lowry and Allen are just. But permitt me to tell you, as I have leave from my steward, so I must beg you will order and command the waggon-men, who run their wag[gons] over the staith or who were the cause of their neighbours' misfortunes, to be discharged without any delay. For, shoud we once pardon this petty treason against us, we shoud always have them plotting our ruin. Wholesome severitys the Torys will allow, because 'tis S[acheverell's] doctrine, and lett us beging here.

As soon as I can gett your letter of H[all's] account from sister Cowper I will personaly wait on my master. Under that pretence, for the following reason, Sanderson has often told me that we coud hope for no better security from D[avid] D[ixon] than the remainder of a morgage your Fa[ther] has of Mr. Widdrington,[388] which I like not. Therefore to prevent any mistakes I will discourse him myself and not trust it to Sanderson.

60. London, Dec. 7th, 1710.

This is the 5th post day that I've had my pen in hand to thank the Vaudois for a letter (of so old a date I am ashamed to mention it) and have still been prevented by compagny or ingagements abroad. My steward, having answerd the parts of your letter that referrd to business, I was, on that score, the more dilatory. I also waited on sis[ter Cowper] to know of her, if coud inform you about the peices of gold your paper of perticulars mentions, but she is so busy a furnishing a little box that's impossible to gett a word with her att present.

You, I hope, desire no publick news. There's little stirring. The Parliament, to dispatch late petitions, have some att the Barr of the

[386] Sir Simon Harcourt was appointed Lord Keeper, when Lord Cowper insisted on resigning as Lord Chancellor.

[387] Spencer Cowper, younger brother of Lord Cowper, was M.P. and a barrister.

[388] ? A relative of William, Lord Widdrington.

house. Stanhope's is one.[389] How happy are we now to have a Parliament not only resolved to redress our grievances, but to prosecute the warr with vigour, and especially in Spain. This is, I hear, what the great Johnny Marl[borough] approves of and what he joyns in. Tho' thanks for his last year's campaign is referrd till he appears in person. A gent[leman] told me the other day that amongst the H[igh] C[hurch] he heard them rail att [Sa]cheverell and say he was madd, he was a fool, and, what Stanhope justly stiled him, an insignificant tool of a party. For he'd left his flock in Southwark to take lodgings in Westm[inste]r, to be near his Parliament, and every day appeard in the Court of Request, and calld himself the sun, and was so angry his suspention was not took of and that he was not made chaplain to the Commons or Lord Keeper,[390] that he hufft att mankind; and that now none but Sir J[ohn] Water[391] and friends spoke to him. If once they beging to dispise this holy man, what are we to expect? The D[uke] of Shrews[bury] has sett up an assembly and I hear the D[uke] of Kent, D[uke] Or[mond], Lord Port[land], Sir J[ohn] Germaine[392] and others are to follow the example. Are we not in an age of pleasure and lead we not merry lives if we like it? I must from this come to the old A[rch] B[ishop],[393] who, as I hear, was sent to from the Queen, to tell him when the Convocation mett, from him she expect'd to have it kept in order. The good old man, as the Town says, return'd answer, that theyr heats woud not concern him. The Queen was the head of the Church and what she comanded, shoud be fulfill'd by him. Is he not meritorious to own a supremer power over the Church? I will conclude all with a horse course, if you've not already seen it, and, as a jockey, you may, if you like, bett. Adieu. I salute your spouse and am . . .

[P.S.] Keep the course to yourself and friends.

61. London. Dec. 12th, 1710.

I readily lay hold this opportunity of writing, tho' it be to trouble the Vaudois, that I may convince him my late silence was no dis-

389 Stanhope stood for Westminster, but was defeated and petitioned. He had to come in by a seat at Cockermouth.

390 The new Tory Lord Keeper was Sir Simon Harcourt, one of Sacheverell's defenders.

391 Sir John Walters, M.P. Oxford.

392 Sir John Germaine, son of a Dutchman, was M.P. Morpeth 1713-15.

393 Thomas Tenison, 1636-1715, Archbishop of Canterbury.

respect. Know then, that amongst all the proposalls D[avid] D[ixon] has made to repay us, none seems so fair as that assigning over to us his part of the Duke's lease, wherein your Papa is concern'd, for a security that in 6 months he shall pay in the mony, in case the master approve of it. Saunderson has therefore writ to Mr. Gowland this post, to desire of him to goe to your Papa,[394] to inquire and look into those deeds, and, with your Papa's permission, to send us copy's of what will be neccessary, which I hope you may venture to interceed for, on our behalfs, that we come to some conclusion with that worthy gen[tleman].

I have no news for you. Therefore I will gett this frankt as the only way I have to excuse the trouble given by the Vaudois' most humble servant . . .

[P.S.] I beg a humble service to your spouse.
[Additional postscript by the Governor.] Honest Jemy, pray thee do me the same fav[ou]r and believe me to be your affec[tiona]te friend, Gov[erno]r. I hope Madame Governanse has recover'd the fright the Alderman putt her in.

62. London. December 21st, 1710.

Since my silence fills the Vaudois' brains with chimeras, I will for the future take what care I can to prevent it, (att least till the Parliament has doubled the price of letters as 'tis at present talkt of). You taxs me with owing a thing I assure you I am ignorant of. So soon may the innocent be thought guilty! Why do you give creditt to all our foolish northern reports, especially to one the world ought to have been weary of some years since. However I have many thinks to return the good Vaudois for his kind wishes. Therefore will not disown that my head these 2 or 3 last years has run much after a lady's, but the person, whom my inclination lead me to think of, was a North B[rito]n.[395] This year he's forfeited my warm heart by voting for the new Lords returned to Parlia[ment] and now I've fixt it on a Whig bully in hopes of better success, tho' his wife is yet living, [being?] I can neither speed with widdowers nor batchelours.

[394] James Clavering of Greencroft, 1646-1722, 2nd son of James Clavering of Axwell, 1st bart.

[395] A Scot, who had obviously voted for the 16 Scottish peers, who were nearly all Tories in 1710.

That part of your last, that relates to business, I will reffer to another opportunity. That's after I have discoursed my steward. So will fill this with the transactions of the Brittish Parl[iament] as I hear them. I will first begin with good Lord Wm. [Pawlet], who in the comittee carried his Election, tho' his councill did what they coud to give him up and my good cosen Grizill said he hoped in God the House woud *root* him, when 'twas reported to them. Lord W[illiam] had near 50 votes the majority, therefore you can't say his namesake was a little partial. The next day the late Chancellour, late Chief Jus[tice] and the two secretarys[396] were roasted on account of the Bewdley Charter,[397] which argued in Chan[cery] before Sir J[ohn] Holt, the Queen and Councill, before 'twas granted , and, after that, confirmed by the last Parliament, by which Comodore Cornwall[398] satt the last P[arliament]. I need only say that Mr. Antho[ny] Lechmere[399] was returned by the new charter and Mr. Winninton[400] by the old. Mr. Freeman[401] of Hertf[or]dsh[ire] open'd the cause and all the rethorick that coud be musterd, was, on this occasion. Att last Mrs. Stotes' Mr Shippen[402] said, 'twas arbitary and illegall and tended to the distroyeing the constitutions of Parliaments, [and] that an humble address shoud be presented to her Maj[esty] to repeal the Charter. This was carried 213 against 53, with leaving out the first word, tho' one certain considerable man shoud say 'twas the most arbitary and illegal proceeding ever heard of, save the business of Edmunds, for which Dr. Harris and poor Piershouse[403] lost their places. The S[olicitor] Gen[eral][404] condemd the Charter, spoke much to the memory of Sir J[ohn] Holt, never mentioned Lord Cowper, tho' he made him S[olicitor]

[396] i.e. Lord Cowper, Sir John Holt, Henry Boyle and Lord Sunderland.

[397] There was a great election dispute in 1710 about which Bewdley charter was valid. *Boyer*, ix, 264 and 268.

[398] See note 230.

[399] Anthony Lechmere, Whig M.P. He was unseated. Brother of Nicholas Lechmere, who had been one of the Whig managers of the Sacheverell impeachment.

[400] Salway Winnington, Tory M.P. Bewdley 1694-1708, 1710-14. Connected by marriage with the Harleys and Foleys.

[401] See note 11.

[402] See notes 33 and 232.

[403] Lord Chancellor Cowper had dismissed Peter Persehouse, as secretary of the commission of lunacy, and also his chaplain, Dr. Harris, for being too officious about a commission of lunacy against Mr. Edmunds of Hertfordshire. He then reversed the verdict. *Luttrell*, vi, 594.

[404] Sir Robert Raymond, 1673-1733. *D.N.B.*

Gen[eral]. Sir J[ohn] Pack[ington] [405] was glad to see the face of a Brittish Parliament, the former one looking like military ones. This reminds me of a pleasant whims of your Richmond representative H[enry] M[ordaunt],[406] who, 'tis said, came into the house and aloud said, "I much [sic] goe into the Court of Request to try if I can meet a face I know, for by [God] I know not one here". The Whigs pleaded hard and home on the behalf of their late friends, Sir Jo[seph] Jekyll,[407] Mr. Lech[mere], &c., and honest R[obert] Walpole, who, when he'd said all he coud, told them, if they past that vote, 'twas branding the memory of one great man, endeavouring to blott the caracter of the greatest living and 'twas to him——, and so made a low bow and satt down.

I am glad to hear my girls are well and, when I've seen my steward, I will answer your proposal. Betty, poor girl, had last Sunday, two violent fitts of her astmah, but is now well again, by the help of the apothecary only. Jacky is come and proves a bully on the Whig side. Give me leave to trouble [you] with a story relating to him. Att Eaton the school is devided W[hig] and To[ry]. Jacky was one day ingaged fighting a Tory boy and Lady Oglethorp[408] came and bid him give over. Jacky pursued his quarrel so she call'd him names, and told him she'd box him if he gave not over. [She] came up, but mist her blow. This, you may believe, fired Johny, who turnd and gave her a severe blow on the face and bid her a Popish hussy, putt her child in the warming-pan and carry it the Queen and make the nation believe 'twas hers. I've scarce left room (to tell you I write to Lady Cla[vering] this post about Mr. Wright's[409] advice) nor to give the services of this family to you, to whom I am . . .

[P.S. In the Governor's hand.]

Pray send to Geo. or Tom Hall and either will settle my account with you. I have not my books so can't inform further than that I am indebted to the concern only £5 this last year.

[405] Sir John Packington, M.P. Worcestershire 1690-95 and 1698-1727. He was a leading back-bench, high-church Tory. For his speech on the Bewdley Charter see *Parl. Hist.* vi, 932-4.

[406] See note 309.

[407] Sir Joseph Jekyll, Whig M.P. 1697-1738. A barrister and brother-in-law of Lord Somers, he was a manager of the Sacheverell impeachment.

[408] Eleanor, widow of Sir Theophilus Oglethorpe, whose son was a Jacobite.

[409] William Wright, chairman of Durham Quarter Sessions, a mine-owner associated with Sir John Clavering at Tanfield. *Hughes.*

63. London. Dec. 30th, 1710.

This is the first week of our having a coach to visit withall (my uncle being but just returnd out of Yorkshire), which business has these 2 post prevented my writing to the Vaudois. And, tho' I'm invited out to dinner, in order to spend the whole day, I will spare some small time to tell you, that if you continue your thoughts of the manner proposed to send our girls, tis was [?what] is approved of here; and whatever agreement you make with the servant shall be punctually performd; and whenever you think it convenient to send 'em we shall be glad to receive them.

As to the purchase you mention, if 'tis what you think convenient, we must acquaint the master. For the court, you know, is to direct us how the mony is to be disposed of. D[avid] D[ixon] now works himself into what is of no use to him. He's angry I am not content, nor don't approve of his menagement, and wish the rest of the mony may be as well account'd of. [He] thinks it a great hard[shi]p, after his services to the family, that I shoud scruple his anuity or charge him more than he likes. I vow I think by his expressions his troubles some time confound his thoughts. As soon as Mr. Gowland give the account of that lease, we shall proceed as farr as possible.

I have no news to send you. The disgarded officers and the D[uke of] M[arlborough] is all the talk. Some say a conformity bill will be brought in soon, but time must prove that. Consider I am to dress, therefore excuse hast in . . .

[P.S.] This family salute you. So do I, my cosen. I am to tell you from my steward that he spends this day upon a dull whisk [sic] invitation, with the gentlemen at the end of the row, if he can gett.

64. London. Jan. 16th, 1710[/11.]

As I have always been famous for contradiction it will be no surprise to the Vaudois to tell him my Christmas rambles begun, when Christmas was ended. I had Turkey feast to attend and a whig play, which occasiond my not sooner thanking the Vaudois for his good wishes and New Year's Day letter, but the telling him also I rejoyce Milly, and now Jenny, are so well gott over those 2 dreadfull diseases, small pox and measells.

You take me, I perceive, to be a new acquaintance of a worthless, I shoud say worthy, divine. Pass not so hard a sensure on me, I desire. I knew so many more of that robes than's good, that I avoid them now as much as possible, but woud sooner goe to hear their doctrines than follow their practice. News, I know, you will expect. I know nothing of Comons. My mind runs after Lords and great men. You must have heard Lord Pe[terborough] is gone to Vienna with the thanks of the Lords for his great services in Spain,[410] and Lord Gallaway,[411] Lord Terlawly,[412] and poor Stanhope sensured, without leave to produce a paper by way of defence. This is not all the surprising scene. The Lords of the Councill are sensure[d] in the same manner, for the advice by which Spain was lost, and consequently Toulon. A majority of 20 against them and when call'd on to deffend themselves their mouth were ty'd, and, without the Q[ueen's] leave, they could not divulge the councills. Upon which the white staffs were detatch'd to know her pleasure, who graciously gave them leave to discover all. The D[uke of] Or[monde] was then a cabinett man, and generously sensured himself. Mr. Harley was then Secretary, and 'twas then a mixt ministry. Lord Lindsay[413] came to the Whigs, when he see the speed the others made. The Bishop of Winchester[414] is with the distresed. Lord Ossulston, the B[isho]p of Litchfield,[415] the D[uke] of Newc[ast]le,[416] Lord Pembroke, and that glorious honest youth, Lord Lincoln,[417] who has nothing but a pension to depend on, and vote for his country. I've heard a bird whisper he woud not loose thereby. Pray God it may be true. Now the managers of this are, as I hear a-visiting, Duke Beauf[ord], Duke Arg[yll], Lord Scarsdale, Lord North, &c.; men of worth, who are indifatigable in the service of there country. Shoud I now be sensure, I should value myself so much, that I shoud scarce know how to behave myself.

Friend, I wish you joy of your idle life. Be of good cheer. What has been, may be, the Torys and papists say. Who knows who may be sensured and who thankt? But I must conclude. Compagny to pass

[410] For the great debate in the House of Lords on the conduct of the war in Spain see *Parl. Hist.* vi.

[411] Henri de Massue, Marquis de Ruvigny, 1648-1720, was a Huguenot refugee, who became Earl of Galway and a general in the British army.

[412] See note 4.

[413] Robert Bertie, 1660-1723, Marquis of Lindsey and later Duke of Ancaster.

[414] Sir John Trelawney, 1650-1721, Bishop of Winchester since 1707. *D.N.B.*

[415] John Hough, 1651-1743, Bishop of Coventry and Lichfield and later Bishop of Worcester. *D.N.B.*

[416] John Holles, 1662-1711, Duke of Newcastle and Lord Privy Seal.

[417] Henry Clinton, 1684-1728, 7th Earl of Lincoln.

the evening are come in. Adieu. My best wishes attends your spouse, and believe me . . .

[P.S.] My uncle and aunt salute you. Duke Richm[on]d, I fear, is a time server. He voted against Lord Gallaway.

65. London. Feb. 13, 1711.

When I've scearcht my pockett and find a letter of the good Vaudois from Richmond, yet unanswerd, I wish for my own [sake] I had not been so exact in looking to the dates of those letters that lye [by] me. However I will pass it by in silence (as there's nothing material in it) and come to that dated of the 30th Jan[uary], in which you complain of want of health. But coud I believe you so much Tory, to passively submitt to the peal, you mention, when you re-turnd from killing a brace of hares, my compassion for you woud sease. Yet, as you have renounced pollitickss and talk so passively, I don't well know what judgement to make. You may, for all that, resist and be for the Church. Tho' this may seem an objection, yet to shew you I believe you still Whig, (tho' you may be raised out of the Com[mission] of Peace) and so moderate in your censure and revenge, that, as you desire, I may joyn with you in taking some on my steward. Lett me know what you propose and I will, if I can, assist you therein. I am concernd to hear you are so perplexd as to threaten some with the Peace. Your reports I think I shall contradict at the end of this letter, and, whenever I do change my name, I shall not disown it. Till then, believe not what you hear. I, perhaps, can guess why all this [torn] and why my friend Vaudois is so teazed. Nothing of that kind, I can assure you, has prevented my not writing sooner. I have been out of order and can't now say I am perfectly well, and holding down my head is troublesome. I hear Lady Clavering gives Doll [Waite] up for author of her news. How comes Doll by the secret, whom I've not seen her, I don't know the day when, tho' I must att the same time own I'm the faulty person? This may serve to convince you, who are a reasonable man, of the little creditt is to be given to the world, who are always making and breaking matches. I'm of opinion, as long as the world marrys me, I shall never change my state of life. Nay, I don't know but I was as near it of my Christening day as I am now.

Charles Sanderson tells me by my steward, for he won't come near me, that he's yet had no account of Mr. Gowl[and] about that lease I writ so long agoe of to you. Now the first, I fears, a canary bird, so wish you coud spurr up the last, that I might see the mas[te]r and come to some end of our affairs. They frett me and plague me to death, for I believe we shall never gett farther. So those parts of your letters must yet remain unanswerd.

I am glad the girls are coming, by which I shall be free of the troublesome questions of those here. As to Mr. Bourchier's gold, 'tis only the peice that lapp'd up and writ on for him. As you've renounced politicks for once, I once take you att your word and so will conclude in assuring you I am . . .

[P.S.] I salute my cosen.

I've lately received a letter from Mr. Poyen, who desires Mr. Bernardeau and he may be chapmen for some lead, which my [sister?] and I agree to. They will speak to you of it.

66. London. Feb. 20th, 1710[/11.]

I had resolved before the Vaudois' came to hand, to give him the trouble of a letter by this post, to acquaint him that of Friday last my steward received a letter from George Hall to desire an enlargement of the time for paying in the mony; that if he sold the estate now 'twould be to great loss, and as he had ever behaved himself with the utmost respect to us all, he hoped we shoud consider his poor family, and stuff to this effect, which did not a little surprise me. Now, good Vaudois, consider 'twas att your intersession I so long forbore, and I now demand of you a hearing. 'Tis not with the consent of the master we have proceeded in this affair. Therefore, as the time of payment is come and the mony no nearer to us than formerly, I will neither lett you nor myself be laid lyable to inconveniences that may attend us on this occasion, and therefore request you to proceed against the said G[eorge] Hall in the most vigorous manner the nature of the affair permitts, for shoud we grant six months longer we shoud have the same request att the end of that time, and so to the world's end. [But], in case when this is read to Hall, he desires a forbearance till he receives Mr. Liddell's answer, this is all he's like to have, for the Gov[erno]r has been a housekeeper near a week and is to ill still to answer any letter. So you must excuse him to that person of so excellent behaviour that must move our compassion, but I will leave him to you, in hopes you'll do us all justice, and tell you, I sent yours to the sick, who, in return, desire his service and to tell you 'tis 10 days agoe since he gave you notice your mares were sett forwards and before this reaches you he hopes they are safe in your custody. I heard a week agoe they were gott well to Stamford. As to other matters you'll give me leave to be silent till I can see and trouble my steward with them; save the girls, which will be heartily welcome and hope come perfectly safe, and prevent the going forward of some people's discourse. Your other directions shall be observd. Had I any news I'd send none to one who stiles himself a Trimer. But will undertake to chide one for never naming wife nor bairns when they write. Adieu. I to your spouse and self . . .

[P.S.] Newc[astle] is now a merry divided town. Their inferiour representative[418] had att supper lately the great Dr. [Sacheverell?] and six other parsons. Their only wanted the old woman to make it fitt for a Gunpowder plott.

67. Feb. 24th, 1710[/11.]

Whether I am my own or your Gov[erno]r's secretary I leave to the Vaudois to determine. I am first therefore to tell you, from that gentleman, your cloths are bespoke. But, as you lately have asumed the title of Trimer, he's took you att your word and made your new habitt of the Church nor Republican colour, but betwixt the two. Now, Sir, I am farther to tell you, if you expect this suite compleat you must send up by the return of the post the mesure of your head, for that, your Gov[erno]r vows, he brought it not out of the north with him.

I come now to my pupill's affairs, therefore shall range the objections in order. As to the fitting out ships, we have parts in, my steward tells me 'tis unavoidable or we must dispose of them. However, I think you'd doe well to call on Mr. Johnson for an account of those ships, we have parts in, and desire att the end of every year he woud bring to account, who we have r[eceive]d profitt of and who not.

2dly, 'tis lookt on here to be the only way to dispose of our keels. The article of repairs, I observe, runs very high. The properest way therefore to dispose of them is to send for a carpenter to purchase them of us and, if he will advance us anything in

[418] The two Newcastle M.P.s were Blackett and Wrightson. The latter was probably the inferior representative.

the price, we shall oblige ourselves to take them of him, for such a number of years as you think fitt, att the common price of keels, and so take out our debt, if he can't pay the mony down. Wm. Cotesworth will assist you in this affair.

3dly, I can but comend the Vaudois for the just objections he made to the negotiating bills. The salary is now so good I shoud have thought that article might have been omitted. But supposing that for the future he will make good the master's notes, we shall allow it. But if he insists upon it, that it is what's allow'd to other fitters, we must complye rather than quarrell, which I think a hard sentence.

Lastly, as for the premium to masters, as our coals were badd this year I fear we must allow it. However, you may cavil a little on that score, but not break and assure them that for the future, as this new seam is so hopefull, no such thing shall be allowd of hereafter.

For the agreement att the Gate, nothing can be done for us there till that affair of the last year is settled with 'em. It woud gett air and turn to our disadvantage, so we must be dormant and wait with patience till a fitt opportunitty. You are desired to be, and [I] advice you to be, cautious of what is said concerning the coal trade. As you will perceive, by the Gov[erno]r's to the Cap[tain], things have already took air that may lead us into trouble, and if Mr. Cotesw[or]th come up, [as] projected, it must be given out he comes upon his own business. 'Tis so late I can only see to add my best service to your spouse, and assure you I am . . .

[P.S.] My steward charges me with his services to you and family. Mr. Gowl[an]d send word our securitty is to be Mr D[ixon's] word, that all the mony shall be paid before May day.

68. London. March 3d, [1710/11.]

As I had nothing material to impart to the Vaudois I differ'd writing till I coud give him an account our girls were safely arrived and in very good plight. [They] had as good a journey as the season woud permitt, and from York had my uncle Allanson's b[rothe]r, who has been kind beyond expression. I've left the 4 sisters together and Mrs. Caverley has took a lodging for Mrs. Milly near her so that my servant or one of theirs shall always be with her.

I must return you thanks for your dispatch to Mr. Gowl[an]d.

In my last I told you the word of a gentleman was to be our securitty. Since then, till this afternoon, coud not sett face of Sanderson and I have rung him such a peal that I believe he won't be fond of coming again. He denyed neglecting us, either now or att any other time, and he'd write to Mr. G[owland] and D[ixon] and demand further securitty or take him up upon contempt of the court. I woud neither hear nor answer, and we parted in a huff. For 'ere I take a resolution on this head I must advise with your Gov[erno]r, who I apprehend will give over writting, in case anybody will ease him. His papa is out of order, therefore your letter is dispatcht to me, that I may tell you the measure of the child's head was not inclosed in the letter as you mention and that caps or hats are cheifly used, but he will waite your further orders as to this commission.

I [am] also comanded from the same hand to tell you that J[ohn] J[ohnson] ought to be gently used in this affair. If it be a thing of moment and worth prosecuting, then doe it, but, if 'tis a triffle, he will take snuff at it and make it a handle to leave the concern. And where are we then? And in regard to G[eorge] Hall, we both agree that if Mr. Hedworth[419] will give us securitty, that he takes the debt upon him, and he shall have ½ a year time to pay it in. This is the resolution here, if you agree thereto.

I can't conclude without telling you I was yesterday surprised with a req[ue]st made to me, to contribute something to burry Dr. Durant withall, who dyed mearly of want of necessarys, unknown to his wife or any friend. She was to come up to him this summer, believing he gott a good living in town. But this is to melancolly a subject to inlarge upon and therefore shall only add my best to your spouse and assure you I am . . .

69. London. March 29th, 1711.

Your last is off so old a date (tho' unanswerd) that I am resolved to overlook it and proceed to tell you Mrs. Milly sett forwards for the County of Durham last Monday. I gave £8. for coach hire and 30sh. for expences and, if that don't do, you are to make up the difficiency. I gave her three guineas for her care and trouble and hopes she was satisfyed with her journey. I am sure she ought, for the girls did rarely with her. They are fine girls indeed, but the confoundest Torrys I ever heard.

[419] John Hedworth of Harraton, 1683-1747, who was a mine-owner and later M.P. Durham County 1713-47. *Hughes*.

In the next place I must putt you in mind, that sometime agoe you told me amongst your papers you found something you fancyd might be of use to us, betwixt Sir John [Clavering] and my papa. Pray lett me know what it is, for the D[uche]ss [of Lauderdale] writ me last post that she'd sent the copy of the account to her cosen Wright, with orders to waite on me, who I believe will not care to come the errant, as I shall intimate to her this post.

The first thing I observe in yours is a civill reproof for twice admonishing you not to quarrell [with] J[ohn] J[ohnson]. Lett me tell you that was not my fault. Your Gov[erno]r dictated, and I writ, and then gave it him to read. I perceive the repitition as well as you. You need compassion in the multitude of business you have. The thoughts of those accounts craze my head and I've fought so long and to so little purpose that D[avid] D[ixon], which is the first thing to be settled. I've given up and your partner must manage as he can, for Sanderson is as much above my hand as D[avid] D[ixon] can be. The latter, you know, is under contempt of the court and, least he shoud slip you, I see but one way I've left, which is to sue the trustees for not proceeding in your affairs. Beware of me. You see I'm a woman of humour and so I am, but as the French say, no penchant for the lawyers and their worse creatures, the attorneys. The Lord, I hope, will reward you for the troublesome and vexatious days you have upon our score.

Perhaps you will blame my silence now in a perticular manner, because of the lottery, but, as Sir Harry no doubt woud acquaint his friends, 'twas so soon fill'd, that the morning appoint'd for the subscription the Book were full and shutt. I doubted not, I say, but this disappointment woud that way reach your ears therefore did not give you the trouble. But to show you I readily obey your comands, they talk of another, and I'll make it my bussiness to inquire after its meritts and acquaint your honour therewith. Now, good Vaudois, explain to me a little that paragraph, wherein you say my foresight's good and that has of late as often occassiond my being named. Pray on what score? Politicks you reject, so shall conclude with my best service to your spouse from . . .

70. Lond[on]. April 3d, 1711.

I was prevented last post by compagny from returning the just thanks that are due to the Vaudois for his good salmon. I affirm it to be good for I've lived upon it ever since and treated my neighbours, who are whigs, with it also. Your health and family's we drink dayly. How sister Cowp[er] will prove I know not. She run away and left it and stays some short time in the country. So you must yet waite with a little patience. Pray, good Vaudois, why will you chide me for not giving you an account of Sir H[enry's] health? During his indisposition I believe a lettre [sic] went to R[obert] C[otesworth?][420] and H[all] every post; at least to the one place so I coud not fancy you coud continue a stranger to his indisposition or recovery. All I can say is that he kept house to receive visitts. We friends in this row went to breakfast and he lookt so well then, I thought might venture out, but he confined himself to be visited, *as he was*, by all the ladys of his acquaintance; and some few days agoe ventured out, to return some of them. So now you may depend he is on the mending hand. The other contents of yours [I] must not answer till I see my steward in the evening.

In regard to the coal trade, Mr. Cotes[worth] is to be sent to the Gate and the result you shall have from either him or your Gov[erno]r. But, consider, this is a time of great difficulty. In your affair I will ingage no further. I avoid it as you do politicks. Next [I] am to tell you Mr. Co[tesworth] is to write to somebody, his name I know not, to press the payment of that mony of Lord B[arnard] before he leaves the country; and if Gibson do not perform covenants we must try if anybody can hold him. As to the map, we readily agree to your proposition and the Gov[erno]r thinks it, as I perceive by him, the cheaper way. The management of Med[omsley] Farm is left to you to do as you think fitt; which answers all the material parts of your letter, so adieu. The Bell is going about, and can only add the service of this family to yourself and spouse, and to w[ho]m I am . . .

[P.S.] The Gov[erno]r is both your servants. A lottery there will be, but nothing is yet come to a resolution concerning it. I inquired.

71. London. April 10th, 1711.

Being alone I begin my letter, tho' I can make it but a confused thing till I've seen my sister about the State Lottery, and Mr. Wright, who I expect att 7 a clock. Therefore in the meantime shall

420 A son of William Cotesworth. *Hughes*.

return the Vaudois thanks for his kind letter by yesterday's post. I need not, I hope, tell him how much I pitty him with the masters and fitters. The though[t] of them perfectly crack my skull, but the word Patience is ever and anon whisperd in my ears as if 't coud have an effect where the signification of it was never understood. But as they fitters are far behond my comprehendtion, as viewing a staith when there's a flood and the like, well may they then saw for a mixture of better coal elsewhere. You are therefore desired to propose to Capt. Liddell, that our fitters take part of Team top coal and mixt with ours so, and all goe by the name of Cla[vering] Stella. That if the mixture shoud not give content Sir H[enry] woud be no sufferer, if otherwise, both partys will thereby receive an advantage, their woarse coals going of with our good ones. His answer to this, return to me, as I doe to you the inclosed Bill, which will not be paid, and am orderd to beg of you to see it deducted [from] the Governor's account, who last post had a complaining letter from both J[ohn] J[ohnson] and Waters.

Sister C[owper] is just gone and bids me tell you that all their mony is on the Land Tax att 9 or 10 p. cent. For the lottery scheme, her master has not seen it, but as soon as he dos she will send me his opinion of it and, tho' he's a disbanded courtier, his sentiments shall be transmitted to you. He dos not perfectly sink the creditt, for what mony he has the Government makes use of it, and I hope he now receives as great a salary, all things then considerd (that then attended his place and now the double interest), as he did then, and has his liberty into the bargain. True 'tis my selling out of the Bank made as much noise here than amongst Torrys, as 'thas done with you; but I mett severall there and adviced them to buy in, for I'd sold, not liking the hands we were falling into. Are you, good Vaudois, weary of an ignorant life that you desire news. Since 'tis your own request I will tell you. The town says Mr. Harley is to be Earl of March[421] and Lord Treasurer, Earl Powlett, Master of the Horse, and the other Comissioners [of the Treasury] turn'd to grass for the summer. Lord Dartmouth[422] is to be P[os]t Master Gen[eral] in Sir T[homas]

[421] Harley was, in fact, created Earl of Oxford and Mortimer. *G.E.C.*

[422] William Legge, 1672-1750, Baron later Earl of Dartmouth. He remained Secretary of State until 1713, when he became Lord Privy Seal.

Franklin's room and Lord Marr[423] marrys Mrs. Hill and is to succeed in the Secretary's place; and after the rising of the Parl[iament] all that ever bore the odious name of Whig must turn out. How I shall laugh then, to see the mungrells, time servers &c., scratting their knavish sow's crown. Revenge is really sweet.

Yesterday I see a letter from D[avid] D[ixon], w[h]ere £100 more was to be paid Mr. Gowland as last Saturday, £100 in a few days, and the rest att Whitsuntide when he receiv'd the mony for his estate att *Shinkley*. I wait to hear the first confirm'd by next post or I'll proceed for his contempt of the court. Give yourself no uneasiness about the monster of mankind as you call him. The Holy Father has been presst to receive him into his Church, but as he'd done a publick benefitt so he ought to have a publick reward, and refused all that spoke in the fool's behalf.

Mr. Wright has been here and shew'd me the originall paper betwixt Sir J[ames Clavering] and my papa. I told him I perceived there was an account of some coals that Sir Jo[hn] refused to pay, and, till that was ended, I coud not order the payment. I made my storry a little confused, but told him as soon as that was agreed [I] shoud order the mony, but must beg the original to be shewn the Master. He told me whenever I pleased to comand he [would] waite on him with it, and so we parted. My papa kept him in mony always. What allowance your g[rand]-father made I know not. You are reffer[ed] to Mr. Poyen about the coal bill *and our mixture*, which was read a second time his day and comitted to a private comittee. I can see to add no more than my service to your spouse and assure you I am . . .

[P.S.] The Gov[erno]r salutes you all. He was inform'd by Mr. Nic[holson],[424] who said he had from good hands heard that you, Mr. Ellison,[425] Mr. Spearman[426] and himself were turn'd out of the Comission of Peace.

[423] John Erskine, 1675-1732, 22nd Earl of Mar. He was made Secretary of State for Scotland in 1713. Later he led the Jacobites at Sheriffmuir. He married (1) Margaret, daughter of 7th Earl of Kinnoul, d. 1707 and (2) Frances, daughter of 1st Duke of Kingston, in 1714.

[424] See note 54.

[425] See note 140.

[426] Robert Spearman, 1657-1728, attorney and mine-owner in Durham. His son Robert lived 1703-61. See *Surtees*, *S.S.* cxxiv and letters 172-86.

72. London. April 26th, 1711.

This I send to your own habitation not knowing which way you design to steer, tho' you say south-west first. In that I resemble our kinsman, who when he was shewd n[orth] and south never knew the other 2 points. However, I hope this may come safe to the Vaudois' hands, that he may know how heartily concernd all here were att the account Mr. Ber[nardeau] gave of your indisposition (and he as much rejoyced to hear of your recovery). Without asking leave of your spouse I must chide you when you coud be so foolish to catch cold with physick. (The next time you undergo that operation I hope your spouse will lock you in your room). What had become of us had you had the ill fortune you've had so fair a chance for? In a just regard to your own young family, *as well as your friends*, and those abroad, you ought to have a perticular care of your health. And by way of punishment for this I will pronounce neither maids, wifes, nor widdows, you merited a visitt of condolance from, as our neigh[bour] had in his long indisposition. He was in your case since and sent us word one day he was very full of pain by the jollting of a hackney coach, and that attending the coal comittee woud undo him. I sent him word by signeur, that in his last illness I pittyed him, but coud not doe so now. Since a hackney coach did not agree with him, he might have kept his own horses and not have sold them, at least till the Comittee had ruin'd the coal-owners. *Upon that subject I am to add att night.* Therefore shall only tell you the fatigue agrees well with Sir Harry. Of Sunday he seem'd to be very chearfull and well. This account I give you because you say can hear seldom of others.

The Bill I received, and your Gov[erno]r has given it to Peter, who has had a letter from J[ohn] J[ohnson] concerning it. Now, Vaudois, in regard to our pupill. I remember in one of your letters you tell me that half micksture is as much as you can allow and some masters are honest enough to own the coals very good, were it not for the outcry att the Gate and I conjecture assisted by the fitters, for in the last fleet some of our own M[asters] were loaded att Team. Some part that, part ours and the remainder Sir J[ohn] Cla[vering's], which I understand not. The Cap[tain], you say, refuses us coals, and Sir Harry, of Sunday, seem'd to resent a little that J[ohn] J[ohnson] sent some of his keels to be loaded att his staith when the Cap[tain] had forbid because he had no coals, and a promise made no keels shoud be sent and yet the next day they went. I coud not help saying, Sir, you've no cause of resentment, for, after all, everyone must own that he's a good paymaster, which some of your fitters are not. The anger shoud be from me, whose hired servant he is, and without whose leave he gos to other staiths. However as Sir H[enry] seems to agree with the Cap[tain] by taking no farther notice of the proposal, I hope, as we can't be servicable to one another in that colliery, it may be soon in our powers to obey Lord C[owper's] pleasure in not mixing coals with anybody. And for Bensham I have a reason to have an avertion too and therefore must inquire what we doe att that staith. The Bill is the devill. 'Tis cookt and cookt till I see coal-burnes are cookt out of the markett for they are to come singly; *that's, I say, not to be sold att all,* if other clauses dos not throw it out the Bill. Adieu. When he's 14 he shall chuse another Madam Guardian, for the complaint to prevent mixtures was made by the Oldners against coalburns and the clause inserted. I'm so madd I care not what's done, so shall reffer till the next post saying any more on that head, save that the fitters are mauld, in case the account passes. I salute your spouse and am . . .

[P.S.] My storry is imperfect, but I'll mend it soon, when I hope [I] may say the Bill is thrown out.

73. London. April 28th, 1711.

I was in so devilish an humour last post I believe you coud not make anything of what I writ. Therefore must not omitt this post explaining my meaning, which is this, the lightermen complain'd of coalburn-coales as what they had been great sufferers by; and the mixing of them, as well as others, was an injury to the publick. Therefore [they] desired a clause to prevent the mixtures att staiths, for the future, which was granted. The good name given us by this must of necessitty, I see, fall very heavy on Jacky and provoked me not a little, knowing how indifferent that colliery is for the markett. But tho' the Comons shoud pass that act as 'tis, I hope we shall make friends that either the masters and lightermen shall be also included or that rejected in favour of the owners, by the Lords, which has given me some quiet of mind for the present. But take no notice of this, I beg.

Of Thursday your Gov[erno]r and I were att daggers drawing about Jack's trade, on the account above mentiond. I told him

I now see since our fitters found the sweat of coming to his father's staiths, so low in the river, and good coals, they were att Team come nearer (if not up) to proportion, and we short. That since we coud have no coals att Team, where Sir H[enry] was soly concern'd, I had my reason to object to Bensham and I was of opinion that Jacky must work his Leadgate so as to make his colliery goe singly of, as long as it coud, and then do as well as possible. The waggon-way woud be saved so farr. And in fine I was so weary, that I'd keep my trust no longer than Jacky was 14, to chuse some other. The same I repeated to Sir H[enry] this day, only with this addition, that I woud sooner serve him than any in the river, but must serve myself first; that I see a small incouragement woud bring my fitters to his service; that when the Gov[erno]r was concern'd for both, I never made any inquiry, I believed him equally just; that now 'twas the Cap[tain's] business to promote his only advantage and, therefore, as we were on another foot, I was obliged to be more cautious in those affairs; that since the Cap[tain] thought it not feasable to take from Team, I lookt upon it as a denial and the more so since he was pleased to be silent on the Cap[tain's] opinion since 'twas 1st mention'd. But without his answer I was not satisfied. "I shoud expect the same Sir," said I, "by any who came to Stella". However we parted without a further answer or resolution, till which I really think our fitters must be forbid Team.

I always forgett to beg of you to keep the account seperate of the expence and profitt of the colliery won, so it must goe into Chancery, that by that they may judge of the reasonableness of our petition and upon what ground they grant us any other. This I shall mention to Peter.

Can you tell me how that £40 dispute on coals is betwixt us and Sir John, and what more we have to deduct, that we may end that account?

I received a letter from D[avid] D[ixon], wherein he says he has paid Mr. Gowland £350 already and had Johnson's hand for paying the 50 in dispute, with the interest, and the other mony shoud be paid in May when he r[eceive]d the mony for Shinkley estate, if I'd forbear him so long. I've orderd Mr. Sanderson to waite on the Master to know his answer, and that shall be return'd him, for I won't make myself liable to the debt indeed. Adieu. The Gov[erno]r is by us. He and this family salute you and your spouse. I am to you both . . .

74. London. May 11th, 1711.

The Gov[erno]r last post woud acquaint you I'd writ as civill a letter to Lady C[lavering] as she did to me, in your regard of your worship, and wherein I told her you shoud conclude the account, that you att once might right Jacky and yourself in matters now depending, which will I fancy grate them, and not a little, and, as soon as I receive my master's order, you shall have it comunicated.

As I'm ingaged tomorrow I beging this the day before, that I may bring it so near a conclusion that my apointement may not prevent my returning you sincere thanks for the favour of your last letter and saying somewhat of the posture of my pupill's affairs, in regard to the well cookt up Bill att present in the Comons house. The advantage of it, the world must plainly see, was only to a few, and as the Oldners did us the honour to name our coals as base mixtures before the Comittee, I can't be so much imposed on, but to think this must be of pernicious consequences to us. Tho', thanks be, the clause is so worded everybody will be sufferers thereby. I'm a true collier and must rejoyce when the shoes pinches any of the trade; and, give me leave to say, as good a lawyer in my own affairs as one you lately conversed with, as to what were distinct collierys, and who, to you, was against that mixing clause, tho' to others of the trade, whose letters I've seen, coud object against nothing but the enacting clause. This I call blowing hott and blowing cold and must form my judgement of him as I've received the severall copies of his. Not having practiced the law I can't penetrate further into the meritts of one I'm not acquainted with. Nor dos hearsay affect me on his score. He seems to think he knows my Lady Ann and has every [sic] since protection time. But I leave him for one we are more concern'd with. Mr. O[rd?],[427] I doubt not, you look on as a sincere friend and the publick happy in his services, but Mr. Cotesworth I admire of all mankind. Since he came to town [I] have seen him but one half hour, and since the Bill. He was never the person that came to ask if I liket or disliket it, or any part, or to say, "Madam, you must look about. Your coals were made the foundation for that clause. I am concern[ed] in general and therefore must not shew myself in the interest of a perticular person, but some care ought to be took". No, I'm a female and consequently not capable of understanding further than that some

[427] John Ord, agent and lawyer and also one of the five colliery directors of 1710. *Hughes*. For coal-trade bill see *C.J.* xvi, 531-687.

one day, betwixt this and Monday morn[ing], he leaves the Town. [I] must receive him and, with some turn, he shall give his thread of discourse. I shoud fancy we have vast obligations, but I've made my silent observations and am intirely convince[d] of what I formerly surmised; so much that my eye shall never be of him and, for his sake, att Xmas next I shall beging, that as we pay punctually, so shall all do to us and then everyone pay the ballance of their account (by which means I shall, I hope, leave you in a good state, tho' you are pleased to make me a great and undeserved compliment on that score). To what I've said will be alledg'd the Gov[erno]r spoke. 'Tis true, he did it att Westm[inste]r &c., but coud any one believe he was to press the thing farther. No, Sir Harry had the prospect then of receiving too great an advantage, for his son, in duty, to appear against it or to espouse warmly the cause of the opposers. I can see traps laid and lying, to swallow undeserving persons in. But I believed your Gov[erno]r so just, when steward to both familys, that now he's out of the one's service nobody shall be able to alledge against him, that by his eagerness to serve his pupill, one may conjecture he's been too negligent of the other. I know few of his honesty in the world, but to prevent what may be said, I desire to manage for my son a little; and a virago I know I shall be call'd, but I care not. I am conceited *this London spoils us* and fancy I coud understand my trade as well as many coal-owners Mr. Cot[esworth] has been with. But as the Bill, they tell me, will be lost, that putt an end to all disputes.

Saturday. This morning Mr. Sanderson came and, as my presence was not absolutely necessary att the Master's, I gave him his papers and full instructions, upon which this resolution was took. As the Gov[erno]r writes me, Mr. S[anderson] has writ a rec[eip]t on the back of the account for Sir John so sign, which gos down this post, and fittage mony is to be deducted, as also mony I've l[ai]d out for my lady. But take your £100 and pay the ballance, I say, and from me tell her I've [no?] interest att the Gate. So I beg the favour of her to return me a bill of £165, to pay of the upholdsterer, as soon as she can, that I may discharge that debt 'ere I goe into Yorkshire and next post she shall hear from me. I've not time to add more, save my service to your spouse, who am the Vaudois' . . .

75. Lond[on]. Nov. 25th, [1712].

I was the last post day prevented returning you my thanks for your long letter by indeavouring to gett advice for you to ease your concience and I hope effected my design. I mett with our old friend, who came to town for three or four days. I laid forth your grievances and received the following private answer. As to J[ohn] J[ohnson], that what he has done won't prejudice the Trustees, for the objections to his account may still be made, and will be allow'd by law, notwithstanding the part he has acted. The rest I give, as you desire, for the good of those employ'd. However you may use J[ohn] J[ohnson's] roguery as [you] see fitt to check him.

I had yesterday from Mr. Ord the copys of P[otter] Newton[428] estate, and shall proceed in that affair. I mett one we always consulted in the matter, who tells me that Atkinson[429] putting himself into gaol, with a design to defraud us, will avail him nothing; that for his villanous actions he adviced the severest prosecution of the law and that without delay; not only as he deserves it, but as 'tis absolutely necessary in our case, to convince all employ'd under us that we are not in jest and neither mean to cheat the infant, nor see him cheated. Johnson's late menagement has not a little surprised me, but if my friend understands the law, that loophole will not prevent Jacky's having justice done him by the law. Now I am upon this topick, lett Peety send me a true estimate of D[avid] D[ixon's] affair, and, if 'tis overcome, lett us proceed to something else. I have not yet received the accounts for the last two years and this is the third year wanting att Xmas. I percieve by you Mr. Cotes-[worth's] account are yet unbrought in, which I've often desired you to solicit. If he's not a good acc[oun]tant, lett Peety help him. I spoke to Mr. Sanderson to mention this to him some time ago, but Vaudois, you can best judge of the delay. Only this I will affirm to you, had you complied to what Lord C[owper] adviced you, when in town, this difficulty had been over. He proposed an estimate of all debts owing to Jacky, by whom and upon what score and of how long standing, and beg the direction of the court in suing the severall partys, or if the time ellaps, you and my Mas[te]r pay the debts to Jacky when att age, for the law will not suffer him to loose it. You best know the reason why you comply not with his advice, but this I will affirm, if you press not the passing of the

[428] Anne Clavering's step-mother, Elizabeth, was from Potter Newton in Yorkshire.

[429] See note 163. He went bankrupt in 1712. *Hughes.*

accounts and the ridress of the complaints, if you dye your family is ruin'd, and if you live 7 years longer you are so yourself. And as you, in kindness to my papa's memory, undertook this, I can't help being concern'd to see [you] act such a prejiduciall part to your young family as well as yourself. If this spurr you not, the Guardian must sew the Trustees. I debated this to Mr. Cotesworth when in town, which he may remember. I wish you well settled in your new house since you removed, but I liked the other better. My Mas[te]r salutes you, &c. I read him yours and as he only neglected answering the part of the Bill, I fancy I may say, 'tis come safe or he woud have spoke. I am to you and yours a most faithfull servant

A[nn] L[iddell].[430]

[P.S.] I will not be excluded serving you upon this remove. I know no more of what you mention than the child unborn and can receive no more prejudice by stirring than Mrs. Smyth, for my illness was a cold I gott by returning late from my aunt's when she was ill and the Dr. thinks madam too consumptive to bear a cough. That's all.

76. London. Dec. 16th, 1712.

I have been prevented two post of writing to you by the hurry I have been in upon the remouvall of your girls to Cosen Waite's, which I accomplisht last Saturday, much to their (and I hope their friends') satisfaction.

I shall proceed to tell you Dan. [Poyen] gott well up after a very ill journey. The particulars you will have from himself, I dare say, so will not mention them and only run on to acquaint you with the cause of my spleen a few post agoe. I had been to solicit Jacky coming to town this Xmas and tho' my answer was ambiguous yet I perceived he had comitted some great fault and that if they took him, *which was uncertain*, he was to have no followers, but the bent rather run upon changing his abode when in town. To this I answerd, the child, and those concernd for him, vary. I was confident sencible of the obligations they lay under to them upon that score, but if his being longer there was inconvenient, those concernd for him must think of some other place for him; and only desired to know the cause of his disgrace, which was a letter he *forged*, *I fear*, last Whitsuntide to excuse his task; but since, as I judge by talk,

[430] Anne Clavering had recently married Henry Liddell, the "Governor".

he's this Xmas to come there, but not to stay so long, which I own I approve, of this I was to say nothing and therefore you must not.

As to the accounts, we agree in the abilitys of one person employ'd, but how those meritts can be of use, when the accounts are so long refused, is the question. I've often askt my lawyer that, and, 'tis on this score chiefly, he recomends you to the Chancery. For when arguments, says he, won't prevail, then the fear of a suit from the court will spurr him on to the delivery of them and prevent the inconvenience for the future. What remains further to be added is, Vaudois, I am no longer guardian and therefore uncapable of serving you. Charles Sand[erson] has so long buss'd it about, it can be no secret and, for my part, I resolve to lay all aside. You must not be surprised when I tell you that seeing the great regard my master has for W[illiam] C[otesworth], I've never made mention of his name near twelve months, and I can but suspect 'tis upon his score my advice to pass the accounts is of so little weight. Besides I've sent so many times to our lawyer to ask that question concerning J[ohn] J[ohnson's] accounts, that I've mett with jesting reproofs, which I believe bear *earnest* with them; and all won't do; that to make all easie I must give over medling. I see I've so much fire and quickness for your sollicitour, which is a great fault. He'd keep you in his hands and I woud have you out. He has a great influence over my Mas[te]r, as I coud demonstrate were you here (but 'tis too much for letter). In the business of Atkinson, which I've been gov[ern]ed by Lord Cowper in, for my mas[te]r won't speak good nor badd to it, so it becomes my perticular province and that I believe must see finisht for you. As to all others [I] am as ignorant as the child unborn.

I am concernd for you and your family, for as you are not in court, if the accounts pass not, you are in worse circumstances than if you'd never desired their protection. My best service to madam, whose comissions [I] shall execute with pleasure and am to yourself . . .

[P.S.] My mas[te]r salutes you both. This letter to yourself.

To James Clavering Esq., att Newcastle upon Tine.

77. Midsummerday. [Endorsed June 24th, 1714.]

'Tis three post att least since I promisst my sister Cowper to interceed with you, in her name and that of your daughter Jane, to lett poor nurse Wear have her house repaired now [there is] this dry weather (and so give no dinial). But your Governor's resolution of going down has so fretted me that I am, as to my own health, where I started, tho', thank God, I now beging to be easy and I hope in some measure prepared for whatever news I may receive concerning him when in the country. For to be plain with you, Vaudois, I know he is so little his own master, that after the journey and the welcomes succeed, I expect not to see him more, or at least in so miserable a state that death were better. But by reflecting I find your letters have more force than my concern (for I never heard him mention it but once) and that 'tis you that, as I hear say, occassions this journey. I hope you then will from time to time give me a true state of his condition. I omitt the word health because I'm confident he can enjoy none. As I shall always be in expectation of the worst there will be no need of disimulation in this as you did when you told me you fear'd such a journey woud be of the worst consequence to him. And as soon as you arrive, send for him. What can have happen'd to make this sudden change when you were expected here again att Michaelmas? Lett what will, be the event, you will ever justly comdem yourself if you stick not to Lord Cowper's advice, for that only will govern Mr. Freke.[431] I wish I had the girls' accounts for I want to pay some things for them before I may leave the town. Adieu. I salute your spouse and am Vaudois' . . .

[P.S.] Madam, from Sir H[enry] I hear, gos this day, but takes not leave of Lady Ann. You may tell your spouse.

To James Clavering Esq., at Lamesley, neare Durham.

78. July 20th, 1714.

I was in hopes to have mett our friend to have inabled me, as you desired, to give you some advice, but all attempts of that sort have hitherto been vain. This day is dedicated to Mr. Kempe and orders, if he comes, to come for me for I want his opinion on Caverley Pinkney's[432] letter also, to comunicate to you. What you

[431] See note 40.

[432] Calverley Pinkney of Dalton, Yorkshire, a London attorney. *Sharp Mss.* No. 11, Vol. I, and *Letter-book*.

say in your last I easily give credit to, for after I have chid you I did not look on you as the sole occasion. I coud but observe (tho' I was not allow'd it) that a more secret reason induced, and if you value a caracter, and if my information be right, you must produce in court all the authoritys you have, upon which you ground your aspersion. For, Vaudois, without you can make out you have [not] defrauded the inf[an]t, your pupill, you'll not have a release speedily. And as you have acted justly I [would] have you now publickly shew it, whatever threats, &c., are used, as you mention, to you. As you ask my opinion I freely give it you, and, as I heard in R[ussell?] Street, you, in your last but one, say something of extraordinary thinks [sic] you've receiv'd from a certain person. Pray what were they for? I'm yet a stranger thereto. The knowledge thereof may be of use to you.

I am glad you've disposed of Lowrey's place to Richard Allen.[433] 'Twas always design'd him upon the like occassion for many years before my poor father died and what I shoud have solicited for him had I known it sooner.

This week your two girls and I go into the country to breath a little fresh air, and where I propose to recover a crazy constitution as farr as can be done by one, who every day expects to hear the northern people have welcomed your Governor to the grave or near it. But this to yourself, for my complaints shall not reach one whose joy upon the intented ramble was not to be exprest. Direct yours hereafter to the Hon[oura]ble Maurice Ashley's[434] house in Bedf[or]d Row and then I shall have them that night or next morning. Adieu. My best wishes attend your spouse from . . .

[P.S.] Sir H[enry] or Mr. Gen. will perhaps intertain you with news of Mrs. Smyth, therefore I shall be silent.

79. Augt. 14th, 1714.

I've many thanks to return the Vaudois for his kindness to my master and for his diligence in giving me an account of his health. I am glad to find that by experience, the advice of using exercise and living regular, he's sencible conduce to his recovery, or his father and all friends, as well as Doctor, surgeon, and apo[thecary],

433 See note 329.

434 Hon. Maurice Ashley, 1675-1727, was a younger brother of the 3rd Earl of Shaftesbury and Whig M.P. 1695-8 and 1701-13.

have so great an esteem for him they woud not have presst anything but what reason convinced them must greatly turn to his advantage. In the terms they did this advice. Pray settle your accounts and come both away, not only to make an end of that troublesome affair, but to intertain yourselves with the coronation of the greatest prince in meritt, the universe can boast of.

I shoud say somewhat to you upon the late accident of your family, but I'm so lost in the satisfaction of this new goverment I can think of nothing else.[435] Jemy Craggs[436] return'd yesterday with the King's thanks to his Parliament and the Regents, and that he and the Prince sett forwards next Wedn[esday] and of Saturday propose to be att the Hague. The Princesse[437] is with child and will follow. Robin Walpole moved yesterday to have the Han[over] troops paid, upon which Speaker[438] declared the motion past with a Latin sentence and then all the vile Whigs laught. They've also inabled the T[reasurer][439] to pay out of the first aids the £100,000 for the Pretender's head, and are to inact it. This I hope will please you as 'thas us all, and my girls say they only want the Supply Bill you promist them to perfect their joy. I'd a letter from Dan. [Poyen] since I'd yours, full of the accounts I sent and some errours I've comitted, but no mony nor mention thereof. That I may always write such news is the sincere wish of, Vaudois, . . .

[P.S.] All round me salute you. So do I your spouse.

To James Clavering Esq., at Stow-House.

80. Augt. 31st, 1714.

Your two letters I r[eceive]d this moment as I was setting pen to paper to acquaint your spouse, I gott Mrs. Ashley to send her, by Robt. Pilin yesterday's the 30 of Augt. carrier, a box directed for Mr. Ralph Mitford,[440] in which is a white popling gown and peti-

[435] The death of Queen Anne on 1 August 1714 heralded the dawn of the Whig supremacy.

[436] James Craggs, jnr., 1686-1721, Whig M.P. and later Secretary of State. *D.N.B.*

[437] Caroline of Anspach, wife of the future George II.

[438] Sir Thomas Hanmer, M.P. 1701-27 and Speaker of the House of Commons 1713-14. *D.N.B.*

[439] As almost her last act Queen Anne appointed the moderate Duke of Shrewsbury as Lord Treasurer.

[440] Ralph Mitford, Newcastle merchant and colliery-owner. *S.S.* ci.

coat linend with a black and white sarcenett, a black and white satin gown for your son Jack. But, as master Tom's vest and tunick was not then come, these first things went in one box, which was no sooner gone than master's things came and were sent in a box by the same carrier and directed as the former. I hope you'll all like them. Calimanco and camblett, I feard, woud be too hott for the children, but if you'd have the two hatts follow, you must send me word. I'm heartily concern'd your spouse is so much out of order. God send her safe in her bed. As to the other particulars of yours I'll return an answer as soon as Mr. Freke comes up, if that will do for you. I'm glad you've begun to meet with some of the errors, and hope this next term will settle all matters to all your satisfactions, for assure yourself it can never be in your power, for the future, to run yourselves into the like inconveniency. When this is once ended you will find yourself intirely att ease.

The 21st Mr. Yorke[441] paid me 60 guineas for the use of your three daughters, equally divided, so place it in their accounts. I shall in a little time call upon your b[rothe]r for this last small bill of yours. All here att home and next door salute you and your spouse. I'm to both, good Vaudois, . . .

[P.S.] Our good and glorious king sett out but yesterday from Hanover. I can just add Lord Bull[ingbroke's][442] office was this day seal'd up by the Regency, but he's not turn'd out.

To James Clavering Esq., at Greencroft.

81. London. August 2d, 1722.

Sir,

My thanks are greatly due for the favour of yours dated the 27th July and shall heartily rejoyce when an oportunitty offers to return you the congratulations. I can easily judge, by the vexations such a delay occassion'd myself, how anxious it must be to you to continue under the same circumstance. And were it in my power to serve you I shoud readily imbrace it, for I had said as much to Mr. Sanderson as I was capable. Elsewhere I've no intrest. I bless God I've paid

[441] Thomas Yorke, 1658-1716, James Clavering's father-in-law.

[442] Henry St. John, 1678-1751, Viscount Bolingbroke. He was Secretary of State, but, as a suspected Jacobite Tory, was persona non grata with the new regime.

K

the outmost farthing. Yet shall rejoyce to hear, and see, our late pupill meets with greater advantages fr[om] his new friends. The services, we've done, are past. I can therefore only advice, as I wish the prosperity of you and your family, that you woud conclude. I fear you are to expect no quarter; and he's now begining with the Cole-Ch. Therefore consider if more vexation may not be raised to you fr[om] thence.

I shall rejoyce to hear your spouse is in a safe way. The window curtains for the wrought bed were not bespoke. Your other bed is ready and your instructions Mr. Cox will observe as to your chairs, &c.

I thank you for your prints and rejoyce to hear our good B[isho]p is well approved. My papa[443] has made himself worse by fretting that he coud not att[en]d. I hope he now begings to mend, tho' very slowly. God preverse [sic] his life, so neccessary to his family. I am Sir, . . .

[P.S.] I'm my cosen's servant.

82. London. Sep[tembe]r 24th, 1726.

Sir,

Your obliging letter of the 18th lyes before me, with the continuance of your kind wishes for me, which deserve my best thanks. I wish as you doe, [but] am yet a stranger to all but what you mention. [I] am heartily concern'd you've mett so many vexations and uneasiness. Pray, what provision can the Baronet make for his lady? When he left us, female talk was, that he woud have enough for her and the sisterhood, and I ask no questions for conscience sake. Nor shall I dare to name to our friend that's reported our pupill is to be more nearly related to her. The discharge of Wheately surprises me, who after doing so much and being so able a steward, shoud quit.

Am heartily glad Alderman Ridley[444] is recover'd and the same for our neph[ew] Tom.,[445] tho' I never refflect upon his education with comon patience. Yet two lives are better than one. Sir H[enry's]

443 Sir Henry Liddell, her father-in-law.

444 Richard Ridley, who farmed at Byker and had mines there and at Dipton. *Hughes*.

445 Thomas Liddell, the son of John Liddell, who was the second son of Sir Henry Liddell. *Surtees*.

picture is drawn and some say design'd for his mama.[446] If my former news was true concerning him, Lady Hal[ifax's][447] death is a great misfortune. Your comands are always executed with pleasure, to the best of my poor capacity, but I can't allow you have any occasion for what you mention. And lett me beg you not to vex so to give you any return of your old complaint. Am not forgetfull of my promise on that occassion, as soon as I can get to see the lady. My service attend my cosen and your young folks and believe me . . .

[P.S.] I thank you for your kind wishes for Isabel. I've just gott her out of her chamber to mine.

83. Oct. 1st, 1726.

Sir,

I was prevented last post from returning you thanks for the fav[ou]r of yours by dining that day out of town. I am heartily concern'd for the difficultys you meet with and the uneasiness the treatment, yours mentions, gives you. I hope you know me too well to believe me capable of doing anything to prejudice my friend at any time; and much more after a caution. The same I doubt not [I] may affirm for Doll,[448] if she has not already for herself. Nay, further, [I] am confident are too well known to be applied to on that account. Nor, when the warmth of words are over, I believe the worst part.

[I] am infinitly obliged to Mr. Yorke for his discourse to the one brother in presence of the other,[449] who is as extraordinary in his way. My service attends him and my cosen. Two peices of news two different papers furnish me with this day. The one is Mist['s] journall[450] with the match of G[eorge] B[owes] Esq. and Mrs. Bright,[451] neice to Col. Liddell, and one with Sir W[alter]

[446] Anne, widow of Sir Thomas Liddell, 2nd bart., and daughter of Sir Henry Vane of Raby. *Surtees*.

[447] Mary, daughter of 1st Earl of Scarborough and wife of 4th Earl of Halifax died in 1726.

[448] Dorothy Waite, née Clavering.

[449] This refers to John and Thomas Yorke, brothers-in-law of James Clavering, who were in dispute at this time as their mother favoured the second son, Thomas.

[450] Nathaniel Mist began his *Weekly Journal* in 1716. As the organ of Jacobites and High-flyers it frequently incurred the wrath of the Whig ministries. *D.N.B.*

[451] Anne or Catherine, daughter of John Liddell, who adopted the name of Bright when he was made heir of his maternal grandfather. *Surtees*. She did not marry George Bowes.

Cal[verley's][452] son and one of Miss Claverings. The other a statute of bankrupt for one And[rew] Dick,[453] hoastman and fitter, and the persons concern'd according to the statute are to applie to J[ohn] Airy.[454] Your thoughts on this will oblige . . .

84. Oct. 13th, 1726.

Sir,

Am favoured with yours of the 8th and am concern'd you shoud return out of order from the sessions. I hope for a better account of you in your next.

The Barr[one]tt[455] came to town on Friday. My Lady, Mrs. Waite, and self, mett him at Stevenage according to promise at parting.

The world might justly condemn any person that did not defend their legal right, but what title has Mr. Bowes to stop our kinsman? I apprehended the coles went through no other grounds than were my old uncle's, which coud be let to others, but no way-leave required on the other side.

'Tis nothing new to have weddings in a [widdow?] head, but at this time to clear myself [I] must tell you I dined that day out of town and that paragraph was read at table, and none else. At the same time some present said Mr. Bowes had shewn resentment, when in town, to the spreading the report.

My adversarys have got an order on Michealmas-day, that their cause may be heard with mine and depositions, took on one side, serve for the other. Dos this look like accomodation?

I understand so little the affairs of your neighbouring corporation that I don't know whether this late choice of a mayor is better or worse for Mr Ridley. [I] am sorry he's so long confined.

I wish yours, and the Long Newton family,[456] joy of this little fellow. You won't own it, but our talk still continues [that] yours is increasing.

[452] Sir Walter Calverley, c. 1670-1749, father of Sir Walter Calverley Blackett. *Foster*.

[453] See *S.S.* cv.

[454] John Airey was the Ellison family attorney. He married a daughter of Robert Ellison. *Hughes*.

[455] Sir Francis Clavering, 1673-1738, succeeded as 5th bart. in 1726.

[456] The Vanes of Long Newton, a junior branch of the Vanes of Raby.

You've told me news, I rejoyce at, about my Lord of Landaff's[457] family. I am, Sir, . . .

85. London. [Nov.] 29th, 1726.

Sir,

By this time I fear you've ranked me in the same class with my female neighbour, tho' I now assure you [I] have been prevented returning the thanks due to you, for your letter from Long Newton, by my winter friend, my cough, which has occassioned my making a perpitual noise in the ears of my friends this three weeks or more. Yet [I] am unwilling to suffer Small[458] to cut my throat least that shoud feed me, for, thank God, I am become so considerable I think myself fitter for a cart than a horse were I to be convey'd any way; and at the same time have had employ in another kind, to be ready for Lord Ch[ancellor] when call'd for (which sort of business you know my giddy head must be clearer at) for they supenead me to the passing judgement, which rowl, I must own, was sent by Sand[erson's] clerck, to whom I observed, all rebukes were not lost on his master.

My female neighbour has been much out of order in a cold and sends me word, in great concern, expecting next post to bring news of her neice Hauxley's death.[459] I can't greatly lament any that are took from so great an uncertainty in fortune. Living upon dependance is to me great misery.

In a letter from the country they write me that you look as well and brisk as ever, which I assure you I rejoyce to hear, tho' am sorry I am so badd an accountant as you seem to prove me.

Our town is dull. Italian plays are all the mode and I don't understand one word of the language so content myself with a twelve-penny amusement, now and then, at the Oratory. Tho', I must remark, [I] am no schismatick for I only goe on lecture days. If you have not yet read two volumes of ficktitious voyages of fairys, giants, flying islands, &c, said to be Dean Swift's[460] and [which] have had a great run here, you may peruse them at leisure, for now the fashion of praising them is almost over. My natural stupidity, which

[457] Robert Clavering, 1671-1747, of Tilmouth, Co. Durham, was Bishop of Landaff 1725-29 and then Bishop of Peterborough. *D.N.B.*

[458] See *Hughes*, pp. 95 and 97.

[459] A daughter of Ambrose Hauxley and Anne, sister of Dorothy Clavering. *Surtees*.

[460] Jonathan Swift. This refers to *Gulliver's Travels*. *D.N.B.*

coud not be moved by education, coud not penetrate the deep design of the author, save to ridicule the depraved taste of mankind in general. Once is [?in] an age my fashion [and] dress come in vogue, tho' here no hopes of success. No, no more than of the number of rabbitts sett forth in the newspapers, and of which a book is printing, with a cop[per] plate of the 17 rabbitts, whole and peicemeal, they say, which must make money to the author, being intirely news. These at present are visiting topicks.

As to what you and I have [oftener?] heard of, give me leave to ask what colliery Mrs. F[rancis] can gain out of Sir F[rancis Clavering's] estate? This is comon chatt. As is, I fear, Lady Cla[vering] bringing up her daughters, and the offer there from our pupill, who I hear is looking out a house in George Street. The post-bells calls. Adieu. My service attends my cosen and believe me, Sir, . . .

II. LETTERS FROM THOMAS YORKE

86. London. 11 Aprill, 1717.

Deare Brother,

I am to give answer to your favour of 2 instant, att the first reading of which I coud scarce believe my owne eyes and, if I was as disposed to quarrell as you seem to be, you have laid a sufficient foundation to ground a breach upon; but I must tell you that my friendship and affection is so deeply rooted that it will be difficult to shake it, and, if yours were established on as firme a basis, you coud never raise such diffidence and jealousy and make such insinuations against me, who never deserv'd the least from you. Notwithstanding you say you do not suspect me imposing on you in the seeds, what can you meane by keeping the dispute on foot, and tho' I have in severall letters declared I charg'd no more then I paid, and that probably you might be misinform'd, for Geo. Waylett, the seedsman att the Wheatesheafe in Leaden Hall Street, over against St. Mary's church, of whom I bo[ugh]t them, who I complain'd to on your first letter, solemnly protested to me that I paid no more then others for the same quality att that time, which I beleiv'd, because he is a man of faire repute, and I did not think he woud cheat me in so trivial a matter. Nay, moreover, he show'd me his book, that he made everybody that then bought of him pay the same, and tho' you have mention'd this affaire in so many letters, and cannot forbeare touching on it, (which, unlesse I was quite stupid), discovers your mistrust of me, and, because I defend myselfe, you pretend to carry it with an air of authority and resentment. To justify myself still more I have given you the name of the seedsman, and where he lives, and do now send you his bill, with his receipt on the back of it, which you may compare with the account I sent you, to see whether I have pocketted; but I desire you'l returne me the bill, which I must keep as a voucher, and, tho' I coud not before satisfy you of my innocence, yett I hope this will, that so may hear no more of this grand dispute of the seeds; and tho' I shall be allways glad to serve you, yett if you, suspecting my integrity, think fitt to honour anybody else with your commissions, I shall be no looser thereby and shall not regrett it. [I] am sorry you have provoked me to declare myselfe in this manner.

I make no doubt but you'l be able to give good reason for your conduct as to polliticks, but you ought not to take amisse if I term Sir H[enry] B[ellasyse],[461] T[homas] C[onyers] [462] and G[eorge] B[owe]s, persons disaffected, for I believe I may charge my memory with remembring that you, yourselfe, have bestow'd those high and mighty titles on them. I never will presume to dictate to you what company is fitting for you to keep, such a magesterial air would ill become me, but [I] must say [I] am sorry that you shoud pronounce yourselfe unanimous in the sentiments with those gentlemen aforenamed.

As for making a second visitt to the wid[o]w you desire, if it were to do you service, I woud readily do it, but to make her another visitt, without any prospect of doing any good for you, will look like making pretensions for myselfe, and may give the world a subject for discourse, which woud be very ungratefull. So I hope you'l not expect it from me.

According to your order in your former you have your account currant; the balla[nce] due to me £5. 14. 3; which I hope you'l find without errour.

I feare my mother will be great a looser by not accepting your proposall, that was last made, for a rent charge, and when she stated to me that she would not comply with it, because she woud not consent to have the entail cutt of, on my account, I thank'd her for the consideration she had for me, but beg'd of her not to forego so great an advantage, as the rent charge woud be, on my account, and that, for my part, I did not in the least mistrust my bro[ther] doing anything unfaire by me, as my mother herselfe can tell you. Who that person is you hint att, that finds his interest in the unnatural divisions between them, you know best. I, att this distance, am ignorant, and, as I am conscious to myselfe of innocense, I cannot impute your insinuation to myself, whatever you may do, for I guesse, as you have made me a rogue in your own thinking in one thing, you take it for granted I am so in everything else. But, whatever you may believe of me, I have labour'd to pacyfy

[461] See note 56.

[462] Thomas Conyers, M.P. Durham City 1698-1727.

and compose matters as much as lay in my power, and, tho' [I] have not been successfull, yett shall persevere in my endeavours.

I hope you will not revive these paper warrs that have of late been between us. I, for my part, offer to bury all in oblivion and to continue that love and affection as inviolably as ever, which never was in the least lessen'd to you by what has past, nor ever shall by any bone of contention that may be thrown between us hereafter.

I am deare Brother, your most affectionate bro[ther] and
faithfull humble servant
Thomas Yorke.

[Appended:—] James Clavering Esq. His acc[oun]t cur[ren]t.

1716.				
June 5.	To 6 night caps and 6 handk[erchiefs]	£1	14	—
Xber 3	To a dog collar		4	6
d.	To cash paid H[enry] Liddell	50	—	—
d.	To a bob wig sent you	2	3	—
1716/17 d	To cash paid James Morris	1	13	6
Mar. 12	To sundry seeds and charges		2	6
		£57	15	6

1715/16.				
March 9	By the balla[nce] of last account	£2	1	3
9 ber 20	By a bill rem[itte]d on G. Handley	50	—	—
		£52	1	3
April 10	By balla[nce] carry'd to your dr. on new account	5	14	3
		£57	15	6

Errours excepted. T. Yorke

To James Clavering Esq., att Stowhouse, near Durham.

87. Londo[n]. 4 May, 1717.

Deare Brother,

I am with your favour of the 28 past. I am as willing as you are that the paper warr, we have had for some time, may cease, what has pass'd be buried in oblivion, and, according to the saying, of the falling out of lovers is the renewing of love. Let us enter into the strictest tyes of love and friendship and endeavour to make the knot so strong, not to be slackned by any accident for the future. Tho' to cleare myselfe of what you cast on me, of being jealous without reason, I must beg leave for the last time to add a few words upon this ungratefull subject, which has given me great disquiet.

You did more then insinuate in very plaine words, which to my poor sense coud beare but two meanings, and that, either I was so carelesse in your affaire, to let myselfe be imposed on, or did impose on you; and tho' att the very first I told you, I did for you my best, and beleivd you paid no more then the just price, and that it was not impossible but you might be misinform'd or that there might be some mistake in it. Yett you, not content with this but [in] letter after letter, I think it is been ever since Xmas, coud not forbeare your reprimands and expressing your mistrust of me, tho' the most it coud be for woud not amount to above a few shill[ings]. Thus I desire this odious subject may have an end and I can assure you, tho' what has happened might have made some impression on an unsteady mind, it has not in the least on mine, and the respect and value for you is as great as ever, which I will demonstrate whenever [I] have occasion of serving you, which, I protest to you, was and allways will be with the same goodwill and zeale for you as for myselfe. As for the topick of polliticks, whether the complaints, you with too much reason make, can be laid more justly on those that are turnd out or those that are kept in, I will not determine. However I may venture to assert, that the grievances and mismanagement, you intimate, was not the reason of that change and that the present gentlemen will not redresse those egregious faults and that such blunders have been committed by this new sett, as sufficiently bespeake them unequal to their businesse and to carry on the grand affairs in hand. If you and I must not speake well of a ministry, because we have not what we ask, tho' we have both perhaps good pretensions; you, by your faithfull services and venturing and exposing your person att your proper charge, and I, by my father's steady adherence to the present government, who desired nothing for himselfe if they woud only give me a small place of £2 or £300. I say, if we must not commend a ministry till they give us each a place, I feare they must never have our good word. I never knew any ministry without faults and I believe the late had their share.

I am glad we agree in the characters of some of your neighbours you associate with, tho', if I can understand your former of 2 past, you woud not allow them that denomination you do now. Do not let the present M[inistr]y have the merit, if 12,000 men are disbanded, because that proposition was made by Mr. S[penc]er C[omp]ton,[463] and to let what was saved thereby go towards the £250,000; but then it was violently opposed by your patriots, and he branded as an enemy,[464] and now in a few days, truly it is become so good an expedient to be putt in practise, as it's said. So things change. I coud mention many more instances, but I'l say no more.

The distraction that reigns in our family[465] is very melancholy to reflect on and I feare there will be no avoiding the sad consequences that must ensue, unlesse my mother consents to leave the matter to be decided by arbitration, which I have earnestly recommended to her, that I wish it does not putt me out of her books, tho' it is plaine that method will be most for intrest. For if, as my brother asserts, he has had the best advice about this case, that her personal estate is his, then, if they go to law, it will all be given from my mother, with costs, besides a vast expence in defending her cause, with the plague and vexation that attends law-suits allways. Whereas, if it is put to refference, she may perhaps be awarded to pay only part. And, as I can safely say I have not given any other then healing advice and tending to compose their differences, I am resolved to continue to act the same neutral part. Yett, rather then heare of their animosity and unnatural proceedings, which is very shocking to me, if I coud have the least incouragement of going anywhere abroad, I professe I woud instantly retire out of England, let it be where it woud, for no other reason then that I might be out of the way, and the hearing, of these fatal discords. I repeate to you, the love and friendship I beare you is very sincere, as will appeare upon all occasions from, deare brother, . . .

88. [Incomplete letter. Endorsed May 28th, 1717. Bro. Thos. Yorke.]

. . . My mother and sister are safe gott to towne. I am just come

[463] Spencer Compton, c. 1674-1743, M.P. 1698-1710 and 1713-28, Speaker 1715-27, and later Lord Keeper and Lord President. *D.N.B.*

[464] See *Parl. Hist.* vii, 439.

[465] Catherine Yorke, née Lister, planned to leave her property to her second son Thomas (1688-1768) and only £10 to her eldest son John (1685-1757) because of his "undutiful behaviour".

from them and they desired me to give their services to you and sister. My mother seems fully resolv'd to defend her right, as she says, if my Bro[ther] attacks her, and will not listen to any advice to heale and compose matters. My bro[ther] has not yett been to visit my mo[ther].

89. Londo[n]. 30 May, 1717.

Deare Brother,

By an accident I did not gett your letter, of the 24 instant, time enough before what I wrote you, p[er] the last post was sent to the post, and, as ill luck woud have it, we have had three hollydays together; the King's birthday, the Restora[tion], and today Asscension Day, on which all businesses is att a stand. And this fine weather drawing people out of towne, I am inform'd Mr. Hutton[466] is in the country, so that I coud not proceed with that expedition in your affairs as I shoud have desired. However, I have been with Mr. Moore, who will send to him to meet us on Saturday morning, so you may expect to have a more particular account in my next, of the answer Mr. Hutton gives.

My mother has been prevail'd on to employ Mr. Waites[467] in drawing up her case, in order to have Mr. Vernon's opinion on severall points, and to be further assisting to her in his profession, which, I think, is one great point gain'd, that she has an honest attorney, that will not hurry her into vexatious lawsuits out of any self-interest; and we take all oppertunitys to incline her to a pacifist disposition.

I am deare Bro[ther]. . .

90. Londo[n]. 4 June, 1717.

Deare Brother,

Mr. Moore and self were to meet Mr. Hutton on Saturday last, but he disappointed us, which made me not keep my word of writing you last post. I have since had the good fortune to see Mr. Hutton, who told me that he had an interview with Mr. Moore, before he begun his journey, who he fully discours'd on the matter, and who made an affidavid to some matters he required of him. As Mr. Moore is on his journey home he will probably give you a better account then I can. Mr. Hutton told me that he had wrote att large

[466] John Hutton, attorney of Durham City.

[467] Charles Waites, first husband of Dorothy Clavering. See note 59.

to Mr. Dixon without having any answer. He seem'd dubious, when the matter came to a hearing, how the court woud take it. As I am a novice in affairs of this nature and little acquainted with the particular circumstances of your case, I coud only talk to him on generalls and recommend your intrest to him in as strong terms as I possibly coud. To which he answer'd me, that everything shoud be done by him in his power to promote your advantage and, as I remember, he said this affaire woud come on on Thursday and he seem'd to think it woud not be against you if the depositions in the comm[issione]rs hands were deliver'd into court; which I thought woud not answer the end, but he overruled me with reasons I coud not reply to. I wish he may make good his professions of sincerity to you and that this affaire may end to your sattisfaction. I am, deare brother, . . .

91. London. 9 July, 1717.

Deare Brother,

I am with your favour of the 2 instant, with an inclosed bill of £110 on Claude Jamineau, to which I shall procure the needfull and, when in cash, follow your orders in taking Mr. Waite with me to Mr. Freke and paying him £100 on account of John Clavering Esq. A suite of gray cloth for 2d. mourning is now in hand by Mr. Turnbull, who has promised to send it to you by the first carrier. He assured me he has your measure still by him and doubts not of fitting you.

If the rancour and malice of your ill-natured ennemies prompts them to attempt more mischiefe against you, may they receive the just reward, that is, be disappointed in all their designs and projects, and be obliged to make submission and pay the costs and charges you may be att.

I beleive my mother has but rec[eive]d little incouragement from her lawyers, that she has been with for advice about her monys. As to all differences I do not find but they stand just in statu quo. On Sunday last my mother invited my bro[ther], Mr. Weddell, and myselfe, to dine with her, and made a proposall to my bro[ther], to give him £500 if he woud give her a discharge for his claime to her personal estate, which he refused and insisted on £800, but that was not agreed to and so nothing was concluded on. Yett I hope a lawsuite may be prevented. Neither of them seeme now very fond of entering the lists, and both of them concurr, seemingly, not to meet att Richmond together, which I hope may prevent fresh differences. As the Parliament will rise in four or five days I suppose my brother designs for the country, not that I have any other grounds but my own bare conjecture, and my mother talks of taking a turne to Bath, if the doctor says it will do my sister Betty good, and after that, if one can judge by her discourse, she does not think of seeing the country very speedily.

I am growne so indifferent as to pollliticks that I never inquire or trouble myselfe about them, for I think I am so inconsidered, that neither anything I can do, or wish, can have any more influence then my endeavouring to stop the tide att Gravesend with my finger. To what purpose, then, is it to vex oneselfe. And, as to Ministers, I have one opinion of them all, and, as long as I heare that King George and that family is secure on the throne and that there is no feare of the Pretender coming amongst us, I am easye, and am, dear brother, . . .

92. London. 6 Augst., 1717.

Deare Brother,

I cannot let slip one post without giving answer to your favour of the first instant. I doubt not but you have received your suite of cloths, the taylor having assured me that they were sent, as [I] wrote you in my former. Your bill of £110 was punctually paid and I was no lesse punctual in the payment of the £100 to Mrs. Liddell,[468] who I went to, along with Mr. Waite, the very morning the bill was due. You'l have perhaps heard that Mr. Freke is deade. I wish with all my heart that all further quarrells and differences between my mother and brother may be prevented, but I much dreade the contrary. I am glad you have againe disappointed the designes of your ennemies and I hope you'l do the same as often as they renew their attempts against you. You wrote me in a former, that the father and mother took part with you against the adversary. I am now sorry to see they have so farr alter'd as to show such uncommon civillitys to your greatest ennemy. As to pollliticks I am of the same opinion I was, that it is trifling for a private person, as I am, to be sollicitous who is in the Ministry, for neither my wishes or inclinations will avail one way or other; and I am glad you begin to come into my sentiments. I am, deare brother, . . .

[468] Mrs. Anne Liddell, née Clavering.

93. Londo[n]. 5 Augt., 1718.

Deare Brother,

I am with your favour of the 31 past, with 2 bills for £235, of which I shall take proper care as to acceptance and payment; but I wonder that Mr. Bernardeau, who professes kindnesse for you, shoud make his bill of £210 att 40 days date, when he knows that you want to have the money soon, in cash here, to pay it in.

Mr. Waite began his journey for the north last Friday. Before he went I was in consultation with him about making the first payment, but since that I am informed, that Mr. Hiccocks, the Master in Chancery,[469] who is appointed by the court to receive the monys &c., relating to this trust, is gone to France and will not returne before the terme begins, so that I shall be glad to receive your order how to comport myselfe; whether you woud have it payd into C[harles] Sanderson's hands, the sollicitor, who I suppose may be trusted with the monys; but then whether intrest will be allow'd from the date he receives it. Pray think of this and let me have your directions. Likewise, if you think Mr. Waite's opinion needfull, I doubt not you know how to write to him, and you may desire him to give me his sentiments hereupon, to prevent losse of time. I note you are making all the dispatch you can to send up the mem[oria]ll of the mony you propose to pay into court.

I am sorry that the young gentleman shoud so misbehave himselfe to loose his reputation and to follow the steps of his sister in what is so obnoxious. I feare you are to expect no favour from that quarter. If you have strict justice done you, without the trouble and expence of law, you come of well.

It is the part of everyone of us, that wishes sister Betty well, to give a helping hand to what will conduce so much to her happinesse. By what my mother wrote me I concluded the matter had gone further then I find from you it has. If my sister has no objection to his person, I wish with all my heart it may be accomplish'd. What I mention'd in my former was expresly by my mo[ther's] directions, and I hope she may be prevail'd on to make an addition, to promote my sister's welfare. I make no doubt but you'l do all in your power to bring it to beare, and I dare say you'l proceed with that caution, prudence and secresy, that if it shoud not go on, to do neither party any prejudice. I meane, if it shoud be made publick

[469] Thomas Hiccock, barrister Middle Temple and a Master in Chancery. *Foster*.

or take aire, and afterwards breake of, Betty may not be blowne upon. And, I fancy you'l agree with me, the best method, to prevent that, will be to learne the utmost limmitts of the dem[an]ds of one, and the offers of the other, before a formal courtship begins, by which you may guesse if any probability of successe. But this I know is needlesse to mention to you, because you know much better than I how to proceed in an affaire of this kind. My service attends the women and I am, deare brother, . . .

94. Londo[n]. 23 [September] 1718.

Deare Brother,

I am without any from you to answer and so am now to acquaint you that I have used my utmost endeavours to procure payment to the two bills hereunder specified, but all to no purpose, and I begin to despaire that they ever will be paid, particularly the note of John Hartley, who says he has no mony, and cannot pay it, and I may arrest him if I please, for in short it is out of his power. So I desire your orders what to do with it. I believe the best way for me will be to returne it to you, that you may recover that mony of the person you took it of, who I hope is an able man. Langley does not give so plaine an answer, but I feare it is not [torn] better with him for my goldsmith has a bill on him that he has [denied?] for this 2 or 3 months. I am, deare brother, . . .

[P.S.] John Hartley's promisory note, in date 21 July att 30/d date, payed to Wm. Kitchingman, due since 23 Augt.

Wm. Langley's promisory note, in date p[ri]mo Augt. att 30/d date, payed to Simon de Landifield, due since 3 instant.

95. Richmond. 1st. June, 1722.

D[ear] Brother,

Hoping to see you either here or att Greencroft before my returne I will defer answering yours, which I just rec[ieve]d before I left London, till I can do it by word of mouth.

I reach'd this place on Wednesday afternoone under the greatest concerne for the sad occasion that call'd me downe, and, as an additional trouble to me, I find new differences and troubles arose here, which I want skill to compose. I wish my abilitys were equal to my inclinations. I will not add further then my respect and service to your spouse. I am, . . .

To James Clavering Esq., att Greencroft, near Durham.

96. London. 28 June, 1722.

Dear Brother,

I left Richmond last Sunday evening and arriv'd here safe on Tuesday afternoone, full of a due sense for the very kind reception I met with att Greencroft, for which I returne you my hearty thanks.

I coud wish that I coud tell you I had left our friends att Richmond in a disposition to promote their owne peace and happinesse. My mother had been told more then once that she coud not maintaine her right to the £500, and I hope time will induce her to resigne up her pretensions to that, and then I hope the maine difficulty is conquer'd and there can be no difference of moment about anything else. I hope you'l continue to cultivate a good understanding, to which end I endeavour'd to contribute all I coud by removing some groundlesse mistrusts.

The coldnesse between my bro[ther] and me was much heightned before we parted. He sett me to Bedale and in my way thither took upon him to catechise me and demanded of me to know everything my mother had said to me, nay, what she had given me, and, because I coud not be so particular as he expected, I tho[ugh]t we shoud have parted in downeright anger. What he means by this I cannot imagine. I am sure I never did him any ill in my life. He takes no care to cultivate an understanding and if you and I follow his steps, for ought I know, we may stand on as bad a footing and have as little expectations. I plainly told him, as I was not a man of ambition, I was very well content with my present way of living, which I coud just support with the assistance I have from my mother, but, if he was desirous of regaining her favour, I woud desist from my application and woud turne my thoughts of making my fortune some other way, and, as I have health I hope I shoud find friends to send me abroad, for I woud not submit to starve att home and cast any disgrace on him and the family. How he'l proceed gives me no great paine.

The most welcome news you can send me will be the happy delivery of your spouse, and am with great truth, . . .

97. London. 4 July, 1723.

Dear Brother,

You telling me in yours of 7 past, that you intended the week after for Scarborough, made me send my answer on the 13th. directed thither. But, not hearing since from you, I am doubtfull whether it has reach'd you, so this is design'd to find you att your owne house.

I went out of towne Fryday last, the 28 past, and was detain'd by a friend that was with me that I did not returne till yesterday, the 3 ins[tant], and found att my lodgings a letter from Mr. Gowland, in date 29 past, telling me you had disappointed him of monys for the fine for your assault on the bro[ther] Gray;[470] that your motion woud come on the 2 ins[tant]; desiring my attendance with the monys to pay such fine as the court orderd. I guesse if you had desir'd this of me you woud not have tho[ugh]t much of the trouble of writing me about it and [I] much doubt your having failed in having made the necessary provision in Mr. Gowland's hands. However, [I] can assure you I have your welfare so much att heart if I had been in towne I woud not only have given my attendance, but, as I am very low in cash, I woud att least have endeavour'd to raise the monys on my credit, which being very indifferent. If [I] had not succeeded I hope you will take the will as kind as doing the deed itselfe. But [I] am glad to find that Mr. Gowland has, by his dexterity, gott a reprieve till next terme so that you have now time enough before you. It will be very good news to me to heare you, as well as spouse, are well, and am . . .

98. London. 20 July, 1723.

Dear Brother,

The receipt of your fav[ou]r of 12 ins[tant] remov'd many gloomy apprehensions occasion'd by not hearing from you so long, and, tho' you do not think me worthy to be advis'd of the illnesse, nor anything else that passes, yet I can assure you I take no small pleasure in the account you give of your recovery, heartily congratulating you thereupon and wishing you a long continu[atio]n of health and happinesse. I am extreamly concern'd to find your spouse labours under so bad health. As she has my sincere wishes for her recovery, I cannot doubt that either advice, or anything else, will be neglected. I shall impatiently long for good tydings of you both.

I am glad you have so good hopes of defeating the malice of your

470 George Grey, 1680-1772, of Newcastle and Southwick, Co. Durham, who was a counsellor at law, married in 1712 Alice Clavering, the youngest sister of James Clavering, *Surtees*.

ennemies. It runns in my head that I had send you some of the receipts for the mony I paid H[enry] Liddell, but I find I have those for the large summs I paid to Mr. Hiccocks.

I cannot imagine what is meant by those irregular and unwarrantable proceedings att the late election of sherifs unlesse the ennemies of our government are forming designs to imbroile us in new troubles and so are resolv'd to have sherifs att any rate that will serve their turne, but I hope, as the administration is aware of them, they will be baffled.

We have had fine rains of late, which I hope has recover'd your aften grasse and done no harme to your corne, and am . . .

99. London. P[ri]mo Augt., 1723.

Dear Brother,

I am with the fav[ou]r of 26 past and do sincerely congratulate you and your spouse on your recoverys and offer up my hearty wishes that you both may grow sensibly better every day till you are perfectly restored to your health.

I am att a losse to guesse att the motive of the excuse you make for denying me the favour of informing me of your health. I hope you have no hidden reasons for resuming that thread of correspondence, which was carried on between us some time since, which, however agreable to you, [I] can assure you was not so to me. I am farr from being inquisitive and neither do expect nor desire to be inform'd of anything that is a secret or not fitt for me to know and all that I am desirous of knowing is relating to the wellfare of yourself and family and, for the rest, it will be time enough for me to heare what relates not [to] yourselfe nor the family when [it] is [made] publick in the world.

I will make a strict search after the receipts for the monys I paid on your account and give you the particulars in my hands, att the foot. I wish you may be able to overcome the wiles of your adversarys and shall be glad I coud contribute anything to it by answering interrogatorys relating to any discourse I had with C[harles] Sanderson and will recollect what pass'd in conversation the best I can, but, as I am to be upon oath and my memory not the best. I doubt not but you will be content with the best recollection I can make.

I am glad the good Bishop[471] met with a reception, so much beyond his opponent, from J[ames] C[laverin]g, who, must loose his

[471] See note 287.

intrest by making use of such popular arts, especially when they do not succeed.

I am sorry for the accident befallen your son and heir and but hope no arteries and sinews may be touch'd, and am . . .

[P.S.] 1715

Janu[ary] 5	A receipt	£100	by Hen[ry] Liddell.
1716			
9 ber 30	—	—£200	by ditto
1717			
July 22	—	—£100	by Ann Liddell.
Xber 16	—	—£100	by J. Hiccocks.
1718			
8 ber 30	—	—£1,000	by ditto.
Xber 15	—	—£300	by ditto.
1718/19			
Feb. 3	—	—£500	by ditto.

I wish when you go to Newcastle you would be so good to inquire of Dr. Bradey, who is heir and execut[or] to Mr. . . . Eyons deceas'd, there being a small summe in the hands of a friend of mine, belonging to the deceas'd, who woud be glad to part with it to any person he can safely pay it to and that will give a legall discharge.

100. London. 29 Augt., 1723.

Dear Brother,

In answer to your favour of 16 ins[tant], tho' I am never better pleas'd then when I heare from you, yett when businesse or the absence from home deprives me of that pleasure, I must submit to it with patience, without putting you to frame an excuse, which piece of formality is better laid aside between us.

As I never look upon anything a trouble to serve you, I do now send you, according to your desires, coppys of the receipts for the severall payments I made, by your order and on your account, for the executorship of your kinsman Clavering. As no man can be suppos'd to spy out mistakes in himselfe, so soone as a standerby, I am perswaded you'l not take it ill if I discharge the office of a true friend, in offering to you my sentiments upon your resolution of making the utmost defense you can in order to expose him. I wish some subtle lawyer has not buoy'd you up with hopes of successe, to incourage you to enter the lists for selfish ends of his owne. I doubt not, because you say so, that you may have it in your power to show that they have been very malicious and base in their proceedings against you, but you forgett that you have also laid yourselfe open by having such a large summe of mony in your hands belonging to your trust and, when was call'd upon to pay it in, was not ready with it, which occasion'd their applying to Chancery. Whereupon the court made an order for you to pay so much half yearly in discharge of principall and intrest, and, in my weak judgement, if you bring this matter before the court againe, they will, in their turn, throw dirt att you, unravel all your accounts over againe, and, if they can make objections to some articles, put you to a great charge, expence and trouble, besides costs of suite, and confirme the former decree of paying intrest.

You may be assured I shall be very willing to serve you, in recollecting anything that will be of advantage to you. Be pleas'd to send me up the letters themselves, that relates to any conversation I had with C[harles] Sanderson relating to you, for without them the chief, I remember, that pass'd between us, was his professing a great friendship to you and his excusing you from any dishonest views in running out the infant's mony, because you so readily came in to make over your estates as a security.

The summe belonging to the late Mr. Eyons is £4. 19. 5, [which] was paid into my hands by Mr. Weddell before he went into the country, which I am ready to pay your lawfull heir, upon a legall discharge of receiving so much from Mr. Weddell by my hands. It is no small concerne to me that you cannot give better news of your owne, nor your wife's, health. I hope you do not let spleen add to your distemper. I cannot doubt the taking all proper care of yourself as well as her. You have my heart's wishes for your recovery, and I beg to heare of you.

I wish the putting yourselfe to the charge of entertaining the Bi[sho]p may answer your expecta[tions]. I feare all great men are alike. I am, with sincerity, . . .

101. London. 28 [Septem]ber, 1723.

Dear Brother,

You, having been so delatory in favouring me with an answer to my last, putt me under malancholy apprehensions, which your favour of 15 instant has now dissipated, and I heartily rejoyce with you that you have att last subdued your troublesome indisposition, and, I hope, without the fears of a relapse. I wish you coud have given me as good an account of your spouse. The gout is a very irksome and disagreable remedy, but it may perhaps be better to undergo some present pains, which are not immediately dangerous, then to languish under a worse illnesse that foreboded instant and imminent hazard. She has my best wishes for her speedy recovery.

I cannot help hoping that both you and your kinsman may incline to make an end of all differences in a peaceable way. Pushing matters to extremity will not answer his purpose, but sure I am, it will not yours in the long. And, this being my real opinion, I coud never forgive myselfe if I did not impart it to you, tho' I know I lay myselfe open to your censure for taking this freedom upon me.

I am highly pleasd to find there is a disposition to accommodate the administra[tion] affaire in peace and quietness. You'l not want your share of applause for the part you have acted to bring it about, and I am perswaded you have too much goodnesse to use the power, you say [you] have, of making retaliation, otherwise then very gently.

It is a further confirmation to me that you are eas'd of your pains, because you are dispos'd to show the wit and mirth. It is very surprising you had not your intelligence earlier and that you shoud be so late in your congratulation. I had however rather be the object of your merriment then your malice and ill-will.

You will, I doubt not, acquaint with the needfull [at] the first oppertunity. I am . . .

102. London. 11 January, 1723/4.

Dear Brother,

In answer to your favour of 24 past I am to thank you for the bill of £10 you send me for mourning, which I have rec[eive]d.

I make no manner of doubt of your being every day more and more sensible of your great losse, for she certainly was a most affectionate and faithfull wife and a most tender and provident mother to her children and, as that weight of care does now evolve on you, I dare say you'l discharge yourselfe as a prudent and kind father.

I am very glad to heare you gave so favourable an account of your health, and I hope you'l continue to recover sensibly every day, which I heartily wish.

Since you inveigh so loudly against the late swearing act you'l find there is a bill bringing in to explaine and amend it, which I hope will pacifiy all reasonable men, tho' it is impossible it shoud all that joine in the outcrys against it. It seems to be confessed the act was pass'd in a hurry and was not so well consider'd as it ought. Humanum est errare, but for a sett of men to clamour att any severe laws that themselfes, by their restlesse endeavours to disturb our peace, have putt the Legislature under a necessity of making for our safety, is very unreasonable; but I think no well-wishers to our constitution shoud chime in with them in their groundlesse and false invectives. That you may injoy all health, happiness and prosperity in this and very many ensueing years is heartily wish'd by . . .

103. Richmond. 8 March, 1723/4.

Dear Brother,

Since my coming hither 4 or 5 days ago your favour of 27 past has been transmitted to me.

I can easily believe, *without your assurances*, the great losse not only you, but the poor children have sustain'd, never to be repaired, for she undoubtedly was a most affectionate, loving wife, a frugall, carefull manager of your family affairs, and had an indulgent, tender regard for her children.

If I was given to be opiniated of myselfe perhaps self-conceit might so farr blind me as to take to myself that purity of thought, which you, to be sure, very seriously woud ascribe to me; but if I woud do you justice I ought to celebrate your sublime way of thinking, which does indeed farr surpasse my poor understanding for I never knew before that vices coud interfere to moderate griefe. I do not pretend to be so pure and undefiled as to be free from faults, but I thank my God, as I am not high-minded and have not those incitements to avarice and self-love, the ambition of living in a grand way above my circumstances, I have not that call to an immoderate desire of wealth, further then in common with all mankind, to take a proper care, as farr as is consistent with strict honesty, to support the way of life I am in, without running out my fortune or putting myselfe to the inconvenience of borrowing of others.

I know by some quotations you formerly made out of Tillotson,[472]

[472] John Tillotson, 1630-94, Archbishop of Canterbury.

that you are well read in good books, but in my low opinion you are as wrong in your application of this borrowed sentence as you was in the other before. He must be more than man to know the motives that directs men's actions and, besides, it is not so very Christian to assigne ill causes, why any man does good. But let us state this quotation and then see in what light it appears.

He that doth good because he thinks himselfe oblig'd to do it, doth it with an ill grace.	He that doth ill because he thinks himselfe oblig'd to do good, doth it allways with a good grace.

As to your services to the government, I will concur with you, they have been great and conspicuous, and I wish with all my heart, they may be rewarded suitable to the merit of them.

I wonder why my wishes and desires, that you make an end with your Chopwell relation,[473] without going to law, shoud stunn you. I am sure it is not the first time, by many, I have said so, and I give you joy and sincerely rejoyce with you, that you have obtain'd an order to your liking, and are now disintangled of that vexatious affaire.

As I am a great lover of peace and concord, and can lay my hand on my heart and safely say I never did delight fishing in troubled waters, never did sow the seeds of strife and contention, never endeavour'd to sett one relation against another by raising groundlesse mistrusts of each other, nor ever made use of indirect underhand practises for selfish ends of my own, so lett the consequence be what it will, I will inviolably adhere to the same pacifick measures, that the world shall have no cause to censure me justly, nor I have reason to reproach myselfe; and if you are dispos'd for any hidden reasons, to commence a new paper warr with me, you shall carry it on by yourselfe.

If I had not had it explained to me since I came here I should not have knowne what you meant by going to Newcastle to be cut. I am truly concern'd for the occasion and heartily wish successe in the operation, a good recovery, and long health and prosperity.

The short time I propose staying here will not permit me paying you a visitt, for I must returne in 10 days. I am . . .

[473] John ("Jacky") Clavering of Chopwell. See note 1.

III. LETTERS FROM JOHN YORKE

104. London. 20th February 1723[/24.]

Dear Brother,

I am duely with your favour bearing date the 13 instant and dare say we do not differ the least relating [to] the administration affair. As I woud be glad to put our case on a good foot we cannot complain of being denied an inventory. What then? We must alledge a sufficient cause to lay a good foundation for our proceeding, to shew we are in earnest and determined to have justice. For my part, [I] am the worst in the world [at] representing this case to counsel and do wish your presence here to put matters in agitation or, if you'l get our complaints stated, I will then consult Mr. Capper.[474] But I think, as brother intends a visit so soon to Richmond, it will be better to rest it till his return, to see if reasonable things will be offer'd. Tho' I declare it's my opinion, nothing will make her comply except filing a bill, I submitt everything to your consideration and better judgement, and shall concur in anything you transmitt to me. Mother has wrote me two letters in an affectionate manner but nothing relating [to] the administration. In her last she desires me to write to Mr. Rudd,[475] that he woud employ some attorney to procure her the £100 she lent Mr. Owen,[476] which I shall decline, having had nothing to do with that affair from the beginning, and put it upon my brother. I am sorry your kinsman runs matters to so great a violence, and wish Lady Cowper's death may make any alteration. I hear Mrs. Liddell made her appearance abroad soon after her death without the least regard or comon decency of dress. I suppose she had no mourning given her. I sent the inclosed to Mr. Gowland, with my request to expedite your affair, who return'd me for answer, that his best endeavours shoud be employed and that he woud come to see me. I

[474] Richard Capper of Bushy, Hertfordshire, a barrister of the Inner Temple. He later married Dorothy Waites, née Clavering. See note 59. *Foster* and *Letter-book*.

[475] John Rudd was seneschal and solicitor-general of Durham. *Hughes*.

[476] Stephen Owen was a lessee of Park colliery, Gateshead, and a gentleman of Gray's Inn. *Hughes*.

always intended making Mr. Rudd a present of his Majesty's approbation, but I did not apprehend the charge woud have been so great. I have only time left to reprimand you for the unaccountable negligence of your own welfare; that I am surprized you continue in that lethargick humour to be deaf to all advice of your friends, besides physicians, and I wish you have not suffer'd already to prevent a cure in time. Your inclosed to Mrs. Waite was carefully deliver'd and your letters have come without any remarks from the post office. When you hear of any good French wine I desire your remembrance of me.

I am dear brother, yours very affectionately,

J. Yorke.

To James Clavering Esq., att Greencroft, near Durham.

105. London. 24 March 1723[/24.]

Dear Brother,

The last night finished the Northumberland election in the comittee, who voted Mr. Jennison[477] duely elected 110 against 58, and I believe will succeed on the report to the House. It's a very intricate business, but numbers will clear it up. Brother was with me this morning for settling the tickets. I ask'd him some interogatories relating [to] his visit in the north; who is very private and begun to be peevish and woud resolve me nothing. I am truly impatient to hear a good account of you and your son, tho' when not hearing from you last post make me hope the best. I am . . .

106. Richmond. Jan. 16th, 1725[/26.]

Dear Brother,

Your favours of 7 and 11 date accompanied me yesterday att 4 in the afternoon and, according to your request, [I] take the first opportunity of returning thanks. I perceive your son remains yet with Mr. Scaife and except you know him to be neglected, I fancy, tho' Mr. Scaife has left of a publick school, yet surely capable and not wanting to instruct Jemy.[478] Otherwise he woud have certainly sent him to his son. Therefore I hope there is no occasion for any uneasiness and in my thoughts it woud be better to have the spring a little more advanced before you place him to any school about

[477] Ralph Jennison, M.P. Northumberland 1723-41. *Surtees* and *Hughes*.
[478] James Clavering junior, who died in 1726.

London. However I shall be ready to do everything in my power, that you may think for the boy's interest, but I cannot possibly call att Cambridge or should I venture him to ride post with me. Tho' when att London he may come in the stage coach and I will take care of his arrival and conduct him to my lodgings, and where you please to order him afterwards. I shall endeavour to follow your directions in every particular and desire you'l joyn a friend with me, for perhaps I may be att a loss how to act for the best. However I pray let your directions be full in all respects. Mr. Recorder and nephew are not yet arrived. It's now past 9 in the evening and no tidings of the post so I comitt this to my neighbour's care, to darling son. I am sorry for Mrs. Clavering's[479] ill state of health, and I heartily wish a good recovery. My true love attend all with you, and I am . . .

107. London. 24 February, 1725[/26.]

Dear Brother,

In answer to your favour, which I could not answer sooner, I take the first opportunity to congratulate you on the pleasures and happiness of a married state, and as I have a very great respect for the Lady I heartily wish equall and mutual satisfaction, long to live and enjoy each other, and desire the tender of my perticular respects in the best manner. I hear no tidings yet of your son. Mrs. Liddell has wrote to his master to know the terms of the school, where att leisure times, I perceive, they learn dancing, French, &c. So [I] desire to know your thoughts, whether you woud have him initiated so soon in these accomplishments. We had last Tuesday an election controverted att the bar betwixt Mr. Collier and Mr. Waller.[480] The petitioner only pray'd a void election, and the sitting member after some debates gave it up to save his friends from the censure of the house. I am . . .

[P.S.] I am very sorry for the misfortune of our friend[481] att Long Newton, tho' [I] am glad the worst is past and hope he will recover soon. I am just going to the House and, if any novells arise, will give you a further trouble.

[479] James Clavering's second wife Elizabeth, daughter of Lionel Vane. *Surtees.*

[480] On 7 February 1725/6 Harry Waller petitioned against Charles Collyear or Collier because of malpractices by the mayor in the election at Chipping Wycombe. The election was declared void on 22 February. See *C.J.* xx, 564-5 and 586.

[481] Lionel Vane, father-in-law of James Clavering.

This day the King came to the house of Peers and gave the royal assent to the land tax bill, the lottery bill for a million, and the bill for punishing mutiny and desertion.

108. London. 3 March, 1725[/26.]

Dear Brother,

Upon receipt of your favour [I] waited on Mrs. Liddell with the inclosed, and, when your son James arrives, I shall be sure to consult her in all respects as I think she will prove an excellent governess to us both. Mrs. Waite is a great rambler, that I have not yet met with her att home to pay my devoirs. What Mrs. Liddell thinks necessary, in equipment or otherwise, for your son, I shall readily order matters accordingly.

Yesterday we had a pritty extraordinary petition from Mr. Hampden,[482] setting forth his inability to pay his debts due to the Crown, when he was Treasurer of the Navy, desiring a composition to pay 10s per round, which was referred to a comittee of the whole house. So I beleive it's intended to save his paternall estate and the publick to make him a present of a sum betwixt £40,000 and £50,000, that he may be enabled to continue his extravagance amongst the females. I perceive brother intends speedily to visit mother. [I] notifyed your marriage to him, that he might make you a visit or at least send his compliments. Please to make my respects acceptable to my new sister; wishing you and family all health and happiness, I am . . .

109. London. 15 March, 1725[/26.]

Dear Brother,

Mrs. Liddell prevented my writing the last post, who then gave you an account of your son, [who], as I think now, is in a hopefull way of doing well, having no ill symptoms, that I hope in a week's time to attend him to school. His master was with us this morning in East street, with whom I had some little discourse, and, on the first appearance, your son approves of his as well as myself, and he likes him the better because he's not in orders; and I please myself that all the lost time will be regain'd by the master's carefull eye and due observance, provided the boy settle well att first and [is] willing in his endeavours. The master signifyed that whenever a lad proves so

[482] Richard Hampden had been Treasurer of the Navy 1719-20 and had been involved in the South Sea scandal. For his petition see *Parl. Hist.*, viii, 513-6.

refractory [as] to be incorigible, and continues so, he always desires his parents to remove him, least his other boys shoud be spoil'd. As he certainly is in the right, Jem shall want no instructions or advice from me and it will be a great pleasure that he answers the end of your care and charge in his education, for now is the very time of making a good groundwork, to enable him for better proficiencys on his appearing in the world. [I] suppose you have already the charge and method of the school and you may be assured I shall act in everything as Mrs. Liddell directs or advises. I expect no good from brother's journey, who is now gone to inspect mother's estate, and I hear after his report [he] intends to return imediately to Town. I wish all health and happiness to yourself and family, which concludes me . . .

110. London. 22 March, 1725[/26.]

Dear Brother,

I am favour'd with yours and a bill for thirty pounds, which I hope will be duely honour'd when due. Since Mrs. Liddell writing you last post your son is better. The feaver is now intermitting, that Jesuits' bark is now applied and [I] do not question in a few days to conquer the feaver, tho' I have my concerne that something worse will be hard to avoid, which is a consumption as the Drs. apprehend. Yet under all events you may be assured no care will be wanting to do everything to restore his health, which time alone must direct to inform you more. I presented your letter to Mrs. Liddell yesterday and then, as well as often before, made your compliments upon the unexpected trouble of poor Jem. If he shoud grow worse or fall into a declining condition you will hear from one of your friends every post. Otherwise be satisfyed there is no occasion to trouble you. We have been under expectation these two days of a message from his Majestie; prevented, as I suppose, by a great minister's Lady falling ill of the small pox; which we shall have next Thursday. I divine it either relates to money or troops, to be in readinesse in case of necessity. I am . . .

111. London. 29 March, 1726.

Dear Brother,

In answer to yours, the lingring indisposition of your son, who in times is better and worse, has given me great uneasiness, that this morning I consulted Mrs. Liddell to have a physician in time, to know the true state of his case. So, on her recomendation of Dr. Hulse,[483] I mett him this evening att 6, who apprehends an impostumation on his lungs, and, if it ripens kindly, to throw up all that nauseous matter by spitting in a plentifull manner, he hopes the poor boy will do well. Otherwise in a gradual manner [he] is affraid [it] will overcome his strength. This being the true state in the Dr.'s judgement. He has prescrib'd some powder and asses' milk, Bristol water for drinking, pudding and fish for his dyet, and prohibited all manner of flesh. Under these rules I have taken some pains to desire his obedience without reluctance, whom I left well satisfied to take everything prescribed. I can only repeat my good wishes and assurances, that no care will be wanting in us to restore health. I do not apprehend imediate danger, but, I fear, if he does not begin to pick up crumbs soon, we must submit to the Divine pleasure; and all will be owing to the irregular life at Hisson, which the poor boy owns, and confesses many of the pranks he comitted there to weaken him, and has had complaints this half year.

I mett with Mrs. Waite this evening in East street, who, being not easily found att home, paid her five guineys by your order. Mrs. Liddell writes you this post. My love and respect attend all with you and I am . . .

112. London. 2 Aprill, 1725 [an error for 1726.]

Dear Brother,

I am with your favour, and take care of the inclosed, and [am] sorry that I can give no better account of your son, who, I fear, daily wastes and except the vomica shoud naturally take place to throw up the ulcerous humour, which is so nauseous that when he throws up anything [it] is past enduring the room, so that I really dispair rearing him up. Under these circumstances he may continue some time, but the doctor disheartens me from any hopes of recovery, and all that can be done att present is to ease him in his pain and cold; and besides he's so refractory taking what is proper for him, that I believe Mrs. Liddell has a hard taske to govern him. The Dr. has orderd him to be blooded this evening and waits on him tomorow morning, where I shall attend and you may depend hearing further the next post either from Mrs. Liddell or self, who am . . .

[483] Dr. Edward Hulse, 1682-1759, eminent physician, created a baronet in 1739. *D.N.B.*

[P.S.] Bro[ther] is safe return'd to Town, but I hear no novels from him. I shall in a short time think of moving northwards, except my staying coud be of any reall service to your son's recovery, and I hope may have your leave.

113. London. 7 Aprill, 1726.

Dear Brother,

We are adjourn'd this day to next Wednesday, which will give me so much idle time to settle my affairs in order to return home, the session drawing near to an end, and if you have any comands I shall be glad to receive them by first opportunity. Since my last your son is much in statu quo, appears brisker, tho' gains no ground, that I am affraid he insensibly decays. As all who are consulted have little hopes of his recovery so that Mrs. Liddell coud wish you to see him and bring up your son Tom[484] to school and carry down poor Jem if he's able to travell, for the Dr. does say their is litle to be expected, except his own country air will restore him. I cannot advise anything myself, not knowing how your affairs may suite such a journey, so submitt Mrs. Liddell['s] advice to your own government. In the meantime shall continue due attendance on the poor child and shall be glad to receive any further directions, wherein I can serve you. I am . . .

[P.S.] My respects and service attend all with you.

114. London. 12 Aprill, 1726.

Dear Brother,

In answer to yours, if Mrs. Liddell's and my letters are come safe to your hand [I] must imagine you on the road or preparing for a London journey to see your son, who languishes daily; and his own impatience to see you, and return home, makes him frett and very uneasie, as he was this morning, which provoked a violent fit of coughing, and the matter he throws up as nauseous as possible, which he has voided plentifully these two days; and it's the general opinion that nothing is so likely to restore him as such a vacuation, which is so corrupt that he can scarce bear the stench himself. For my part [I] wish him att home or that any way could be contrived without hazard, for I am sure he will be under no government except you are

[484] Thomas Clavering, born 1718, succeeded his father as 7th bart. in 1748 and died in 1794. *Surtees*.

with him. Therefore Mrs. Liddell thinks it absolutely necessary, if [you] can order your affairs att home, to loose no time as well on your son's account as Sir James Clavering,[485] who is thought to be in as dangerous a way. I can only remark that, as the poor boy complains of the uneasiness in a coach, as he takes the air sometimes, I am affraid he will scarce be able to undergo a long journey especially in the stage coach and, besides, no passenger will be able to endure his coughing, &c. I am . . .

[P.S.] My respects and service wait on sister and the lads.

115. London. 15 Aprill, 1726.

Dear Brother,

Not hearing from you last post I continue writing to Greencroft, tho' I could wish you here upon many accounts, as now I am affraid your son will not survive many days. I found an alteration this day att noon. [He was] in great pain, working inwardly, and very low spirited, inclinable to slumber, and said litle. So we sent for the doctor, who prescribed something to ease him, but has not the least hopes and says, that the first warm weather will go hard with him.

Attended this evening att 7 to use my perswasion [on him] to take what the Dr. order'd. I found him something better, but woud by no means submit to a glister to cool his body, not having had a stool these three or four days. Till at length, after an hour's intreatie, on condition that I woud buy him "Robinson Crusoe", he woud suffer it. Upon which he grew very outrageous and woud not keep the glister two minutes so it coud not have had the full desired effect. Yet he found some benefit imediately. Mrs. Liddell, as well as myself, have had no litle trouble and concerne, on this refractory disposition, to do himself good. I have little more to add except to prepare you to submit to the divine pleasure, which must be all our fate's sooner or later. If it shoud please God to preserve life till you see him it woud be a great satisfaction and pleasure to us all. Otherwise, for want of directions, I shall consult Mrs. Liddell in everything for the best and I beg leave to conclude with true concerne . . .

116. London. 19 Aprill, 1726.

Dear Brother,

In answer to yours [I] shoud be very glad to give you a more

[485] Young James Clavering, 4th bart., son of Sir John Clavering, died in 1726, aged 18. The title then went to his uncle, Francis. *Surtees*.

agreable account of your son's state and circumstances, in which an unexpected turn has happen'd since my last, which gives great reliefe and made him abundantly better; that is a humour fallen down to his foot, which the doctor says this morning is the gout, and proceeds entirely from his irregular vicious life att school. It may do great service if it can be prevented from returning to his body, provided he will be governable and leave of his outrageous fits. I wish this humour woud grow and swell more to a head and then burst, as there is no hopes left without an extraordinary evacuation somewhere. It's certain he's much eased att present, more lively and brisk, but continues very weak, besides his lameness that he canot point the ground. I consulted the doctor, for his returning home, who gives no encouragement to endure the journey with safety, tho' says he can do him as much service att Greencroft as here, in corresponding about his case from time to time. There is no immediate danger att present, but God knows how soon it may happen. Therefore if you coud continue to undertake a journey hither it woud give equall satisfaction. I am sure [illegible] to yourself as well as your friends as I hope you'l make no longer delay.

I hear mother threatens much after the session is up, that the decree is not serv'd and obey'd. So something or other shoud be done. If no accomodation is to be met with, we must submitt to everything or I shall joyn with you in any measure you think proper. I am affraid nothing is to be expected from brother. I believe the best way is to instruct Mr. Rudd to form a mediation and desire him to make a purpose visit, that matters may not depend in this maner, to be liable to any advantage of the law against us. I pray you duely to consider as you do not know how she may be hurried on, and I believe Mr. Rudd may bring matters to an accomodation and I will abide everything agreed on amongst you. I am . . .

[P.S.] I beg my humble service to sister and all yours. I shall wait your answer and then think of returning homewards. Shoud not Cappers be demanded and paid of, who has not yet return'd me my settlement?

117. London. 3 May, 1726.

Dear Brother,

I have yours of the 29 instant and do assure you am now heartily weary of this Town and nothing but the love and respect I bear to you and yours coud have detain'd me thus long, tho' God knows att this juncture every day appears more melancholly when I see poor Jem in such pitious and languishing a condition. Nothing that he has taken these 3 days stays with him, and [he] is now in the weakest state to live that ever poor boy was, and the sooner God is pleased to take him the happier, for he has endured more than can be possibly imagin'd. What relates Mrs. Liddell's servants, if I have no perticular order from you, I shall desire to consult Mrs. Waite and, as far as my cash reaches, I shall freely employ it to discharge all demands on this unhappy occassion and I hope the account will shew that nothing has be[en] unnecessarily expended, tho' we are unfortunate in our best endeavours. I am going this evening to take my last farewell and I believe Mrs. Liddell writes this post, to whom I refer more perticulary.

I have been twice att Mr. Capper's for his account, as I was this day, which yet wants to be drawn out. I gave him a cover to write you this post. Whatever you and Mr. Rudd agree on I shall readily concur and am of opinion that its none of our interests, since the proceeding begun, to have it lie dormant in this manner. An unactive suit often brings the greater charge att last and do not know what advantage mother may receive from it, either by attachments or extents against me, for I woud not willingly be in her power or agents to be under any difficulty (notwithstanding I know my priviledge). Yet nobody knows how indiscreet the master may be in his abounding wisdom and I am apt to believe [I] do not stand well in his good graces. I am . . .

118. London. 7 May, 1726.

Dear Brother,

Yours came duely to hand yesterday and I believe that some or one of your friends have been constant writing to you every post. However, if your female correspondents perform'd what they promised or intended, [I] may safely say for this last month we have not omitted one post, so probably miscariages has happen'd some way. I am surprized you could entertain the least hopes of your son's recovery or long continuance, who lingred on beyond everybody's expectation, as you had the melancholly account from me last post. Also the funeral intended for tomorrow att nine in the evening, which I hope will be perform'd in every respect, to have your approbation. On which occasion [I] can add no further perticulars to my last, except that Mr. Richardson[486] refuses to take his fees, and, calling to mind the family's constant civility and respect to you and yours, so we think proper to compliment the doctor, son and daughter, with scarves. I had a letter from brother in answer to mine, giving some hopes of his attendance. Yesterday Mr. Capper visited me when I had company [so] that we could have no private discourse, that I desired, if he had brought his bill to leave it with me, which he did, tho' litle unwillingly. I find he has seperated the charges. He acknowledges to have received on your account £25-5s, and the bill charged to you amounts in the whole to £44-3s-9d. The bill charged to me in the whole is £15-14s-2d so that your £25 being deducted from the whole brings it to £18-18-9d, which I will discharge if you please, tho' I think it very extravagant and many articles superfluous to aggrandize it. I shall call in all demands next week and do my utmost to discharge everything, but I hope by that time you may send bills. I shall certainly wait your answer to this by returne of the post and do my utmost to shew you that I am with sincerity . . .

[P.S.] As to mother, what you think proper to do I shall most heartily concur in, only that things may not sleep in this manner.

119. London. 12 May, 1726.

Dear Brother,

In answer to yours I have litle to say since my last, to which refer you, as everything was perform'd on Sunday, that decency and respect required, and I hope nothing can be deem'd amiss, when I have the satisfaction of seeing you. Indeed I owe great obligations to the two ladies for their kind assistance on all occasions, especially to Mrs. Liddell, who had it more in her power to be serviceable; and friendship when tried, to find it reall, is an inestimable jewell. Upon your letter to Mrs. Waite, she consulted me what to give Mrs. Liddell's servants, in which case I own myself no judge, but she thought guineys a piece woud do well. So I gave her three guineys, desiring her to distribute it. I have now discharged all demands upon poor Jem's account except Mr. Small, who to me declin'd making any demand or bill, but woud leave it to myself. So truly I was affraid trusting myself in giving more than what he deserved. On

486 ? Rev. Robert Richardson, vicar of Atwick, Yorkshire, 1680-1728. *Foster*.

this consideration [I] have prevail'd with Mrs. Liddell to undertake him, who I doubt not will manage for the best. When I have your answer shall make provision and discharge Mr. Capper's bills. I propose, God willing, on Wednesday next to leave this dusty town, either in the Stamford coach, which goes in one day, or take post att hand, and hope to lie in my own bed the latter end of next week, where I shall be glad to hear a good account of your wellfare, being concern'd for your present indisposition. I think [I have] never yet mention'd my correspondence with Sir Wm. Lowther,[487] on your late servant's account, who has put me of from [time] to time in hopes of the money, and yesterday [he] told me that he had discharged the man and did not care what became of him. He's maried and lives somewhere in the neighbourhood about Swillington. I am, dear brother, . . .

[P.S.] My respects and best wishes attends you and yours.

120. Richmond. 20 May, 1726.

Dear Brother,

On receipt of your favour I was in some hurry preparing for my journey the next day, which [I] perform'd very well to this place yesterday in the afternoon tho' the heat was violent and the dust troublesome to bear. I hope Mrs. Liddell woud plead for me, which shortens my apologie. I am truly concern'd for the continuance of your ill state yet I am of opinion that moderate [exercise] on horseback is the best phisick and I advise you not to neglect such gentle means in time. As to your omission of the rings I found there was no hair saved, and indeed my time so short, that I could not have them done before leaving the Town. Besides, you did not mention whether male or female, for your two friends in the country, so that your direction was a litle lame to have acted upon such an occasion. As to myself, [I] desire you'l not think to be att any charge and I think it unnessary and beleive it not expected from you to the family by London Wall, whom I waited on before I left the Town, but found only the Dr. att home. [I] paid my compliments and return'd all due accknowledgements upon your account. You may send other things what the country affords, which, in my thoughts, will be more acceptable, as he hinted some obligations to you in that way. Mrs. Waite,

[487] Sir William Lowther of Swillington, M.P. for Pontefract 1701-29.

when I consulted her about the rings, she advised that Mrs. Liddell might have a ring of £5 or £6 value, if you thought proper, and refused any such thing for herself. I promised to comunicate her thoughts to you on this subject and submit it to your animadversion, for there is no haste required. My neighbour's come in to visit me so I must hasten and can only add that I answer'd all demands on your account, by bill or otherwise. [I] likewise paid Capper's unreasonable bill and shall be glad to receive any further comands, wherein I can serve you. My respects and service waits on sister and the lads, who I hope keeps well. [This] concludes me . . .

[P.S.] I hope [I] shall see you shortly. However [I] expect you att our races.

121. Richmond. 27 May, 1726.

Dear Brother,

I have your favour and thank you for the kind inquiry, [to] which my letter this day 7 night woud give some satisfaction. The disbursements on your account, upon severall occassions, which I hope shall satisfye you att meeting, amount to £94-9s-10d. Whereof [I] do accknowledge to have received a bill for £30, which reduces it to £64-9s-10d, tho' Capper's bills are not included in this account, and, if I understand you right, money is scarce, by meeting with disappointments. So far is it from my thoughts to put any inconveniency upon you to straiten your affairs, that I propose this expedient, if it's approved of, to make up the debt [to] a hundred pounds, into your own pocket, and to account with you till matters are accomodated or ended in Chancery amongst us. If you please to give your bond or note for this purpose, I will order the remainder sum into your hands when you please, tho' I beg your early answer, that I may provide accordingly. I am truly concern'd for the continuance of your ill state of health, which makes me very uneasie till I have a better account. I wish you woud try [a] change of air and let me see you, which I promise myself will not be long. However I do engage you att our horse races.

When I left London [I] put mother's bill and my answer in Capper's hand and he assured me to comunicate [to] you what he thought best to be done, that we might consider and confirm. I beg my humble service to sister, &c., and am . . .

122. Richmond. 27 December, 1728.

Dear Brother,

In answer to your favour, [I] hope you will give me proper notice if you expect my meeting you att Thornton for I intend, God willing, to see the opening of this session, if the weather and ways will allowe, for we have fresh and deep coverings of snow, and likely to continue, that I am afraid the inhabitants upon the moors will suffer greatly. I am glad to hear of the wellfare of your young men and that they make so good improvement att Kelloe, which I wish may continue to your satisfaction. I propose moving to London about the 14 or 15 of next month. I beg my respects and service to all your fireside and I am . . .

123. Richmond. 23 Augt., 1730.

Dear Brother,

I defer'd answering your favour, dated the 19 of last month, intending you a visit att that time and really was now fix'd to wait of you on Tuesday next, but finding yours of the 17 upon my return yesterday from Yarme races, I wish this reaches to assure you of not failing to salute you att Thornton on Thursday noon, the 27 instant, and accompany you hither that evening. Brother and his spouse decamp'd last Wednesday 7 night for London, but [I] have heard nothing of their arrivall. I beg my humble service to sister, and, if Netherdale is famous for whiten yarn, I will endeavour to procure the best that can be got at my next going over. Adieu, to our meeting att Thornton, and I am . . .

124. Richmond. 10 Nov., 1730.

Dear Brother,

By your favour I am glad to find the affair with Sir Francis[488] is in so fair a way of being accomodated. [This is] much better, in my thoughts, than the hazard of a London journey. The unknown expence, and the plague of sollicitation in such a cause, would be too troublesome to undergoe. So I wish you a favourable determination without any further law, which tho' instituted for the preservation of the subject, I am affraid the practice has grown too much otherwise and become a generall grievance. The news of my nephews' recovery after their illness is very wellcome and abates my concerne

488 Sir Francis Clavering, 5th bart.

since they are so well to go abroad, and I hope continue so. I have been severall times prevented waiting of you, but the next week if possible I will endeavour to kiss your hand. Tho' the season is so far advanc'd, that if the weather will not permitt, I hope you will excuse me till next spring. I am . . .

125. Richmond. 18 Dec., 1730.

Dear Brother,

Att the time of my writing last to you (notwithstanding the litle regard shewn to you) I thought proper to give you the earliest intelligence of mother's circumstances and how affairs stood, by my neighbour Wilson's going to Newcastle, who drop'd my letter att the Red Lyon, which did not require so immediate an answer as I must accknowledge your favour this day by the post, and, since my last account, [I] do not think mother much alter'd in appearance, but doubtless much weaker tho' she has a strong appetite and will eat what she pleases. [She is] sometimes very restless and uneasie and cannot lie in bed and dozes in the chair. This afternoon, with much difficulty, we prevail'd to send for Dr. Johnson[489] of York, but I cannot conceive any hopes of her recovery; that the least disorder must carry her of, as she will not be govern'd and woud have nobody in time but poor Nan Dike, who does her best. I am happy att present, being restored to mother's favour by her blessing and I could wish, before her departure, she woud be in peace with all the world and not make such reflections about her funerall. These two days she has said litle about it. Brother has been with me since Sunday at bed and board and I think it woud be hard to quarrel with me, when everything goes according to his owne desire, and I hope he will be easie upon all accounts. My love and service attend all about your fireside. I am . . .

126. London. 27 Feb., 1730[/31.]

Dear Brother,

I have yours dated the 18, which came to hand the 25 instant and [I] believe [I] am not mistaken in what Mr. Boothe[490] told me. Tho' I am far from blaming you [for] accepting of these terms, for peace sake, rather than run the uncertain fate of the determination, atten-

[489] Dr. James Johnson of York, later Bishop of Gloucester. *D.N.B.*

[490] Thomas Bootle, attorney, who in 1733 was appointed attorney-general of Durham. *Hutchinson*.

ded with unknown charge and inconveniency, but I think [I] may venture to say the judge has not proved your friend as he promised. Yesterday you send me to an ale-house, where I mett with the scarlett oak acorns. I found them extravagantly dear and not very fresh, that I only purchased a hundred att 5s., which I send in a litle box by Monday's carier, directed to Mr. Gatis[491] in Newcastle. I shoud advise you to steep them in water the night before you sett them. As to the true pitch tree and as you say some ceries of a firr unknown, [I] suppose you mean species, were all sold and gone.

The Lords have put of the pension bill to next Tuesday, when it is said Lord I[slay][492] will demonstrate that the bill, intended to prevent bribery and corruption, will effectually establish it. So there is litle hopes of success.[493] By letters, yesterday from Richmond, give me a melancholly account of mother; that they dispaird her surviving two or three days, which sett Brother forward (as he intended before) this morning of his own horses, but I fear she will be gone before his arrivall. I am no further inform'd of her will than when I wrote you from Richmond. We have been told lately from a great man that we shall soon be put on a new foot both at home and abroad, so I hope our trade and manufacturers will revive and flourish att home and abroad, and [be] establishd'd upon a lasting foundation. I am told we shall have a lottery, which I must oppose, totis viribus, being the most pernicious and infamous way of raising money. I am . . .

127. London. 20 April, 1731.

Dear Brother,

I am oblig'd with your favour yesterday, dated the 15, and return you my thanks for your care of me, which, if the clarett proves really good and strong, without art [I] shall desire a third part and wish you woud send it to Richmond the first opportunity, before the warm weather advances, well pack'd in strong short-neck'd bottles. By brother's account yesterday, mother is in very deplorable, melancholly circumstances. She has now Dr. Metcalfe[494] joyn'd to Nan Dike, who has prevail'd to consent to have some issues put on her back, which no doubt will give great releife and prolong her time.

491 George Gatis, shop-owner of Sandhill, Newcastle. *Arch. Ael.* 3rd series, V.

492 Probably Lord Islay, brother of the Duke of Argyle. See note 297.

493 The pension bill was passed by the Commons and rejected by the Lords. See *Parl. Hist.*, viii, 789-98.

494 Dr. Theophilus Metcalfe, 1690-1757. *Foster*.

Brother presses me to return home, to which [I] have answer'd, if mother desires and my presence is acceptable. I propose to pay my duty &c., the first week in May, having taken [a] place already in the York coach for Monday the 3 of May. [I am] to accompany a young lady, who is going to spend the sumer with her sister, Mrs. King, att Bewerly. So if you have any further comands you know the time of my residence here. I think [I] do not want a gardiner att present, but I am told now the secret of my old gardiner leaving me, having got one of my maids with child. That, I believe, made him uneasie to scamper in time, which I guess'd att was the case why he gave me such short warning and left me, as he pretended, upon account of more wages, when I was sure he never woud have the same given him. But this is the fate of bringing youths up to buisiness. The Game bill, I beleive, is not intended to pass, being so clogg'd with instructions to be received att the committee, as perticulary a penalty on persons killing woodcocks. I beg my love and service to all your family and I am . . .

128. Richmond. 16 May, 1731.

Dear Brother,

I am with your favour this day, wherein I perceive my third part of clarett is arrived att Greencroft. As I wish you coud get it brought to Peircebridge and appoint the time and place, I woud sent my cart to convey it hither. I propose to move into Netherdale tomorrow morning, where I shall stay 5 or 6 days and shall be very glad to kiss your hands here any time afterwards. My humble service waits where due. I am . . .

129. Richmond. 4 June, 1731.

Dear Brother,

I am with your favour of the first instant and I think now it is very evident that packing bottles in a sheet is much safer than the cask, by which I am a sufferer, and, as you tell me I have more bottles than your share, I do assure you mine are as litle as ever Andrew Kenedy[495] sent me. I am very sorry that the misunderstanding keeps up betwixt you, which I heartily wish otherwise and in my power to serve you. My invitation to you both was with a good intention, and tho' it is not agreable to your inclinations, I hope [I] may be happy with your company att our races, but I really fear affairs will pre-

[495] Andrew Kennedy, a Newcastle wine merchant. *Hodgson*.

vent me from attending you att Newcastle, which I beg you will excuse if they shoud so happen; and my inclinations or endeavours shall not be wanting. My love and good wishes heartily attend all with you and I am . . .

130. Richmond. 18 June, 1731.

Dear Brother,

I have your favour dated the 15, with the advertisement of your diversions, in which [I] am sorry [I] coud not be a partaker to have your company, hoping good fortune, &c., attended your meeting. The next rendezvous is att Richmond on Wednesday the 30th coming. I am obliged to be in Netherdale[496] latter end of next week, but shall certainly return home on Monday, the 28th, to salute you and make you and company wellcome. I beleive now we shall soon have Spain come into our measures of the Vienna Treaty, but how long they will continue our friends I dare not say. I beg my humble service to Mrs. Smithson. With my love and good wishes attending you and yours, I am . . .

131. Richmond. 5 September, 1731.

Dear Brother,

I am obliged with your favour of the 26 and I hope by this time you are freed from any apprehensions of suffering from your late fatigue and diversions upon the moors, in taking proper care in due time. You seem to give me a short hint that I must own you have very good intelligence, which I hope pleads my excuse of not waiting of you att Greencroft. For as I had my thoughts long ago to change my present state and condition, I have again repeated my desires, which yet is only a distant prospect; but I shall shew my constancy and my endeavours to obtain, and, if all goes well, I will take the first opportunity to acquaint you more personally. I beg my humble service to sister; that I have had the thread by me these six weeks and only wants an opportunity for a safe conveyance. Pardon bad writing and haste, and believe me . . .

132. Richmond. 22 October, 1731.

Dear Brother,

Since the 13th past I have been att Bewerley Court[497] keeping, &c.,

[496] Netherdale was one of the Yorke family's estates.
[497] Another seat of the Yorke family.

and return'd home yesterday. Otherwise [I] shoud have acknowledged sooner your favour of the 12, for which now please to accept my best thanks as I am very glad to have your good thoughts and concurrence of the present treaty on foot (having had the lady long in my mind, to renew my former addresses), which I heartily wish may be so happy to effect, that it may be a greater inducement to see you and yours oftener att Richmond. Lady D[arcy][498] does me great wrong to credit any reports, being without the least foundation and what I am sensible of to the contrary, as I hope now she's perfectly satisfyed of my innocency, &c. I am sorry this fine weather shoud cause so much irreligion in your neighbourhood to break the third commandment. Tho', as a constant Churchman, I beleive you mean the fourth. I ask pardon for my forgetfullness of the thread, which gives me some concerne now to forward it safe to you, because I am affraid [I] cannot promise to see you before my intended journey to London, fix'd for the 25th of Nov[ember] next, which on so good an occasion [I]hope you'l have the goodness to excuse and believe me with sincerity . . .

133. Richmond. 9 Nov., 1731.

Dear Brother,

I have your favour this day and am very sensible of your good wishes to me, as I am very glad my choice meets with your approbation. [I am] hoping to succeed att last with the lady I have long admir'd and coveted, but I am not so fortunate yet to know the time for my happiness. [I] must see London first and depend upon the favours already received. I am expediting everything, by the assistance of Mr. Rudd, to clear the way, and I hope before the end of the approaching session to give you a good account and salute you with a new sister. I am sorry to hear the ill news of loosing any of my friends or acquaintance, but we must all pay that debt to nature sooner or later. I perceive the colliers are become very uneasie and troublesome. I wish we have not reason to complain of the farmers before Mayday. Tho' I have no apprehensionson my own account I am very unwilling to leave the country without seeing you, and if I could for one night, I woud gladly undergo the journey, but in case I am disappointed [I] beg you'l excuse and accept of my good wishes

498 Probably Margaret, widow of James, 1st Baron Darcy. He died 1731 and she died 1758.

and inclinations to you and yours. There is an account betwixt us. If [it is] convenient to you, please to make it up and inclose it and draw on me for the ballance att London, which shall meet with due honour. I am, with true love and good wishes to you and family, . . .

[P.S.] It is agreed to leave this place on Monday 7 night.

134. London. 7 December, 1731.

Dear Brother,

I hope my affair in hand will plead sufficient excuse for not accknowledging sooner your favour of the 19 of last month. For tho' I move my graduall paces, yet I presume they will prove sure and successfull in a litle time. Yet [I am] impatient for my approaching happiness. I had a most agreable pleasant journey, the weather and roads very favourable, and, by God's providence, landed the ladies safe in this town last Wedensday; who are both well after their journey and begin now to be ready to take wing, and, when my fair one is fully satisfy'd with the diversions of this Town, I hope she will think and give me leave to take her by the hand and receive the usuall blessing. I shall be glad to hear that peace is settled amongst the colliers; as I wish likewise justice to be duely administred, that might may not overcome right in having a proper regard to trade in generall, that your neighbours may receive some benefits from your impartiall determinations and agreements. I shall be very ready to observe your comission in what you want in this Town, and when I have the proper dimensions of the chimney peices [I] shall imediately order them; and please to give me full directions to prevent any mistakes. I am . . .

[P.S.] Direct for me as before.

135. London. 21 December, 1731.

Dear Brother,

In answer to yours, I hope mine is come safe to your hand. My affair is still depending tho' I please myself with the thoughts of being a happy man soon that I think everything may be ready by latter end of next month or begining of February. As to the sale of your estate att Morden and other places, I remember well the condition of my consent of being concern'd in that act of parliament and how it was forgot and an absolute sale made without me. So I hope may be now as well excused as then, having the same love and regard for your children, to do nothing prejudiciall to their interests hereafter. I can assure you no deed was ever left with me, to consider of, on this occasion. I beg my love and service to sister and nephews, wishing you all a merry Christmas, &c. I am . . .

136. 15 February, 1731[/32.]

Dear Brother,

I am not sure whether I am debtor to yours of the 31 and, having but little leisure on my hands, am determin'd however not to loose the present opportunity of returning my due accknowledgements. When you are pleas'd to intimate the wine is bottled and ready, I shall immediately trouble you with a messenger. I hope one shiling in the pound for the present year proves agreable, especially when it is said the landed interest will be further considered. So happy times are approaching; but in lieu of this the duty of salt is reviv'd which I fear is to continue and prove a very heavy burthen, besides the ill consequences that may attend. This day the comittee, appointed to enquire into the abuses and notorious villainy of the charitable corporation, mov'd for severall of their officers to be taken into custody, for fear that they shoud escape examination as some of them already are gone into parts beyond the sea; also that they might have power to examine evidences in the most solemn manner. The world has a very good opinion of this Comittee, that justice will be done without fee or reward, and I hope the session will be long enough to finish their enquiry to the satisfaction of the world, for I do not apprehend anything else can put a stop to such unparalel'd iniquitie. I am call'd upstairs to the ladies and my wife comes in, who desires to join with me in love and service to yourself, sister and our nephews, who, I hope, are all well. I am . . .

137. London. 23 March, 1731[/32.]

Dear Brother,

I am obliged with your favour and [I am] glad the innocency of my mind produces so much mirth, but did not imagine anything coud want recourse to a dictionary. [I] am sorry to understand my old friend declines so fast. Yet I hope the spring will revive him, but we must all yeild to nature att last. When you are pleas'd to advise my share of the wine is ready, I will imediately dispatch a carrier of it to you, that it may not suffer as I hope it will please your taste when I have the satisfaction of your company. The Salt Bill was read a third time last Tuesday, and litle debate on one side, but numbers pass'd it. If you judge me right I can never be a courtier, inconsistent with thoughts of my country's interest. The report from the Comittee on Lord Derwentwater's[499] estate is appointed to be printed and taken into consideration this day 7 night and, if justice take place, some of our members deserve to be expell'd. I desire you'l be pleas'd to say what you woud have your turnover made of and how much an ell of Camruck or muslin. [I] suppose you do want stocks, otherwise you woud send me an exact measure. As to tea and snuff I will endeavour to please you, and pray tell me by what carrier or how I must send them to you. I am in great haste. I have directed Vanelia and Vanella under cover to severall of your family . . .

138. Richmond. 11 May, 1732.

Dear Brother,

I am extreamely obliged to your favour of the 7th and kind wishes to me. [I] arrived here the second of this month after a most agreable journey; the roads very good and the weather favourable. Whenever it suites your conveniency my wife and I, who salutes you and yours with sincere love and respects, will be glad of your company. The bearer has with him your comission to me and my present to my nephews, which I wish may please and prove acceptable, and desire you will put under his care the wine design'd for me and dispatch him with conveniency; hoping it will be carefully pack'd to arrive without any loss. I am . . .

139. Richmond. 12 Nov. 1732.

Dear Brother,

I have been from home for this last week, with my wife, visiting our friends at Marske,[500] which I hope will plead my excuse not returning thanks sooner. I do not know what weather you have had of late, but I can assure you [we] mett with nothing terrible in Netherdale, not even to force a riding coat and I do not remember any frightfull days here. I have had a letter from Mr. Stephenson[501] without any name to it, who charges half a hogshead of wine with

[499] John Radcliffe, 4th Earl if Derwentwater, inherited the estates of his father, the attainted Jacobite. He died in 1731 and his estates were claimed by his uncle Charles, 5th earl, who was also an attainted Jacobite.

[500] The Hutton family of Marske. *Surtees.*

[501] See note 199.

other articles £9. 11s. 8d, which I think very dear. [I] desire you'l pay him and make the best bargain therein. I canot call it so good but that I have better in my cellar. The sturgeon my wife complains of much, not being firme and fresh. You mistook me in the quantity as I only desir'd a ran. I beg you'l be pleas'd to discharge that note for me in the best manner.

The yarn you mention [I] intended it as a present and beg my sister will please to accept of it. I propose going into Netherdale about the middle of next, and, if any of the same sort can be had, I will bring it with me. Otherwise I shall bespeak it. My wife calls me upstairs and downstairs to supper, who joyns me in love and respects to you and yours, and I am . . .

140. London. 17 February, 1732[/33.]

Dear Brother,

I am obliged with your favour and kind enquiry. [I] left home the 4 of this month and laid att Wetherby that night. I thank God [I] have no reason to complain of my journey, for I got safe to this place on Wednesday the 7th and found no waters anywhere troublesome except att Boroughbridge. The late flouds have done me great damage and I believe it will prove worse than a Land Tax to the north riding, where a great many bridges are demolish'd. I am concern'd you give so bad an account of yourself, but I hope you'l take care in time and not ramble. The distemper is much abated here. It has swept of a great many old people and young children. The spring coming on, it's to be hoped [it] will do no more execution. Excuse my haste and I am . . .

141. London. 6 March, 1732[/33.]

Dear Brother,

Your favour of the first instant came duely to hand and am glad you give so good an account of yourself and wish you may perform your journey well and that I may hear a good account of you att Richmond, where I am sure you'l find one, who posseses me entirely, to make you welcome and will take care of you. The late inundations will prove very chargeable to me in many places and it is very well we have only one shilling upon land and no new fund or tax to affect us this year. There is a great debt upon the navy, but I do not know how that will be supplyed. We shall have a full house next week when the new excise laws will be communicated, which has occasion'd so much clamour. Then the world will be judge of the monster as it is call'd. I know nothing of the Were bill miscarrying.[502] [I] shall make some enquiry and find out the true reasons. I rejoyce my nephew continues well and good, which must afford you great comfort and satisfaction. I beg my service to the old justice when you see him and I am . . .

142. London. 20 March, 1732[/33.]

Dear Brother,

I am obliged with your favour of the 11, and tho' we have had variety and uncertain sort of weather yet no covering of snow, which must do good. The justice has no reason to complain of me, having paid him the last visit, and I shoud be sorry to loose the friendship of my good neighbour. I hope it is no crime for man and wife to possess each other and the more entire, in my thoughts, [the] greater is the happiness, which I please myself will always continue a blessing to me, and I heartily wish the same to all my friends and acquaintance. I recomended Lady Darcy to your horses and I perceive she's determin'd to have them at your own price. My wife tells me how kind you was by return of her servant, for which my thanks. Last Wedensday was a very fatiguing day when the scheme for preventing frauds in tobacco, by way of excise was open'd and fully debated; divided yeas 265, noes 204.[503] I got not to bed till 4 that morning and upon the report of Friday we had another laborious day and detain'd as late, and divided to agree with the comittee yeas 249, noes 189;[504] so that a bill is orderd to be brought in according to the resolutions, and, if the regulation of wine comes on to cure those frauds, I see no end of this session. I perceive the River Were bill is thought convenient to be dropt on account of the City of Durham petitioning to have the navigation lengthen'd to Durham, which alarm'd the coal owners, who do not like it or their aldermen to be made trustees, &c. I beg my love and service where due, and I am . . .

143. London. 7 Aprill, 1733.

Dear Brother,

I am obliged with your favour of the first of this month, hoping

[502] See *C.J.*, xxii, 28.

[503] The vote is given as 266-205 in *Parl. Hist.*, viii, 1307.

[504] The same votes as in *Parl. Hist.*, viii, 1328. For the whole debate, see *ibid.*, 1268-1328.

now your health is perfectly reestablished. Last Wedensday we had a very long day upon the first reading of the Tobacco bill and divided whether it shoud be read a second time, yeas 236 noes 200; so that it is a nice point att present to judge what will be the fate of it. The budget of the wine affair is put off to Friday next, that some think it will be further adjourn'd. By advice from home, that you disappointed our Recorder in your visit to Richmond, I venture to address you att Greencroft. We have now charming fine weather to make one weary of this Town that I wish to be att liberty to sett my face northward. [I] desire to know what price you woud have your Bohea tea bought for and how it must be directed and whether the carier woud not be the better way. I am . . .

144. Richmond. 6 June, 1733.

Dear Brother,

I have defer'd my accknowledgements, for your favour of the 25 of last month, till the bearer gave me an opportunity to send for the wine; who is very carefull so I hope everything will be ready att his coming. I shall be glad to hear that my nephew George is perfectly recover'd of his misfortune, having no ill consequences attending it; and that your tea is safe arriv'd and proves to your liking. Brother and sister are detain'd in their journey hither by Mr. Weddell's falling ill of the gout. I fancy your meeting att Newcastle races was thin, wanting so many great men. My wife joyns with me in respects and love to yourself, sister and the young gentleman, and I am . . .

145. Richmond. 6 Nov., 1733.

Dear Brother,

I have your favour of the 30th of last month to accknowledge with my thanks, and rejoyce to hear the wellfare of the lads, whom I wish well plac'd. Eaton and Westminster you do not like so cannot recomend any to you. I am sorry for Alderman Rudstone[505] and the misfortunes attending, but I hope you will be no sufferer.

I am extreamly obliged for your care in providing some claret for me, never had bad from you and wish for your company to taste the last cargo before it is all gone, for which I am your debtor, and

[505] Francis Rudstone, a merchant shipper and a Jarrow mine-owner, who was mayor of Newcastle. He was declared bankrupt in 1733. *Hughes*.

desire to know how accounts stand. War is now proclaim'd for this County against the ensuing election. Sir G[eorge] Savile[506] declines; Sir Miles Stapylton,[507] att the late meeting att York, was put up by the Tories and Sir Rowland Winn[508] by the whigs, and both have declared by sending circular letters. Only the latter joins interest with Mr. Turner,[509] which I hope will make the former drop his pretensions att this time. My wife joins with me in due respects, and I am . . .

[P.S.] By a letter this post bro[ther] and sister with their little girle, after an agreable journey, are safe arrived in town.

146. Richmond. 18 Nov., 1733.

Dear Brother,

I have your favour of the 13th and am sorry for your congratulation, as I fear Sir M[iles] will be hurryed on by party rage without any probability of success. I do not hear Mr. T[urner] has lost any interest upon his conjunction except your friend B[owes],[510] who will be remember'd if he persists att your county-Election when opposition happens. We are here unanimous as ever against the Tory in[teres]t, which I hope will prevail no more. I wish the times do not put all tenants to their shifts, but some endeavour to take all advantages without a cause, which may be your case, as certainly are not desirable and better parted with, without loss, when opportunity serves. The fine weather continues yet, that I will not be without hopes of seeing you. I am concern'd for the ill news from Sedgefield. I heard Mr. Fletcher[511] intended to start from London last Wedensday. My wife joins with me in love and good wishes to you and yours, and I am . . .

147. Richmond. 21 December, 1733.

Dear Brother,

Having been abroad for a week past I hope will plead my excuse

506 Sir George Savile, 7th bart., c. 1681-1743, M.P. Yorkshire 1728-34. *Foster.*

507 Sir Miles Stapylton, 4th bart, c. 1708-52, M.P. Yorkshire 1734-50. *Foster.*

508 Sir Rowland Winn, 4th bart., later M.P. Pontefract.

509 Cholmondeley Turner, c. 1686-1757, M.P. Northallerton 1715-22 and Yorkshire 1727-41 and 1742-47. *Foster.*

510 George Bowes was elected as M.P. Durham county 1734.

511 ? A Newcastle merchant adventurer. *Hodgson.*

not answering your favour of the 14 sooner. The six pound of tea, &c., is charg'd att three pounds fifteen shilling and sixpence, which I please myself will rectifye and sett the account upon a true ballance; and if you had not given me hopes of seeing you here, from time to time, I had certainly visited Greencroft, tho' now must dispair of that pleasure till my return from Parliament. Our Recorder gave us great satisfaction. How bravely your constitution holds out in the service of your country. I wish we were to be as quite as I find you are likely [to be]. I shall be very ready to do my best service to the memory of my old friend, when call'd upon. Am sorry to hear that he left his circumstances so bad, which perhaps shortned his days. Sir Miles Stapylton came to Town this evening and intends tomorrow, being Saturday, to try the affections of the good people here, who I beleive are all pre-engag'd, except seven or eight. [I] wish it may give a check to his future proceedings and stop in time to save his pocket and trouble, for I cannot conceive the least hope of his succeeding, but I fear party rage is too predominant in him. I thank you for the favour to be a partaker of your wine. When it is bottled [I] desire your notice to send for it, if it cannot be brought hither by the carier. I hope the three young gentlemen are arriv'd in good health. As my wife joins with me in love to you all, wishing you a merry Christmas and many happy ensuing new years, I am . . .

148. Richmond. 29 January, 1733[/34.]

Dear Brother,

In answer to your favour of the 24, I am now preparing for my journey to Parliament, hoping I shall be excus'd upon the call of the House, this day order'd, as I intend, God willing, to sett forward next Thursday; and shall be glad to receive your comands directed to Mr. Williamson's, stationer by Gray's Inn Gate, Holborn. For my part [I] am not so deep in politicks to judge of peace or war, but I can scarce think we shall enter upon the latter, contrary to the interest of the nation. I am this moment interrupted by Mr. Wharton,[512] a noted Attorney of Newcastle, who is playing the same game here, upon the D[uke] of Richmond[513] account, as was done in my father's time, and I hear he's a very proper person to stirr up such dead controversies. I have order'd Tho[ma]s Furnis to send you six stone of soap, and when I hear of any chaps [I] shall recomend your

[512] William Wharton, who was also a receiver of the stamp duty. *Hodgson*.
[513] Charles Lennox, 7th Duke of Richmond, 1701-50.

coach geldings. You'l now be so good to excuse [me] paying my respects att Greencroft till next summer; and, with mine and my wife's love and respect to you and yours, I am . . .

149. Richmond. 21 June, 1734.

Dear Brother,

I am favour'd with yours of the 17 and fear the late rendezvous att Newcastle was thin, that the History of the 4 Kings was not regarded, or that cash runs low. Saturday prov'd a day of rain here, without intermission, and made great flouds, which saluted my walk without doing the least damage, except leaving a litle wreck behind. I am sorry your neighbourhood has suffer'd so much. [I] do not hear of the like damages here. I beleive Mr. Clennell[514] is not much lamented. I had such a misfortune lately in a visit returning from Mr. Metcalfe's of Nappa.[515] My horse fell with me and laid upon my foot, who crush'd and bruised it severely, which keeps me att present under confinement, but I hope to be att liberty to take a journey next Wednesday to Bewerley, where I shall stay two or three days. I have a letter from Brother this day, who tells me [he] will be att Helperby with his litle child latter end of next week [He] proposes to spend one day here and then returns cross the country to his wife and girle att Worcester, and, about the latter end of next month or begining of August, brings them to these parts to breathe Yorkshire air. I please myself with the thoughts of paying my respects att Greencroft sometime next month, but, when you can transmitt the account betwixt us, you'l oblige . . .

[P.S.] My wife sends you her best repects.

150. London. 6 Aprill, 1736.

Dear Brother,

I must now return my accknowledgements for your favour of the 21 of last month, and, as you expect no wine this year, I shall provide elsewhere and wait till I can partake with you. The thoughts of reducing nationall interest from 4 to 3 p[e]r c[en]t has caus'd a great run upon the Bank by artfull men, which is now over. Happy for us that there is a law to prevent stock-jobbing, otherwise people's properties woud have suffer'd greatly att this criticall juncture, tho'

[514] Thomas Clennell, a Newcastle barrister, who died June 1734. *Hodgson*.

[515] Thomas Metcalfe of Nappa, Yorkshire, who entered Gray's Inn 1708. *Foster*.

it's beleived, upon the first reading of the three p[e]r c[en]t bill, engines will be sett att work again. I pitty the female world, if the bill takes effect, to be reduc'd of a quarter part of their income, wherein there are many hard cases. I hope the weather with you is now much chang'd for the better as we have had lately several fine days. We are adjourn'd to Thursday next week and I fear a long session. I am . . .

151. Richmond. 6 August, 1736.

Dear Brother,

I have your favour of the 30th last past and congratulate your safe arrivall att Greencroft, as I am glad your expedition prov'd so pleasant and agreable. The melancholly account you give of the great destruction and scarcity of game, I fear, is become too generall in all places, that the species must certainly be lost if timely care is not taken. I have now an indictment depending att the present assize against a notorious offender, which I wish may deter others from the like idle and pernicious practices. I was the first day att York races, where I found a thin appearance and the worst meeting since the establishment. I dispair now seeing you till your assizes are over and your usuall diversion with your friend Bootle. I could wish the time fix'd to be att home, having promis'd to make Mr. Fletcher[515a] a visit att Hutton, and, if you'l make one of the party, I beleive it will be the begining of next month. Will Shirrington is order'd supervisor att Morpeth. [He] pass'd by here yesterday and fancy he will call att Greencroft, either going or returning to Skipton, when he removes his family. Our love attends your whole self and I am . . .

152. Richmond. 5 Dec., 1736.

Dear Brother,

I am obliged with your favour of the 2d ultimo and [I am] sorry to be deprived so long of your company. I have no thoughts yet of a journey to Town, which I shall defer as long as I can. I thank you for procuring me some clarrett from Newcastle, but I have no imediate want, that I can easily wait till your h[ogshea]d arrives, if it is the vintage of 1736. The gentlemen in this neighbourhood have taken a fancy for an oven on the back of their kitchen-fire, which is call'd an

515a Henry Vane Fletcher (1689-1761), of Hutton-in-the-Forest, Cumberland, brother of Lady Clavering.

everlasting oven, and they say saves great quantity of coals, [is] very serviceable and immediately usefull to all sorts of baking. The operator is performing one for me and will be at Whitworth in ten days time. If you approve of the invention you may send to him thither. He lives att Leeds and his name is Francis Storer. My wife joins with me in true love to yourself and fireside, when they arrive. I hope Tho[mas] keeps well att Hackney. My brother is now att London, raising some money for an intended purchase. I am . . .

153. Richmond. 27 February, 1736[/7.]

Dear Brother,

I have been long in expectation [of] hearing from you, in answer to my last, some time ago, that I fear you are laid up with some indisposition, which [I] shall rejoyce may prove the contrary when you make me happy with your favour. I am now upon the wing, to make my journey to Parliament, proposing to decamp hence next Tuesday. I perceive there was warm and long debates in St. Stephens last Tuesday, the consequences of which, I dread, will create too much ill blood, to the advantage of our enemies. I hope all my nephews are well and that you have a good account of them. My wife joins with me in love and good wishes to you all, and I am . . .

154. Richmond. 17 May, 1737.

Dear Brother,

I got well hither on Saturday last, and this day brings me your favour of the 12. As I am sorry to find you continue yet uncertain in favouring us with your company here, which [I] wish may be soon for [I] fear [I] shall be upon the ramble next month, in making visits to stay from home. I have bought you half a dozen turn overs and two p[oun]d of Spanish snuff, which I wish may please, and shall be glad to know how to convey them. I have been under apprehensions some time for my kinsman, who, I fear, will not be a man long in this world. I am concerned for poor George. Tho' he wants the doctor's advice, my love and best wishes attend him and his brother; and I am glad you was so well diverted att Hex[h]am races. I am . . .

IV. MISCELLANEOUS BUSINESS LETTERS

155. London. 19th Aprill, 1712.

Dear Sir,

Your kind p[re]sent of ale and beer on Wednesday last came safe to hand, for which I return my most humble thanks and can only say, I wish it may ever be in my power to doe you or family any the least service. I account it an unhappiness, my being placed at so far a distance from him, who conversation I so much delight in. I hope long 'ere this, you are p'fectly recovered from the indisposition occassion'd by your fatiguing journey home. The continuance of your health is what I very sincearly desire. Mother hath had a very sevear return of her fever. Wee hope she is now past danger. Her thanks I am commanded to give your Lady for the salmon, tho' she has not as yet received the same. We expect news of the ship every tide. Father wrote Coz. Clavering three or four weekes agoe, to let him know the ship call'd the Newcastle Gally, Jonathon Jenkins, in which the harness and coach wheeles were (the former packt up in a hamper) sett saile for Newcastle or Shields the day before the date of his letter. Since which, not haveing had any answer, makes him uneasy for fear of a miscariage. When you see of that or Coz. Roger's[516] family, be pleased to give our service. Praying that the same may be acceptable to yourself, Lady and fireside, concludes me. Sir,

Your most obedient humble servant
Geo. Richardson.

[P.S.] This moment is bro[ught] home the kitt of salmon. The master acquaints us that the first was, by your order, taken out and a fresh one in the room of that sent abroad. The ship has been att sea about 8 days only, so no question but the same will prove very good Mother is ashamed she should occasion your Lady so much trouble. It's reported that the Queen has been pleased to give order to the

[516] John Rogers, whose father John had married Elizabeth Clavering, aunt of James Clavering. *Surtees.*

Attourney-Gen[era]ll[517] to prosecute the Duke of Marlbro[ugh] on account of the 2½ p. cent. His Grace has retained for His Councell Mr. Lechmere,[518] Sir P[ete]r King[519] and Mr. Dods.[520]

To James Clavering Esq., att his house in Lamesley, near Newcastle.

156. Novem[be]r 27, 1713.

Honer'd Sir,

I have taken a veiw of the Leadmiln and comput she will take aboute £8 to putt her into order. As she is, [she] will not be fitt for noe busness. So I woud not do anything aboute her till I advise you of the charge; and as you direct I shall observe. I thinke we shall gett as much proffitt by smelting the slags as will double answer the charge. Then she will be ready for any other business that falls out. The tryalls att Whitefeild-Moorgate and the falls all offer pritty faire att present for good cole. But if your worship designe to give five to the score, I thinke we must defarr working them and take worss. I heartily wish you and yours good health and am

Your worships most humble and most
faithfull servant
Edw[ar]d Weatherley.[521]

[P.S.] The bearer is our schoulemaster. I have telled him what you ordered and if you aprove of him. I fancy he will accept your offer. Vale.

To James Clavering Esq., att his house in West Gate, Newcastle.

157. Leadgate. Oct. 26, 1714.

Hon[ou]r'd Sir,

According to your order I have reduced Coleburn pitts to 2½ tenns a week for each pitt till the pay. Then, God willing, shall bring them to 2 tenns a weeke and noe lower they cann be brought. The beerers pitt is a very troublesom pitt and more incident[al] charges lys on hir then the other two. So if your worship please to allow him 3 tenns a weeke, it woud doe well. If it cannot be allowed I

517 Sir Edward Northey, 1652-1723. *D.N.B.*

518 See note 399.

519 Sir Peter King, M.P. 1701-15, a barrister and later Lord Chancellor. *D.N.B.*

520 Samuel Dodd, 1652-1716, counsel for Sacheverell. *D.N.B.*

521 Coal-agent for James Clavering. See *Hughes*.

fancy he will not cary hir on, so leavs it to your worship's pleasure. I understand by younge S[pencer] C[ompto]n, that he woud take 14s p. tenn and thank you too. I rec[eive]d a letter from Caleb, by which I understand the bargain I let, when last up, proves very well, gets both in sinking and driveing, and he greatly hopes it will turne to account. I have alsoe a letter from Martin Furnace and he says they gett very good oar and hopes they will gett as much of itt as will defray the charge. So I hope the disbursing of the other £50 will bring us in what we have disburst from first to last, which I shall be very glad to see. If your worship have rec[eive]d a letter from your brother Yorke touching my Lord Pawlet's business, I beg the favore to know the contents.

I thinke your worship did tell me this day seaven night that you were for Yorkshire shortly. If you be, pray let me know sometime before, and I will send for the man that gave me the account of Sq[ui]re White's[522] leadmine. If his reporte be true it will be worth our while to looke after it and therefore woud have you to here what this man cann say, before you goe. I am with all sincerity . . .

Edw[ar]d Weatherley.

To James Clavering Esq., att Stowhouse.

158. London. Jan. 16, 1717/8.

Honered Sir,

I bless God I got safe to London Tuesday gon fourteen days. Yester night wee had a meeting att my master's lodgings touching Mr. Johnson's account. Mr. Bernadeau in his objection says that Mr. Johnson was not to have the ½ p. cent cha[lder] after the increase of his sollery. He says the advance was not for quiting the ½ p.c. chalder but for the answering of bad debts and the returning of the bills into cash. So my master desires you to lett him know upon what score the advance was given, and likewise if you received £22 od money of him for the by vend of my Lady Clavering's coales. I heartily wish you and all yours a good New Year and many of them. My h[um]ble service attends you and am with all sincerity your worship's most obedient servant.

Edw[ar]d Weatherley.

[P.S.] My master gives his service to you and family.

[522] Matthew White, Mayor of Newcastle and a great merchant and colliery owner. *Hughes*.

159. Jan. 27, 1718.

Dear Sir,

I receiv'd both yours and have seen one from Mr. Gowland to Mr. Will[ia]m Lee[523] of Chancery Lane, in which he proposes that this dispute shoud at last be left to Mr. Rudd and himself. What my Lord will think fitt to do, I know not, for I fancy the Mowbrays[524] are now preparing him for the engagement; and a cruell disappointment to them it will be if this tryall at law shou'd be prevented. But I must confess I extreamly admire at your appointment of a Reference for determining betwixt you and the other freeholders. When I had made such proposals as must have been more advantageous to them (and with good authority too, notwithstanding all that Mr. Mowbray can say to the contrary) then the two New Referees I am sure coud make. The time now for applying healing methods is allmost elaps'd, and therefore I will make this only one proposal more and if it is rejected, I will never concern myself farther in the matter. You insist upon having your boundaries enlarg'd to Redwells which will never be agreed to. I daresay it never will. Now if you will be satisfyed to make a division of the moor or common that lyes betwixt Salter's Syke (the first boundary) and the Redwells, and take the half of it by way of addition to your first boundary, I hope my Lord and the freeholders may be brought to acquiesce in it. I have no more to say but that I wish you may not stretch your demands 'till you loose your opportunity, for I am truly perswaded a fair tryall at law will leave you far short of what is now offer'd. I am sure I woud not upon any account wrong you of one pile of grass that I coud beleive of right belong'd to you. I have been extreamly ill of a cold, which has brought a fitt of the gout upon mee, of which I have been confin'd allmost a fortnit. My wife[525] joines with mee in respects to your good Lady and beleive me, I am d[ear] Sir

most faithfully and affectionately
yours J. Eden.[526]

[P.S.] *I am sorry to hear you go on so violently against the Waltons, for I find all the neighbourhood have high resentments of that matter.*

[523] Sir William Lee, c. 1688-1754, barrister and bencher, then Lord Chief Justice in 1737. *Foster*.

[524] The Mowbrays were long-established Durham attornies. *Hughes* and *Surtees*.

[525] Catherine, daughter of Mark Shafto of Whitworth. *Surtees*.

[526] John Eden, 2nd bart., M.P. Durham county 1713-27.

160. Nov. 11, 1718.

Dear Sir,

I have writt to my Lord Crewe[527] by this post to know his Lordship's disposition in your affaire. I shall allso write to Mr. Baker[528] and Mr. Stevenson, &c., to know what it is they insist upon, that, if possible, wee may prevent any further expences and make a good agreement amongst you (if possibly it can be done) when I gett into the country again. Therefore I desire you'll stay your hand a little till I hear from them, and be assur'd no body will be more glad and ready to serve you, then, Sir . . .

J. Eden.

[P.S.] Wee have after a long debate voted a warr with Spain. My wife sends her service to yours.

161. Nov. 22, 1718.

Dear Sir,

I shoud not forgive my self in hast, if by advising you to stay your hand, I shoud lead you into an errour that might have such ill consequences, but I am apt to think the proposals I design to make will appear very fair and desirable to all the parties concern'd.

Suppose then to make peace betwixt my Lord and you, that wee allow your claim to a mannor; will you be pleas'd with a boundary from Chapman's Well to Stanley burn head, thence to Salter's Sike and from somewhere thereabouts directly over to the Lowd house, joining upon the wall of your own inclosure? It is true, this is something less than what Sir Will[ia]m Williamson[529] insisted upon, but I woud fain hope you'll be contended with it; and if my Lord can be prevail'd upon to give leave to the other freeholders to divide and inclose the rest (or some part) of the Commons adjoining to your boundary, I woud hope that might satisfye them to all intents and purposes, and upon so good a footing, I might have the pleasure to see a lasting good agreement and friendly correspondence once more establish'd amongst you. If this shoud take effect, I shoud think it but reasonable that the freeholders, who have leave given to enclose, shoud pay a little matter for each acre, yearly, towards the improve-

[527] Nathanial, Lord Crewe, Bishop of Durham.

[528] See note 241.

[529] Sir William Williamson, 4th bart., of Monkwearmouth Hall, sheriff of Durham 1723-47. *Surtees.*

ment of the living of Lanchester, and my Lord will have no other consideration for parting with the Commons, but the patronage of Lanchester Church. If this scheme meets with the general approbation of all the parties concern'd, I will hasten it as much as I possibly can, that it may without the least loss of time, be finished. I desire you will consult your friends and neighbours concern'd and let mee have your Answer as soon as conveniently you can. I will write to Mr. Baker by this post to the same purpose and I hope you'll have a meeting upon it and send mee your resolutions upon it. My spouse joins with mee in respects to your good Lady. To her and you, Sir, I am . . .

J. Eden.

[P.S.] I woud have this proposal kept as much as can be from taking air, 'till wee know how your freeholders will receive it. You must discourse upon it with them freely, there's no avoiding of it, but to others—silence.

162. [Endorsed: I received this Dec. 13th, 1718.]

Dear Sir,

I receiv'd yours by the last Saturday's post, which I must confess gave mee but little satisfaction. You could not be more pleas'd to have your desire in this affaire then I should be in contributing my best wishes and endeavours towards it, but it happens at this time that I cannot gratifie the friendship I have for you, and do justice to the trust reposed in mee. If the bounders, which I propos'd, will not please, I believe some farther concessions may be obtain'd, if reasonable ones will content you, which may be referr'd to the commissioners to be appointed by the Act of Parliament, which must be had, if the division goes forwards. Or if you had rather have it so, the present referees may determine that point this next spring or early in the summer. But unless your demands are very much contracted I cannot hope to see any other end put to this troublesome affair, but what an expensive suit of law must give; and 'tis very probable (whatever you may hope for from a tryal) you may be oblig'd to sitt down with a much less share then is now offer'd to you. I can tell you too, your neighbours seem better inclin'd to an accomodation then you think (as appears by your last letter), tho' they are far from apprehensions of being worsted by you, in case it comes to a tryal, but you may be sure, they will insist upon it, that after a boundary is consented to, and settled, that you shall not afterwards make any new pretensions to any farther share of the Commons, upon any claim whatever.

I cannot forbear taking notice to you, that I hear you give it out that I had positive orders from my Lord of Durham to put an end to this matter at the Reference upon any terms, which I do assure you is very false for I neither had message, nor letter, from his Lordship relating to my conduct in that affaire before I got to London; and it is very absurd to imagine any such orders could be given to predetermine my judgement in the matter. I can only say farther, that if his Lordship makes any concessions, it is not from any diffidence of his cause or of his success if he can have justice, but meerly for peace sake.

I shall be glad, if what I have propos'd in this, has your approbation; I shoud think myself very happy in being instrumental to restore peace and good neighbourhood amongst you, which is so valuable, that a great many acres upon the barren commons can never be a sufficient recompence for the loss of it; and, give mee leave to add, from the sincere friendship I have for you, *that I wish you had rather pardon'd generously the Walton's for a fact committed so long agoe, then prosecuted them with so much severity. I think, it would have been much better upon more accounts than one.* Pardon my honest freedom; let mee hear from you, and putt mee if you can into a way to serve you and rid you of this troublesome affaire, which will be more acceptable to no man living then to, Sir, . . .

J. Eden.

[P.S.] My spouse joins with mee in respects to your good Lady and yourself.

163. Dec. 20th, 1718.

Dear Sir,

I receiv'd yours by the last Wednesday's post, and am sorry that I cannot, at present, give you the satisfaction you desire, it being impossible to make any right judgement of what farther concessions can be made, without a map; but if you expect any great matters more, you'll certainly be disappointed. I wish you would not think too well of your own pretensions, which may prevent all endeavours to end this affair in an amicable way, and prove a fatall errour to you at last. You seem to think I have a commission to make an end with you upon any terms, which I do assure you is a grand mistake. My Lord may make some small concessions for peace sake, but take my word for't, he'll stand another tryall if you putt him anything hard to it. I could give you a convincing proof of it, if it were not improper to trust it in a letter. If boundaries can be fixed to please you, you may expect all that can be done to make you safe in your possession of it. But till the first point is settled, 'tis to no purpose to trouble ourselves about the other. I will only say, that excepting my Lord's death (which I hope is yet a great many years distant), you need not have any apprehensions of being made uneasie, or of being disappointed, by staying till I get into the country. I'll write more in a post or two, and at present have only time to give my wife's respects and my own to your good Lady and to assure you that I am, with great sincerity . . .

J. Eden.

164. Dec. 25, 1718.

Dear Sir,

You must either have more patience or I doubt it will be impossible to give you that effectuall security which you so earnestly press for, in so hasty a manner. My Lord's death, if it shoud happen soon, may be very inconvenient to you, take what method you please in this affaire, either by tryal or reference. Can you propose any method yourself for your own security? Or will you refer it to Mr. Gowland to draw up an agreement in the strongest terms that can be conceiv'd, to bind the Bishop, yourself, and the freeholders, which when approv'd by Mr. R[obert] Spearman[530] on behalf of his friends, may be sent to my Lord for his approbation? Your boundary must be particularly sett forth in it, as consented to, by my Lord, and when you have all set your hands and seals to this agreement, it may be a foundation for an Act of Parliament, which must be had for dividing the Commons. Now when you have my Lord's and the freeholders' hands and seals to such an agreement, you may wait with less uneasiness for an Act of Parliament. For tho' such an instrument may not bind my Lord's successor yet surely it will bear a very great weight with him and incline him very

[530] Robert Spearman, 1657-1728, a Durham attorney. *Surtees*, and see letters 172-185.

strongly to approve of what has been done, and to suffer it, to be perfected according to that design. I will write to Mr. Rudd about the farther concessions to be made, for I think he will understand mee, tho' I have forgot the names of the boundary marks, and, since you are so hasty, let him try to adjust that matter 'twixt the freeholders and you. I must only put you in mind, that you are to be concluded by this agreement from making any farther claim in respect of the pretended mannor of Iveton. If by Mr. Gowland's assistance you can invent any tyes strong enough for the B[isho]p and his successor, I hope you will let us have them and make your self and your neighbours easie, which I heartily wish may be speediy affected; and it will not be more to your satisfaction then to the pleasure of . . .

J. Eden.

165. Feb. 28, 1718/9.

Dear Sir,

I am heartily sorry to find that there is so little hope of accomodating this difference betwixt the Bishop and you. I thought the last proposal so much to your advantage, that upon my word, I was more apprehensive of meeting with objections on my Lord's part then on yours. I was so desirous to bring you to an agreement, that I ventur'd to make a bold push, and acquainted my Lord with it afterwards, and to tell you the truth, (tho' I doubt not but he would have confirm'd it, because he had given me authority) he seem'd to mee not very much to approve it. And since you have refus'd it, I give you fair notice, that if you should take a fancy to accept it, I will not undertake to make it good.

You mistook mee in the mention made of the referees—I meant not that you had taken any new ones in the case twixt my Lord and you; but in that betwixt you and the freeholders—and I thought the kind and beneficial offers made to them from my Lord, by mee, were better then could be made by any other hand without my Lord's authority.

I grant too, that you never in your letters may have mention'd your consent to contract your boundaries to Redwells, but 'twas what was offered by Sir Wm. Williamson at the reference, and Mr. Rudd, I think, has hinted something of that kind since, in a letter to mee and I thought they might have had your consent to doe it. I lately saw a scetch of a bill, for determining this dispute by commiss[ione]rs to be appointed by the Parliament. It was to be sent into the north to be jointly consider'd by Mr. Rudd and Mr. Gowland to see what they cou'd make of it. Pray lett mee know if you have heard any account of it.

The noise has been made about the Pretender's being taken proves to have been groundless. But there is a Bill to be brought into the H[ouse] of Lords on Monday next, which is of an extraordinary nature. It is concerning the estate of the peerage of Gr[ea]t Britaine; and by it, they say, twenty five Scotch Peers are to have the priviledge for them and their families of sitting in Parliament, and all the other Scotch peers to be excluded, and be disabled from ever serving as peers there. The King will have power to make six English peers more but after that, to create none 'till the number of them is below two hundred, which they are not afterwards to exceed.

My wife joins with mee in hearty respects to your good Lady and pray beleive that I am with great sincerity . . .

J. Eden.

166. Sept. 28th, 1719.

Dear Sir,

I have seen the articles with your amendments, to which, I find, the Freeholders not in the least dispos'd to consent. They are surpris'd, (and not without reason) that you shoud think of having two acres in lieu of those you leave open to the Ivesteners; since tho', taken from your Greencroft mannor, they will be added to that of Iveston. You have forgot, I beleive, the first articles of agreement, when you demanded an alotment for Burnhouse for you were to provide for that and Whinny Garths and Nunshouse upon condition of having 80 acres, which was agreed to. Then you propos'd to take twenty acres (instead of 80) if they woud take care of Nuns House which was agreed to. Thus the case stood and therefore you cannot in honour insist upon that point. And your having your alotment made by the Commiss[ione]rs *in the first place*, is what they refuse to comply with, insisting upon the general division alltogether. I wish to see you at Whitworth, where I shall stay till Thursday morning to accomodate these differences, which I think not very material. I had almost forgot the 2d p[e]r acre, which the Ivestoners are resolv'd never to agree to, and truly Mr. Rudd and all of us, wee think it too hard that you shou'd have both the 20th acre, and 2d p[e]r new [Tons?] too; I am sorry these new difficulties shoud be started and perhaps there are some others which I do not now think on. I am . . .

J. Eden.

167. Jan. 4th, 1719/20.

Dear Sir,

I should make some apology for not having answer'd your obliging letter sooner, but I am confident your friendship will doe it better for mee then I can for myself. I am surpris'd the Waltons[531] should stand off with so much obstinacy, and whether they mislead, or are themselves misled, the difficulty of making them *accede* will be equally troublesome, yet I am not without hopes, that when I get into the North they may by proper methods be persuaded to hearken to reason. My Lord Wm. Pawlet has been often with mee, to desire my assistance in fixing his boundary, and when that is done, there will, I think, remain no pretence for them, to give you any farther disturbance. The conclusion of your letter has something of the riddle in it where you tell mee *if I follow not a laudable example in coming down, &c.*, you know who will be blameable. I fancy you will not think mee blameable for keeping to my post in my country's service, when for ought I know, my attendance may be more necessary then ever. Deserters may plead some merit with the enemies of their country; but never surely with those whom they have forsaken. If you have a dissolution in your thoughts, I can tell you, wee have allmost given over thinking on't here, and I woud not alarm my friends in vain.

People are everywhere making different conjectures upon what my Lord Stanhope's journey will produce. It is said, there is a peace upon the anvill twixt France and Spain, by which all those valuable advantages in trade which were lately in our possession will be given to France, and wee shall have so many moneths given us to consider on't, if we'll come into 't or not.

I can't yet guess how long this session may last but if wee are to enquire into the state of the fleet and some other matters it may perhaps be a long one. I am told there will be a call on Thursday sennit, and no favour to deserters. I have the satisfaction of Mr. Shafto's[532] and my bro[the]r's company, which makes mee easier

[531] The Walton family of Lanchester, Durham and Ripon, Yorkshire.

[532] Mark Shafto or his son Robert. See note 111.

then I shoud otherwise be from home, and my good neighb[ou]rs. We often remember you and your fireside. My respects to your good Lady and pray beleive mee . . .

J. Eden.

[P.S.] I wish you all many happy new years.

I hope you have taken care of the highway for which my word is engaged to Mr. Stephenson.

168. Durham. 4 March, [1719/]1720.

Sir,

This afternoon Mr. Spearman, Mr. Hunter, Mr. Stevenson junr., and Mr. Whittingham[533] sent for me to the posthouse, and there show'd me a letter from Mr. Denton,[534] the sollicitor, and alsoe a letter from you touching the Art[icle] about the Comons; and after some introductory discourse they told me that most of their adherents had now deserted them or at least so farr as to refuse payment of any proportion or share of expences; and that Mr. Bowlby[535] might be sent up to prove the signing of the agreement. Therefore, to discharge that and alsoe the fees in both Houses, it was necessary to raise £120: in this manner—the said gentl[emen] £80, and you £40: or otherwise the whole affair must consequentially cease. I told them this seem'd to me an unequall contribution and noe way conformable to the agreement, which was to raise the expences rateably according to the value of your estates in the Book of Rates. To which they replyed that all p[er]sons but them refuseing and you receiveing the greatest share of the Comon. They thought the above method was just enough. Thereupon I took leave, informeing them that I would (as they requested it) give you an account thereof, which Mr. Spearman alsoe promised to doe this post. Your servant called this morning and told us your Lady's family at Stow house were well. We are mere strangers to the p[ro]gress of your Art[icle]. My father is and soe I am, Sir . . .

Ra[lph] Gowland.

[533] Timothy Whittingham, who owned Holmside Hall, Lanchester. *Surtees*.

[534] ? Alexander Denton, Whig M.P. 1708-10 and 1715-22, who had been one of the barristers for the Aylesbury men and also secretary to Lord Wharton in Ireland.

[535] Thomas Bowlby, a Durham solicitor and father of Peter Bowlby, later registrar to the Dean and Chapter of Durham.

[Appended:—] Durham. 13 March, 1720.

Sir,

I rec[eive]d a letter last post from your son giveing an account that his Bill had past the House of Lords, but he was now under a great uneasiness for Mr. Ord's[536] son's takeing from Mr. Pit's[537] counsell (as he said by your order) the Tanfield writeings, which hath soe provoked that gentleman and given him such jealousy of unfair dealing that he's for declareing void the bargain, which will be the greatest in kindness that any can propose to doe to the family and the poor children must think as well as he, who are innocent and unconcerned in the family prejudices. I must tell you that I cannot beleive this to be by your order; nor shall beleive it; untill I have it from yourselfe. If you have any reason to give I wish that you had first writ it to me and I should certainly have mediated the matter to your mutuall satisfaction. If this bargain be obstructed by any evill counsellors they will not be able to answere to God or man the miseries that may attend his family, which I beg of you to prevent. It is in your power and have not that to answere for. I am soe concerned that you must excuse my expressions, which are the p[ro]duct of true love for your family. I can't think that Mr. Grey[538] gave any such advice, but I doubt you are fal[le]n into other hands, that I should never desire to be advised by.

I beg of you write without fail tomorrow to alter this hindrance and to carry the writeings where they were. Otherwise give me a good reason against it that I may not alter the good opinion I alwaies have of your integrity and uprightness.

My service to Mr. Grey and his lady[539] and Madam Anne,[540] and am Sir . . .

R.G.

169. Durham. 14 March, 1720.

Sir,

Yesterday morning I went to wait upon Mr. Spearman touching the money to be raised for carrying thro' the bill about the Comons and discoursed him upon the proportions; the result whereof was

[536] John Ord a coal-owner, who was one of the five directors (with White, Clavering, Liddell and Wilkinson), who formed a group in 1710. *Hughes*.

[537] George Pitt, an M.P. from Dorset, leased a colliery at Tanfield Moor. *Hughes*.

[538] James Clavering's brother-in-law. See note 470.

[539] James Clavering's youngest sister, Alice.

[540] His sister Anne, who died unmarried in 1750.

this, that many had [unhinged?] departed from the agreement and all refused to pay their contributions but 4 persons vizt. Mr. Spearman, Mr. Stevenson, Mr. Hunter and Mr. Whittingham and that they proposed that you should advance £40 and they £20 apiece, but after a little reasoning he thought it an unreasonable imposition for you to pay double and therefor he would agree to £20. However, in his usuall obscure way he said, if it was not done the bill must drop for they would doe noe otherwise. Just as I am writeing this Mr. Spearman's clerk is come to tell me that he hath this post rec[eive]d a letter from you and that Mr. Hunter and Mr. Whittingham will be in town in the afternoon and desires I may meet them at the posthouse, which I shall doe accordingly, and so write underneath what passes.

Above you have a copy of my father's letter sent this morning to your father. If we receive any answere it shall be imparted to you.

I am just come from Mr. Spearman and Mr. Bowlby, who were [torn] but the other gentlemen expected did not come; therefore Mr. Spearman [torn] the matter thus—that you should be bound with the four gentlemen, above named, for the sum to be advanced, and that the same shall be raised out of the moneys collected and to be collected by vertue of the agreement, and in case of less the obligors are to contribute equally. Mr. Spearman will send for those four gents. to be here on Thursday and I shall send for the Lords to be here the same day and then endeavour to reconcile the difference and if he be satisfyed I think your bill will be in noe danger. Mr. Bowlby proposes to goe in the coach on Friday if he can take a place for that day; but on horseback he dared not venture because he is much afflicted with the gravel. My father is, and soe am I, Sir, your very humble servant . . .

Ra: Gowland jnr.

[P.S.] Mr. Hopper[541] being from home I could not search the office for the recovery with which I acquainted Mr. Wilkinson,[542] who told me he had noe letter about that affair nor heard nothing thereof since you went to London. I congratulate you on your bill passing the House of Lords, but doe not find it in the votes this p[os]t as I expected.

541 Humphrey Hopper of Black Hedley, 1677-1760, who owned land at Rookhope and Barnard Castle. *Hodgson.*

542 See note 273.

170. Durham. 25th April, 1721.

Dear Sir,

This day Mr. Carr of Cocken and the Lady Margaret Paxton[543] (the beauty) were married. I knew nothing of it till near 9 in the morning.

I rec[eive]d yours and know not where to lay the superlative fault of not looking into your title. Could any man imagine but that had been known before you entitled? Ralph desired of Mr. Grey an abstract of the deeds, which he refused him. That Mr. Pit hath made Ord his sollicitor must be plaine; that he's what I writ to your father that his advisor was. That letter makes me out of favour with old and young of them.

The [packet?] will be sent when post [horses?] comes from Northumberland.

I am sorry for your ill usage, nay barbarous, and advise you to bear under the oppression with an humble submission to the will of God and despond not.

Why are you angry with my son? If the other side will not imploy us would you not have us before for those that will? You know my principal and practise and soe it follows, to act for our clients with more zeale than for ourselves and not to betray them and surely then wee lay noe foundation for reflection that can be called just. I think he doth what he ought to doe and what I shal encourage him in to act vigourslу for his client. You dropt him in your bill and got another, and in this he's not, nor was, any way concerned for you or any of those who are for the division bill. What your friends or others without just cause reflects on him, will neither hurt him nor me, and if he or I was concerned for you and not in the house of Lords surely he may be there for those that never opposed you; but will readily agree that you have what is allotted to you. If Jack Hunter had not been what he is and refused the men their known right, they had never opposed it. Why should not Sam[ue]l[544] openly appear and how can the miscarriage of that bill reflect on him? He hath reasonable p[ro]posalls sent him from my clients this post, which ought to be embraced if not. Then wee cannot be blamed.

Inclosed you have Raw's bond. The charges are of three; judge-

543 Ralph Carr of Cocken, who married Margaret, daughter of Nicholas Paxton, 25 April 1721. *Surtees*.

544 ? Samuel Gowland, eldest son and heir of Ralph Gowland snr. He entered Gray's Inn in 1708. *Surtees* and *Foster*.

ments, [illegible] and outla[w]ry £91. 5s. 10d. besides what the sheriffs and gaolers' fees and entering satisfaction on the judgements. His wife was here to know if I rec[eive]d your order to discharge him. I am very weary yet am Sir . . .

Ra. Gowland.

[Appended:—] Durham. 25th April, 1721.

Sir,

I can add that I have done the utmost in my power for service and had not I been more active therein than some others I can tell the length it would have gone. I have been an instrument as much as possible to mitigate and lessen Ro[bert] Hunter's[545] demands and brought him to this proposall for peace sake, whereof noe advantage is to be taken if not complyed with, vizt., that he shall have a quantity of the wast in proportion to the book of Rates in respect of his freehold and other lands and tenements, and the like quantity to be laid continuous thereto in respect of his mannor and for his consent alsoe and the mines under both the allottments and if this is secured to him by an additional clause he will agree thereto. I am heartily concern'd for the obstructions you meet with and think you have been abominably dealt with and wish you speedyly extricated from all difficulties and am . . .

Ra. Gowland jnr.

[P.S.] N.B. All treaties or proposals were rejected here by Mr. S[amuel] and Mr. H[unt]er.

171. Durham. 5 May, 1721.

Kind Sir,

I thank you for your congratulation. I shall rejoice to hear that the counsell agree with you and Pitts. I am much concerned at your uneasiness.

When you and the Moor Ma[ster] Hunter and the others had come to an agreement and you had all signed, and your boundary set out therein, in the bill before the house, and all agreed to the sole conduct of Rob[ert] Spearman and Hunter and [sent?] to the Tory sollicitor above, and wee all laid aside, surely wee might be for the two lairds; and you know, when here, that wee were soe concerned,

545 John and Robert Hunter were brothers, who owned land at Medomsley.

if you had then desired wee would not, I should have sit stil for anything but a great trouble that I shal get by it or my sons either, for I doe not take them to be generous and considerate clients. But having undertaken it and when readily agree to your bound[ar]y what can wee now doe?

I did not suppose that Sam[ue]l doth appear for any but the Lairds, for the sollicitor for those that carry in the bill solicits for the whole bill to pass and not for their parts exclusive of yours, and, if soe, if that bill pass it is for the whole and sure in that you are included, and if soe then Sam[ue]l doth not sollicit for you and the Lairds too. That would be inconsistant, if you oppose them, tho' they will agree for your allotment to stand unimpeacht by them, but then that, I doubt, must be on a new bill and not this joint bill. Assure yourself John is the sole p[er]son that occasions their appearance. He owns them Lords of the Mannor, but that the mannor doth not extend beyond the dike stakes. Then the moor can noe way belong to the tenants as appurtenant to their several inclosures; for if the moors be the comon appurtenant to their in grounds, then they are parcell of the manor, and to talk otherwise is greatest absurdity.

I know Cot[esworth] is their great advisor and was present when Ra[ndolphs?] kept their last Mich[aelmas] Court. Whether I or any of my sons had been concerned or not wee should not have valued for anything that wee shal get by it.

What p[ro]posal was writen to you was soe reasonable as none but John Hunter would oppose, he having the B[isho]pp's lease. He would extend that to the cole mines on Medomsly fell, and soe extend the B[isho]pp's bounder further then it ought, and if the B[isho]pp have the mines there, he must be Lord of the Mannor, not the Hunters.

I doe not know what you mean by—biding you look to yourselfe—I cannot see and could wish that any can use the least argument to shew our being for the Hunters is dishonourable. If I apprehended it soe, I would soon give it up.

If they come about Raw's matter I'll pursue your directions. You must setle the account for principal interest and costs and send me down, that I may know what to take the security for.

I think our justices acted with prudence like good protestants and friends to King George, not to be governed by Tories, tho' the City T[homas] Conyers hath prevailed on, they being wonderfull ingenious, considerate p[er]sons and well affected.

Sir Wm. Williamson and his side offered to address the King by congratulation on the birth of the prince and then petition him for justice on those miscreants. But to address the Comons was imitating '41, to set the King and people by the ear. They were for hanging the robbers, if it could be by law, and I think I gave you my judgement before you went hence, that they should be hanged if it could be and all their estates forfeited and added to the South Sea stock; and that wee are all for. I understand not-quiting the seven millions—nor doth any of the papers explaine it. I am weary yet alwaies would approve myselfe to be . . .

Ra. Gowland.

172. Durham. 7 Jan'y, 1719[/20.]

Worthy Sir,

The resolution taken at our last meeting, not being putt in execution, occasions you the trouble of this to reminde you thereof (least you should impute it to my neglect) I have enclosed sent the forme of a summons usuall in those cases (as I'm informed), which I submitt to your correction you being the properest judge thereof. If you and Mr. Stevenson thinke fitt to signe it, or to gett it signed by any other you thinke proper and sent forthwith to be served on the party before the Sessions that in case he refuses to appeare thereon wee may then meet and come to further resolutions about our business. I take it the summons is to be sent by the Justices themselves otherwise would have saved you that trouble but since the charge is to be bore by the publicke I hope you'll excuse . . .

Rob. Spearman.

173. Durham. 26 January, 1719[/20.]

Worthy Sir,

I had the favour of yours, for which, and the news it brings, I returne you due thanks; and when you and Mr. Wright[546] have agreed of a day to meete here, if you please to let me know your day I'll attend you and in the meantime I thinke it may not be amisse to give Mr. Hunter and such other of the freeholders as you judge p[ro]per notice of the day and place of meeteing that they may bee present (which may take away objections which may be raised) and give an opportunity (when together) to forward matters which I take

[546] See note 409.

to be a necessary point, which is wholly submitted to your prudent management by Sir . . .

Rob. Spearman.

[P.S.] Since the receipt of yours I had a letter from Mr. Eden, which says my Lord Pawlet is very pressing to have a copy of the agreement betwixt my Lord of Durham, you and the freeholders, of which your thoughts are desired if p[ro]per to be done.

174. Durham. 30 January, 1719[/20.]

Sir,

In answer to yours I have not a copy of the agreement ready, but shall order a copy to be made on Munday when it shall be ready if you please to order one to call for it in the afternoone. I take Fryday next may be a very p[ro]per day to appoint to meete on when you shall be attended by . . .

Rob. Spearman.

[P.S.] I retorne you Mr. Wright's letter inclosed.

175. Durham. 1 Feb., 1719[/20.]

Worthy Sir,

Inclosed is a true copy of the agreement which cannot but be well taken comeing from your hands, since a copy was denyed here. I am . . .

Rob. Spearman.

176. Durham. 7 February 1720.

Worthy Sir,

I had the favour of two letters from you, which I deferr'd answering till now, in hopes of hearing from Mr. Eden, but he being silent I conclude nothing is to be done with my Lord. I therefore writt to Mr. Eden by last post, to let him know that it was the opinion of those here not to attempt the bringing in of the Bill without my Lord's consent, soe that we are wholly at a stand at present and I finde nothing can be done unless Mr. Eden and you can prevaile with my Lord to joyne with us, which be pleased to try againe that we may once more have peace and quietness in the parish, which is what's desired by . . .

Rob. Spearman.

To James Clavering Esq., at a Painter's in Bedford Streete, near Bedford Row, London.

177. Durham. 25 February, 1720.

Worthy Sir,

I doubt not but you rec[eive]d myne by last post, which would give you an account of what happen'd at our last meeteing.

This day Mr. Stephenson was with me and brought the inclosed (which has no weight in it) and he has p[ro]mised to endeavour to get me a copy of the obj[ections] made by Mr. J. Hunter of Billingside and the other freeholders.

He tells me that Major Nicholls, Mr. Sandford[547] and several others of the substantial freeholders are for opposing the Bill, and that their cheife objections are the want of a comon-quarrey in that quarter, and that they have noe better allowance for working the colemines and wayleaves in their grounds, and for makeing, keepeing and repaireing of gates, soe that I doubt we shall have a sore strugle to get forward, unless my Lord Wm. [Pawlet] espouse it heartily.

I have got a letter from Mr. Cotesworth to tell me that he had rec[eived] the copy of [the] Art[icles] but had not time to p[er]use it, soe as to send it, by last post. Therefore he onely told me my Lord he had rec[eived] it and named the £200 charges which he left to his Lordshipp to explaine. I am Sir . . .

Rob. Spearman.

To James Clavering Esq., att Stowhouse.

178. Durham. Aprill 30th, 1720.

Sir,

The day appointed for meeting to settle our Bill is Wednesday next at the Post house here, between one and two in the afternoon, where I hope we shall have the happiness of your company. I see Mr. Hunter and Mr. Whittingham this day and acquainted them therewith, so that I doubt not but they will attend accordingly. I take this opportunity to present my service to yourself and good family and am with all due respect . . .

Rob. Spearman.

547 Son of John Sandford of Collierley, Co. Durham. Died unmarried in 1723, aged 38.

179. Durham. May 14, 1720.

Sir,

In answer to yours rec[eive]d by the bearer, the Bill is perfected and sent away to be filed and I expect the [spas?] down in a post or two, and, as soon as they come, shall gett them served.

For dispatch of the business in hand I take 'tis necessary for you to give instructions for your answers that they may be gott drawn and sent up in time. The copy of the Bill is by me which you may see when you please, and your presence will be absolutely necessary here to make application to those concerned for the Bishop in order to have his answer drawn and filed, and, to that end, if you please to appoint a time when you can be over I hope to be able to attend you and in the meane time am Sir . . .

Rob. Spearman.

180. Durham. 4 June, 1720.
4 a clock.

Sir,

I have just now received a letter by a speciall messenger from Mr. Eden to acquaint you that his affairs are such abroad, that he cannot possibly meet on Monday (as he designed). Therefore I send this to give you an account thereof to prevent your journey that day. I have desired Mr. Eden to appoint another day (as soon as conveniently he can) and give me notice thereof in time that I may lett you know the same. I am Sir . . .

Rob. Spearman.

[P.S.] Upon receipt of Mr. Eden's letter I writt this in hopes of getting it sent by your servant (who I sent to enquire after) but he being gone I sent the bearer on purpose herewith. You are to pay the bearer nothing, for that I will discharge.

181. Durham. 3 August, 1720.

Worthy Sir,

You enclosed receive an account of what was done att our last meeting. Mr. Cotesworth promised to send the same account to my Lord by the first post after and to lett me know my Lord's answer so soon as it came to his hands. When he sends it you may depend of hearing further from . . .

Rob. Spearman.

182. Durham. 24 Dec., 1720.

Worthy Sir,

I shall observe your directions relateing to the Petition. I had noe letter from Mr. Eden (which I am very much surprized at). I was to waite on Mr. Cotesworth, who told me, that, in case my Lord P[awlet] laid his comands on him, he would still be ready to doe the best service he could. I enquired of my Lord had answered his last letter, which he said he had not, but p[ro]mised to let me heare from him when he did; and soe we parted. I heartily wish you a good journey . . .

Rob. Spearman.

183. Durham. 26 Dec., 1720.

Worthy Sir,

By last post I had the favour of a letter from Mr. Eden, which is to the effect following—

That my Lord Wm. [Pawlett] and he should have mett last Wednesday night (by my Lord's appointment) but the house sat soe late that he desired another day soe that he fancyed on Thursday they would have a tryall of skill. But my Lord says he will not retreate from any of his demands and Mr. Eden tells him he cannot comply with them and thinks my Lord seemes unwilling that it should be broke off.

Please lett me know how I may direct a letter to you at London least I should have occasion to write.

I wish you a happy Christmas and many . . .

Rob. Spearman.

184. Durham. 28 March, 1721.

Worthy Sir,

I can onely tell you that our partners came here yesterday and signed the bond. I have by this post sent Mr. Denton a bill for £80. As to the objections you make to the notes you signed, I doe not finde but you'l be made easy in it and if we can but keepe together as I hope we shall I doubt not but we shall gaine our point, if the Parliament continue sitting any reasonable time, which is what I most doubt . . .

Rob. Spearman.

[P.S.] Since the sealeing of my letters to Sir J. Eden and Mr. Denton to whom I have writt by this post. I have an account from Mr. Bowlby from Ferry-Bridge by letter from thence dated last night that the waters are soe out that he will not reach London till Saterday next.

To James Clavering Esq. at a painter's in Bedford Streete neare Bedford Rowe, London.

185. Durham. 5 May, 1721.

Sir,

Yours of the 25th past came to hand with one inclosed to C[uthbert] Johnson,[548] which I sealed and dispatched to him, and I had an account by Mr. Hunter that it came to his hand, but cannot heare that he tooke the least notice of it to his neighbours.

I have had another letter from Mr. Denton for more money, wherewith I acquainted our partners (and that it may not be awanting at this juncture). We applyed to Mr. Wilkinson, who got us £100 of Mr. Wm. Norton for which we have given our bond, wherein your first named, and is to signe (as we p[ro]mised) and I doe not in the least doubt, but you'l doe it, but to satisfy the other p[er]sons concerned I have by this post sent a note or memorand to Mr. Denton, which will informe you more fully of the matter and which your desired to signe before him and Mr. Hunter; and when done to returne it and I shall get the rest to sign it. The last note you signed, relateing to the money got of Mr. Randolph, is yet in Mr. Gowland's hands and must be deliver'd up to you when you returne tho' signed. You see Mr. Burton[549] is come in, which will ease us; and to satisfy him we have undertaken the said memorand shall be signed by you and the rest. Please therefore dispatch it.

I returned by last post £80 more to Mr. Denton and the remainder of the £100 went to discharge our debt to Mr. Wilkinson and at the posthouse. The expence above is thought to be very great, soe that it's desired you'l be as frugall as you can, for I finde it will be a difficult matter to raise more money here unless we have good success upon hearing the petition already preferred (to prove which Mr. Didsbury[550] went post from house last Tuesday).

[548] Cuthbert Johnson of Ebchester and Medomsley. *Hodgson*.

[549] ? Mr. Burton who was agent at Streatlam. *Hughes*.

[550] ? Godfrey Didsbury, a yeoman farmer of Stanhope. *Sharp Mss.* No. 13, vol. III.

I am informed that when Lord Hunter's[551] petition was preferred we had not one in the house to speake for us, and that in case any had opposed it, it had beene throwne out as irregular, which news I was surprized to heare. I hope better care will be taken ag[ains]t the petition be heard or we throw our money away and shall be laughed at.

I had by last post a copy of Lord Hunter's petition, upon which I have made some observations which I have by this post sent to Mr. Denton. I heartily wish you good successe upon your hearing for all here will thinke it long untill they have an account thereof. I am with all due respect . . .

Rob. Spearman.

186. Durham. 9 Septem[ber], 1721.

Worthy Sir,

I send this to reminde you that the money borrowed of Mr. Randoph will be due the 18th instant, soe that a meeting some day next week is absolutely necessary, that it may be got raised against the time, for by what I can finde, their will be no overplus of the money returned to London and therefore Mr. Randolph's principall and interest must be made up amongst us. Please appoint a day [the] latter end of next week and let me have notice thereof in time that I may get notice to our partners. I am Sir . . .

Rob. Spearman.

To James Clavering Esq., att Stowhouse.

[551] For Lord Hunter's petition see *L.J.*

V. LETTERS FROM HIS WIFE, CATHERINE.

187. Lamesly the 3 of Dec. [1705.]

My Dearist,

I can'te posible express the satisfaction I take in the receite of your oblidging letters which makes me not dar to omite a poste returning answer, thoy [i.e. though] myn be of little Consequence, for feare of discouridging so greate a kindness, nothing being of pleaser to me with out them. At this time [it] is my only divertion, Sister Nancey is all my Company. Uncle Harrey went of fryday to Greene[croft] and I imagin is gon to Richmond to day. A mane is Come hear on purpose to let hime know that the Ellection is of thursday, so I think I must pay hime because it is upon your accounte. I am exstreamly glad you meet with so maney good frends and espesholly amongst the bishops, where I the most fear'd. I hope you need be in no manner of dispute in the matter of succsess. Your obligations is very much to the Lady Wood for so greate sevillitis, and myn no less for her noble present. Pray tell me if you think it reqesit that I should send her thankes. I asure you it will be very acceptable to me. I wounder to here Lady Clavering is so sturring [a] Ladey. I never took her to be a stickler upon any accounte. I think she will get no greate credite by following the Lords to the hous you mention. It may be matter of concerne to all Sir James' frends to here he gose on in such a course. I heartily wish you may be victoryous in your persute and soune at home againe. The latter, I feare, I wish much more sencearly than you doo; you that meets with so maney divertions and good frends [it] is no wounder if they take your hearte. For my part hath nothing to diverte my thoughts from you. You write me exstrodnary news aboute the queen and her parlament, which we have all reason rejoys at. I wish for the longe continuance of it. I thank you for the printe you sent me. Charles say he hath not accation for any beans of any sorte. If you have a mind for flowers he will write what sorts. For my wantes

[I] am unwilling to trouble you with further than I have accation, knowing London is very expensive. Pardon my nonsense and give my duty and servis were due, wishing you good health and succsess

Dearist

Yours intirly Affectionate

wife Ca. Clavering

[P.S.] If you can get some pickles cheaper than here [I] would think it not amiss to buy some. I sende this day to Hebbron for the wine it being of. Cosen Ellison is very ill.

For James Clavering. No address.

188. Lamesley the 6 of Dec. [1705.]

My Deare,

I would not have you be uneasy upon my accounte for I'me now pretey well againe and am concern'd you should take advis of the docter at London. It is only so much mouney thrown away. However [I] must returne you my best thankes for your greate care and kindness over me. I am really takeing what Mr. Heslop prescribed, which, with my being blooded in the arm, I don't feare but may do me good for the present. For the sack you was so very kind to order me to take, I fullfilled very faithfully till my bleeding begun and then I asked Mr. Heslope whether it was fite for me and he said "No". You might be assur'd I would persue your request in drinking it, thoy I thought it much too good for me. I rejoys exstreamly that you keep your health in the perpituall hurry you are in. I shall longe for some news of your business, that may give me hopes of seing my Dearist, for whom I so much desire the company of. I have not yet hear'd of the mouney Mr. Pinkney[552] was to bringe me which hinders me paying Mr. Dubleday's[553] rente. I beg you'll buy me a paer of wourstid stockins of aboute 6 or 7 sh. a paer and bring them with you, and be pleas'd to sende me down in a post letter half an ounce of french quiltin cotton, which trouble I hope you will pardon and beleive me Dearist . . .

[552] Calverley Pinkney of Yorkshire, who became a London attorney, or his younger brother George, 1690-1749. *Sharp Mss.* No. 11, vol I.

[553] The Doubleday family, of Alnwick Abbey and Jarrow Grange, were yeoman farmers at Butterby. *Sharp Mss.* No. 12, vol. II and *Surtees*.

[P.S.] My obligations is very much to Mrs. Hebburns and I'm in a very greate dispute with myself what to make her a requitall of; wether to send her something or to desire you to make her present of a guiney. I should be glad of your information of. Your mayre that was ill is very well again and all the rest of your horsis and doges.

189. Lamely the 8 of Dec. [1705.]

My Dearist,

I dare not but persue your commands thoy you give me no manner of incouridgment to it by your example. A larger epistle from you would have been much more exceptable to me than all the docter's prescribshons, which I nor sister can reade wone word of, so must rest satisfyed without the enterpretetion of till seas you. 'Tis french to hus. I live in hopes you wonte keep hus long under that ignorance by the sight of my Dearist Jewill. Which newes will be [the] pleasantist thing to mee you can posible send me. You say you had not a letter from me in your last. If you had given me the satisfaction of answering won, you had sertainly been troubled with my nonsense. I am sorry to perceive by my Brother of Sir William Blackitt's[554] Death. I have greatle of compasion for the mallingcoly lady, [who] without dout is so. Uncle Harrey is not yet come from Richmond but we are in expectations of hime. Mr. Davison[555] and Lady was here yesterday to make a visitt. I longe for the time that may bringe hus some news of your business which my good wishes atends a longe with your wellfare am . . .

[P.S.] Sisters gives their servis.

190. Lamesly the 10 [Dec. 1705.]

My Deare,

Since the receite of your laste, [I] hath been in so extreame concerne for to find your anger so vyollent against me, that makes me scarse know what I either say or do. What ever reason I have given, I'm sertan death it self would have been much more acceptable then that unwellcome letter, and I don't know to what purpose I

[554] Sir William Blackett, 1st bart., M.P. for Newcastle 1685-90 and 1695-1700 died Dec. 1705.

[555] William Davison (1673-1735) or his brother Thomas (1675-1760). See note 47 and *Surtees*.

should make any indeavers to preserve life or health for wone that valuys them at so mean a rate as I do, since I am so wretshed a creater in your thoughts. My greive is insuportable. I can only say I beg your pardon, and as for the accation that ofends you, was my desire of hearing from you, which I shall never name more I asure you. Let my ill-natur be what it will, you are the first that ever accus'd me of it. I don't know what you would have me dow in gratifycation. I think I an't [haven't] been wanteing in my thankfullness where due, to the best of my poor [ability] to any of your relations. I am suer I would dow it much more to them then to my own. For my wants, what you think fite to bestow upon me shall be very acceptable, be what it will. You are very wronge informed in my negleckting writeing to my mother. I'm sertane [I] was indebted to her won letter. My Uncle Harry came from Richmond of Saterday. Mr Shaftey declines standing at Newcastle. Pray let it be my request to you, if you have any regard to my happiness and satisfaction in your absence, that I may [torn] your esteem and favour. 'Tis the only thing I desire in the world, and if that may not be granted me, it shall be my petitions a silent grave, which I been prety nigh wons since I see you, thoy I have so little pitey from you in your last. Pray give my duty to father, whom I am very much obliged for his kind letter and beleive me . . .

[P.S.] Father is here to night and gos away to morrow. Sir Harrey Liddle summon'd hime and Uncle Harrey to meet him at Newcastle today. We are invited to dine with the parson tomorrow, and Uncle Harrey is invited to Lord Catchisside's funerall.

191. Lamesley the 17 [Dec. 1705.]

My Dearist,

If that I did not desire to aquit my self of what you continually charge me with, [I] would not give you the trouble of my epistle this post, as sister Alice[556] writes. Your daily accuseing me is a concerne that I can not lay any thing [of] but you call it reprimanding you, which I know nothing of, nor I hope ever shall. It's fite you should be your own master and take your libertey for me and from henceforth [I] will never name your writeing in any kind, since it is such a crime. It is my parte to write as oblidgingly to you as

556 Alice, youngest sister of James Clavering.

I am capable, and I think have don it to the best of my poor [ability]. Indeed myn is not in so good a still [i.e. style] as I could wish but I hope they may be accepted as comeing from an affectionat senceare harte as the more refined. So I beg it of you may have no more angery words and I promis shall have no reason I can prevent. For the latter parte of your last letter, I wounder why you should imagine it to be a pleaser to me, since I never gave you reason to accuse me of imodisty of all faults. If you had seen me read it [you] might have observed a greate maney blushis, which it provoked exstreamly, without any greate satisfaction. [I] shall now reliefe you from my nonsense, believing me . . .

[P.S.] Cosen Pell is come tonight for news. Refers you to sister Alice, who is better at giveing you it than myself.

192. Lamesley ye 20 of D[ec. 1705.]

My Deare,

Pursuyant to your commands [I] will take all your reproves and reflections upon me with patiens, and without nameing it further, hoping the same from you. Thoy I asure you it is no little concerne to me, and I need nothing to be an adition, for my mallingcolly is suffictionat, being quite abondant of all company except master. He and I is like two forlorne peaple these long nights and ill whether. We desine not to endure it longe next week. The latter end of it, will go to Greencroft, it beinge the soonist cane be ready, Master haveing to aquiep [himself] of new Cloths. I dare not stay for your orders in them so hath chose a drukitt for hime, being advis'd to it for the winter. Must have another at easter. Hise wantes is from tope to toy, which I shall suply as well as I can. For your buying hime anything at London, we think it needles for a growing boy and you know his way of wearing them. What he wantes may be got as good here. He is very well and ollso good, but hath lost his reading most exstreamly. I make hime reade wons a day. Can't read one verse without miscalling his letters and puting in words of his own, nor can turne to a Chapter. A greate deale of pains must be taken with hime to come to it right. I tell hime must write to you. I beg you'll get me some threed, a quarter of a pound of 6d an ounce and the same of the rest, 12d an ounce, and 10d, and 8d an ounce, and 2 ounce of 2^{s}, and 3^{s}, and 4^{s}, and a hundreth of needles, small wons. I write yesterday to Mr Hall for the mouney. I have Charles to pay out of it which makes me fear can not pay little master's master what you orderd. I shall longe to here of your hereing of your business that may give me hopes of seeing you. Wishing you success in it and a merry Xmais and happey new year; in hast am . . .

[P.S.] Our clothes wife dyed yesterday of four days illness. You may direct your next to me here.

193. Lamesley the 22 of May
[Endorsed 22 Dec. 1705.]

My Dearist,

I received your most charmeing and affectionat letter with all the joy imaginable and I wish I was capable of returneing it as deserves. I can assure you I thought it the most delightfull thinge I have seen since parteing with my Deare, for whose absence nothing can diverte but your kind letters. Your last hath revifed my mallingcolly drouping spirits, which for wante of company gave me constante opertuniteys to think and lamment being deprived so longe of my greatist happiness in [torn] world, my dearist Jewell, whose company alone I pref [torn] before all the pleaser upon earth, and am glad to find yours is not much less and shall promis you nothing shall be wanteing in my parte that may purchus those great blessings ever so much desired by hus both. Knowing it to be a disatisfaction to you, hath accationed me meney an uneasy hours upon that account, which you have not suspected. I would willingly ly my life doon to procure won of those comforts that woude be happiness to you. I did not imagine Dr. Colbatch his prescribtion had been any way tending to my better health in that perticiller, or otherwise should not have been so backward in takeing them, but now will be no longer an enemy to myself in it, for I will resolve to persue it, and since you are so kind to say will get them for me, I chonce much rather to have them therir than here, so will give you trouble of the inclosed. I find you are much the better fichisshon [i.e. physician] than I am, for I never thought my illness had been so fatal against children as you say. For the other part of the letter, I hope you will excuse me in disobeying you in not nameing what you request. [I] shall be more obedient at meeteing, for your little son is very well. He's my bedfellow. I have got hime parte of his nessarys. He gives his duty to you. He calls me "Mamay". I have got my box with all my things which I like exstreamly, and mighty cheape every thing, and much sooner than I expected all things. I must beg you'll pay her and will give you an accounte what it is. Mrs. Hebburn says my father hath payed the owld score. I desire to send her something by sea. Last night with my letters I had won came directed for Mrs. Yorke at Newcastle, franked by my Father. I thinking it for me, open'd it and found it from Bro. Jo[hn] thanking M[other] for her present and had send her a barrill of oysters. I seelled it and send it inclos'd. Pray don't mention that I open'd it. I was this day informed that cosen Ellison payse for his wine now at Xmais and that your part comes to £5 6s. and shall I send the money [to] Hebbron or what must I do? I fear comeing shorte of money and their is non to be had to spare. My time being now expir'd for sending the letters must bid my dearist adue . . .

[P.S.] Uncle Ha[rry] is just come and gives his servis. I have been in expectation of hime this 2 days and hereing nothing from Greencroft was just a sencing to know how they did. Pray pardon all mistakes for I'm just started of cowld.

194. Greencroft 29 [Dec. 1705.]

My Deare,

I received your last at Greencroft. I came last night and I have no opertunity of answering yours by the next post so I hope you'll excuse this not comeing sooner. I am very much greiv'd to find myself so unfortunat to have disoblig'd you againe by not wateing of sister's home. If I had known your minde, I desired, [I] should certainly have don it, thoy never so inconvenient to myself, for I never am better pleas'd than when I have your abriabation in all things. As I have often towld you it is my wholle indeaver to do what is most exceptable to you and cheife care to make you as happey as lys in my poore. I came of horseback behind uncle Harry, who was very carefull. You might been assured I should have paid Chas. as you order'd me if I'd had moneys from Mr. Pinpney, which I towl'd you before [I] have not, thoy you accuse me of not doing it, which makes me feare [I] have commited a misdeamener. I am straited in it for I have paid Cosen Ellison. The advise here, as we both desir'd Cosen Mitford's care of the things that comes by sea, the better way to go to Newcastle. Sir William Blackitt's corpes is buryed today as they say.

Jack Leabon has a new coffen [i.e. calfing] cow that he would be glad to give any bodey the use of till Mayday, and we being in sad wante of milke, with your leave and aproveing, would take her till that time. I hear since the begineing of thise that Cosen Mitford is very ill. The Dr. say 'tis an ague. I wish you well of your cowld and maney happey new years and that we may see you soon, which is the constant wishis of . . .

[P.S.] I am come to a lose, hath lost wone of the buckles you bought me. [I] must desire you to get me another of the same sorte and then will give you no further trouble with my wants. I have given Sir Harrey Liddle my watch to carry up to get clean'd. Poor mane, I am mightey sorey to see hime so much out of order. All here remembers them[selves] to you. My little spark gives his duty. He is very good boy. I hope he will write by the next post. Pray my duty to father.

195. Greencroft. 3 [Jan. 1705/6.]

My Dearist,

I'm sory to finde you surpris'd with my inclos'd. I hope you will pardon it. You gave me so greate incouridgment to send the Docter's note, if I was willing, that I thought it needles to delay time. I am allwais very backward in endeavering my own health further then what conduceth to the procureing that wished for happiness by hus both, being ignorant that the use of those things was for that intendes or otherwais should have imeadiatly got them interpreted and put in execution, never imagineing my bleeding did me any prejudice that way. The reason I was so hastey in paying Cosen Ellison [was that] I was inform'd that he was to pay for the hogshead of wine this Xmais and knowing I should not have so good an opertunitey whille here to send it. I am now quite of takeing Jack Leabon's cowe, being poor and not worth the keeping. I am very glad to here you was so diverted the hollidays and entertain'd and should rejoys you could tell me was perfickly well. I never here anything from father. Pray tell me how he dus. This inclosed I beleive will aford you a good deversion as it hath don me. Master Landlord's sone came to see hime, so master maid him [h]is inditer, which is very comecall and I was unwilling to give hime the trouble to write another. He is a very good boy; I think improves in his reading, wantes nothing but pracktis and being minded. His master never herse hime but wons a week read and scans that he says. He and his sisters entertained hus with being dres'd in boys close and him in gerlles. Melley desires you'll receive for 2 geanes [guineas] of wone Mr. Slinger,[557] who will come and pay you for it, which is all from . . .

[P.S.] Will. bids tell you he hopes you'll remember the Dutch mastife for his cotch pox [?coach box]. Father was at Sir Harrey Liddle's Ellection; imagining sister Alice giving you an accounte of it, will not give you the trouble of any more noncence, which I hope you will pardon.

196. Greencroft the 10 of J[an. 1705/6.]

My Dearist,

Yours is ever very acceptable to me and I think it my cheifest happiness now in your absence to be oblidged with hearing from you so frequently, which deserves my best thankes as ollso for your care you are pleas'd to express over me in my journey hear. I beg your pardon sencearly if I interpreted your words to a wronge sence, as I think I did only in answer to yours. You are very diverting with your mane George. It seems he is of vallue in his own eyes. I wish he had behaved himselve so as might have been servisable to you. Any way of comeing down is too [torn] for hime. For your linning I took a note of them before we [torn] what you have increased. I hope you remember your orders that pretious spark shall perform. When I named a buckle to you I imagined you had not forgote the buckles you bought me which I lost wone of, to my concern. Sir Harry Liddle left Newton for his London journey to day, as we beleive. He, not being certain himself, leaves both his sones in the countrey and takes stage coach at Yorke if he cane. My little sweet harte wente to scooll of tusday to his greate greive. Would gladly go to New: castle scooll and come home every night. He had not got his task, and, with out a good wiepping now, will never get it. All the arguments [he] could use was in vane. I did not pay either his master or landlord, haveing not mouney. The last account had of cosen Midford [was] that she was better since Saterday. That day [she] was very ill. When I came hear I sent a box with a couse [i.e. goose] pye and some bounges in it, to go by seay for M. Hebron, whom I might requit

[557] Tempest Slinger of Dunnow, Yorkshire, who entered Gray's Inn in 1702. *Foster*.

some way for all the trouble I give her in buying my things. I can not expect she should dow it with out a gratuity. All people that is imploy'd is gratifyed some way or other. This being what I thought for the charge. I fear it will have the same fate of my Mother's, because beleive it goeth in the same shippe I here you are concerned for M[other], so begs you'll take the same care of myn. Shall inclose the not[e] with the name of shipp and master. This night hath heard a peace of very ill news which is a trouble to me now in your absence and feareing it will be so to you makes me unwilling to name it. Nancy the cotch maer dyed last night. Will., haveing caryed her to New : castle that day to bring home some otes, not observing her ill befor Codding was laid upon her and then laid her self down severall times and expyred that night, which is all the account I can give of her illness. Pray be not concerned at it. If you prosper in your business [it] will ballance that, which I heartilly wish you may and that you may continue your health is the senceare prayers of dearist . . .

[P.S.] Pray my d[ea]r, let me intreate thee to take it with pations and courage what way ever fortun gives the cause.

197. Greencroft the 11th J[an. 1705/6.]

My Dearist,

My greate joy and pleaser is to here from yourself, that you keep well with all the hurrey and fiteek [i.e. fatigue] you have had since we parted. God continue it till our meeting againe, which I feed my self with hopes will not be longe now to that happey minet we shall meet. You don'te tell me what I must dow with Georg when [he] arrives for your linning note I have in my closit[t] at home, and can'te tell how to come by it. Milley I gave leave when I came here to go see her Father and Mother and is not yet come back. I think it will be the same thinge when you come down to compare notes. I have thoughts of going home of tusday senite. Stay to hear either good news or bad. We are betwixt hope and despare. I wish it may succseed well, or otherwais fears you will be mightly discouridg'd after so much pans and charge you have bestowed. I am glad you tell me Father and sisters is well. You was very kind in going along with the latter to make that visitt, which I desir'd they would dow. I here Uncle Rogers is lame and keeps his room and his mane, Beney, they think wonte live. They say Cosen Midford is better but very weak.

Their in hopes will recover. In peruseing your letter again I find we shan'te be honour'd with the sight of George, so when goeth home will send you the note of your linnings. All here presents you with what is due and desirse the acceptance of my duty to father and your dear self, who is nameless in myn, believing me dearist . . .

198. Greencroft the 15 [January 1705/6.]

My Dearist,

Thoy you tell me I need not write, yet [I] can not forbear, knowing it will come to you in time befor you leave London, which rejoys me very much to perceive by yours to me, that I was in some liklehood soon to see you, but where quickly vanquished by the sight of Unc[le] Harry's letter, which gives very little hopes either for your soon comeing down, or the cause. If we be so fortunate to here good news next post from you, shall assuredly performe your orders. I was in greate hopes the latter end of the mounth would bring you home, and I think you kinder to my relations at Newbey than they deserve, abundently. [They] can come so often by hus and never call. I can't say but poor sister Betey is rather wours. She hath a mightey desire for some Scarbrouhe watter. Father sent Tick for some, but is not come back. I heartilly wish it may dow her good. If you write to me by next Saterday's post, pray direct it hear, for I think shall not be gon this day senit. Being in hast, can only wish you health and a good journey, if comes next week, and am the [sic] inclosed your note of linning.

Dearist . . .

199. Lamesley the 25 M[arch 1708.]

My Dearest,

Will, with yours, was the most wellcome sight I have seen since you left me, after so long a parting without hereing from you, which was a greate mortifycation to me. I write to you by fryday's post in hopes it would come to your hand being directed to the Black Swan, but I find it has not, which I am sory for. I'm mightly concern'd to here your journey hath dealt so ill with you. Indeed what I fear'd [was] that it would returne your pains for we had fevear whether here last week. I think it's much to be fear'd, with the greate fateags you have had, it has brought what won't easley be cast of. I beg of you to take care of yourselfe and to make it your cheif business to preserve your own health, which will be my pleaser.

Since you have not got myn [I] must indeaver to call to mind the business in it. Cosen Midford I prevalled upon to stay till Wednesday, who, as she wente home, call'd to see the Ladys at Ravensworth and they, that night, came here to make a quarter of an hour's visit, and of Sunday in Church time [went to] see Mrs. Ard and send for me their and Cosen E[llison and] me to go to Mrs. Johnson the next day, which I did. But sister never inquir'd nor wente to Cosen Collior's thoy Cosen Ellison was with hus, who is so kind to stay with me. Sister Carry's mightey nise; never takes any notis of me, but I find it is the same to all people. I perceive they was to go of Wednesday to Hebbron, but I cante [know] wether they kept their resolution, haveing not seen any of them since, nor the gentlemen since they came from Durham. Upon counteing my mouney since you went I find but £10 besides the debts you paid me. I understood by you it was £20. Pray let me know which it was. I desire to put up master's linning in a box and send it by Saterday's carryer and directed it as the other was and put some tins in it, if it will howld any, for tea. Since you went the fessond [pheasant] henn is dead. Was found tralled to a sink and half eaten with some fermine. Your butten is found. I supos you lost it in coming from Greencroft on Giblesworth [Kibblesworth?] lane. A boy found it their that Saterday and he brought it to me the other day. Since the begineing of this, Mr. H[enry] L[iddell] and Mr. Beach and severall others came here. The latter being for London I give him the trouble of Master's lineing, which saves me the sending of a box. Our duch cow is just colfen and I desire to know how the colfe must be dispos'd of. I hope you wonte forget to buy candles this week and me a pair of worstid stokinn. I fance by this you are suffishontly wheryed and am suer I am very sleepey myselfe, being late and can'te think of any thing more. Hopeing this will find you have arived at London, with my best wishis for your and servis to Master and my brother. Duty to Father. Pray pardon all my nonense . . .

[Endorsed: Mar. 25 1708. Spouse.]

200. Lamesley. 29 [March 1708.]

My Dearist,

Since you are not so kind to write to me yet I can'te forbeare dowing it to you, to inquire how you have preformed your journey this desined day, for myn proves so very rainey that I have defer'd it till tomorrow, in hopes it may be more fortunet, and my missing the post tomorrow pute me upon writeing to day, being desirous of constant hereing from you. Pray let me know in your next how my father is for I have not long. I donte find that John the groom has any business, so if you pleas'd to order hime he might help the gardiner. They came to me for the fees and window mouney, which I have paid. Sister Liddle is gon to Hebron. It is report'd she desires to come to Ravensworth again to stay the next week, not to returne to Greencroft. Pray my duty to father and servis to my brother and intreate your care of yourself. Haveing no news must conclud myself . . .

201. Richmond the 2 A[pril 1708.]

My Dearist,

I am glad you have got well to your journey's end and am sory you reprove me so sharpley for desireing your care of your self and ollso that I am so very ridicullas and foolish for being sivall to your relations. I hope I did nothing that made me apeare so or that expos'd me. [I] should be very sory if I knew it. Out of kindness to you is my inducement to make me carrey as oblidging as I cane to all your relations, which I should hope might not be ungrateful to you. I would do nothing that where so, I'm suer. I goe here of Wednesday, sadly wheryed after a seveare journey of two days. My sisters gives their servis and desirs you'll remember your promis to prevall with my Father to buy them close. I'm concern'd my Father is so unfite for his journey. I have pleased my self with the hopes of your comeing down with him, which you don't mention. That makes me not know what to think. The fans is non of myn as I remember. They belong to Greencroft. Pray give my duty to my Father and thanks for his last, with servis to my brother and sister and am to your dear selfe etc . . .

[P.S.] I am very sory Master's linning cloth did not prove right. My mother gives her servis.

To James Clavering Esq., att Lamesley, near Durham.

202. Richmond the 6 Ap[ril 1708.]

I am mightley concerned and surprised to find my Dearist dus not come down with my Father, which I alwais expected, being it is the longest time you pleas'd me with that you would stay. I thought my sister would be ready against your time, because she has had so long a warneing, but I shall never beleive your promisis more. 'Tis you I fear that's loth to leave London as you're free of poor me. I woud have my cloths send to Lamesley and for coffey and tea you know my wantes. I was in hopes you would have taken care for that. If you please if coffey be reasonable three pd of each. I'm glad to here you keep well. I beg you'll let me here from you every post, which I have been depriv'd of more than I desir'd. Pray give my duty to father and servis to sister and brother and I am . . .

203. Richmond the 8 [April 1708.]

My Dearist,

To morrow being the horserace day makes me write to day, to tell you of my greate lose, which I'm in greate afliction for, having lost my pritey pug. By an accident [it] was killed, and without your help [I] must mourn for it. So I must beg of you to suply me with a nother if you cane. Get a pretey little won, other wais let it alone. Pray be so kind to endeaver to grante my petition and you will oblidg me mightly. If [you] cane get wone befor my brother comes down pray send it by hime. I know you will arayn and conteme me of carlessness, but first know the matter of fakt. Pray pardon thise trouble. You don'te let us know wether Mr. Partridg be dead or no. If you see Mrs. Heburn befor my peteycot be don tell her the lenth of my peteycote is yard ¼ and naill. I wonte detaine you longer from your divertions, than to give my duty to my father and servis to frends. I am, my mother and sisters is your servants. Pray remember the latter's close. I have just got yours and have not time for more than to tell you I got it open without a seale upon it . . .

204. Richmond the 11 Ap[ril 1708.]

My Dearist,

You are not so kind to keepe your promis with me in writeing every post, which I towld you would be the greatest pleaser I could have in your absence. I fance Thursday is some busey day with you. I am glad you will have so good company to come down with you, as Sir H[enry] Liddle, but I am in greate fears he won'te keep to the time you mention, for he is seldom in haste to leave London. I must satisfye my self without seing my dearist thise longe time, which is a greate mortifycation to me. Will. tells me he desirs the hind wheells may be an inch hyer than these. My sisters gives you their servis, and joyne with me in thankes for your petition to my father, which I beg you will still continue, with my duty to hime and servis to my brother and sister, wishing you all the pleaser and devertion that London cane aforde and am . . .

[P.S.] I had a letter last night from Mrs. Ann N., who is mightey angery and fas that my mother towld her, that I said, that Mrs. Millmankes [*sic*] had intised Grace away. Pray remember to seall your next letter to me. Mr. Place wone the horse race plate. I thank my F[ather] for his last letter to me and I wish hime a good journey.

205. Richmond the 16 [April 1708.]

My Dearist,

Yours puts me into a mightey consternation what to think, being you name your sudden comeing down, but I don't perceive it is before the time you propos'd with Sir Harrey Liddle, nor the reason that puts you in so much hast, that I am perfictly in a miste. Neither can I tell why you should give me such a hinte as rash judging, and I am sory to be unfortunet in only haveing a sight of you after so long a absence, but if it be your mind, [I] must submite to it with all the resignation I can. You never towld me any thing of Master's illness, which I am sory to here. The cotch wheells I write you word of last post. I desire you'll get me three bottles, wone of Hungery watter and another orinch flower and houney watter, and ollso to send me down in a post letter, a knott of this, to string my pearle nekless, of the smallist that is to be had, and a pearle needle, which must be both got at the jewiller's. If these things be not tow much trouble [I] shall be thankfull, and should have thought it an obligation it would have been so kind to a got me squirill, but can'te expect it now since you are [in] such a hurrey. I hartilley wish you a good journey, whenever you take it and to where, with my duty to father and servis to my brother and sister and conclude me . . .

206. Lamesley. 15th Jan. [1710/11.]

My Dearist,

It was with pleaser I received yours to here you got well to Richmond. I have lived my owld retir'd live since you left me till Sunday [when] I had cosen Tayler's[558] company at dinner and she has

[558] The Taylor family had once occupied Stow House.

invited your son Jemey and myself to dine with her of their birthday. I am much concern'd to here of poor C. Blackitt's death. I wish it may give my sister Nancy warning not to be her own distroyer, which I am much afraid of since you give so ill an accounte of her. My calfe was sowl'd for 12sh. of Thursday and Will. went with the cows of Fryday to Jos[eph] Kells[559] and wente to Greencroft, but I had no sparaygrass worth sending. My two boys is both very well and I hope to see you of Saterday thoy you discourig me, which will be very agreable to . . .

207. Richmond. 6 July [1711.]

My Dearist,

I am very much rejoys'd with yours, which gives me hopes you are well, thoy you say nothing. I am sory that your stay here has been any inconvenincey to your business and no less trully concerned that I am the unfortunett occasion of any fresh quarills amongst your relations, which I am as perficte a stranger too as the child that is unborne, in what I have given ofence in word or deed. I am afraid it will never be otherwaies as long as I have live remaineing and after that you may expecte what is desireable from relations. Here is no news. Your boys is very well. Concludes me dearist . . .

[P.S.] All here joyns in servis to you. My father and brother is gon.

To James Clavering Esq., att Lamesley. To be left att Mr. Cotesworth's shop in Gatside.

208. Rich[mond.] 30 July [1711.]

I am oblidged to my dearist for his kind letter which was very agreable to me. It is the greatist pleaser I can now meette with. My illness strook me last week with surprise and concerne, not knowing what might happen, me being brought to the very brink of miscarying, thoy have escaped and now pritey well againe, but weak and dare not venture to move myself. I hope the latter end of next week or the week after I might ventur home, being very desirous knowing how much my affairs must wante me. Pray beg of Cosen Midford to get me three or four quarts of mushrooms and tell Bettey to pickle the cowcombers and to boyll courans and plums with suger and put

559 A yeoman farmer of Hebburn Grange.

into potes and to dry marreycowlds and whatever she thinks is usefull to get it don. I write thise with so much uneasiness that I can't inlarg further then giveing what is due from this familly to you, and wishing all happiness may attend is ever the desire of . . .

[P.S.] Your boys is well. Mr. Cotesworth will tell you the newes [of] seneyor, I have not seen yet. Mr. Hook and Ladey was here in their road to Durham and she promis'd to see me at Lamesley. If I dont contraydict it, let the horsis come against the time I mention, if convenient [for] you.

No address.

209. R[ichmond.] Aug 3d. [1711.]

My Dearist,

Thoy I here nothing from you this post yet I cane not forbeare observeing your orders in giveing you a line with the inclosed which came this day. The best accounte I can give you of myself is that I am very much out of order and I cannot say gathers any strength. Some days I am much better and others as ill, that I am mightilly discouridged and wish myself at home, but I must submitte to providence. Docter R[atclif] write an accounte of brother Tomey this post, that he has a high feaver attended with a vyollent looseness, but he is not at the hight yet, that we can not judg how he may be dealt with.

I can not perceive Lord William [Pawlet] knows his own mond, whether he goes into Bishobrick or no. My b[rother] John is gon towards Yorke today. Don't send the horsis for me till you here further from me. My fa[ther], mo[ther] and sisters send what is due, and your boys is very well. Pray excuse all faults, which the uneasy poster of writeing makes me commite from . . .

[P.S.] Pray let me know how Cosen Smithson dus and make my excuse for not answereing her letter.

210. Richmond. 11 [August 1711.]

My Dearist,

It was very wellcome newes yours gave me of seeing you and Cosen Smithson. It is a favour and kindness I cante expecte from her. Nor can I beleive her comeing till I see her. I hope you wonte leave me behind you, for I am now so well I thought to have desir'd the horsis to have comd the week after next for me. I desine going down stairs tomorrow. Pray bring with you some nottes you will find rowl'd together, what Milley laid out for me at London. They ly upon the shellf in my closit, and bring my black furbeycond scarf with you. I perceive your little neace is to be christned tomorrow thoy you say nothing. I wish you a good journey hither. All here gives their servis. Our boys is very well and to my dearist I am . . .

211. [Oct. 22, 1718.]

My Deareste,

I can not forbeare inquireing after you, being under all the trouble and concerne that a poor creature can be under at your going away in so much pashon and anger, and especially so sad a rainey dark night. I hartilly wish you may have taken no harme by it. I am very sory to give you occasion by any word of myn, which was spok very undeysignedly and without any thoughtes of giveing you offence, which I am suer woud not have either respecte or kindness, for which addes mightilly to my affliction to perceive. I sencearely beg your pardon and wishis I could say anything that apease your wrath, haveing no other end or way, but the desireing your favoure and affection and that we might live happily and comfortable together, which would be the cheife happiness of the world to me. My care shall allwais be to performe my duty and to discharg a good consciones and hopes nothing criminall will ever deserdly [be] laid to my charg and that God allmightey will suporte me under whatever he sees to lye upon me. I should be glad to know how you are, which would be very acceptable to . . .

VI LETTERS TO HIS SON, GEORGE

212. Whitehouse. Saturday, 5th April 1740.

Son George,

Enclosed will receive a bill for £30 to make good your next quarter, and neglect not, by return of the post, acquainting me with the receit; it will be punctually paid. I am glad to hear you are well and that your face is as formerly and that you have not dryed up your issues, which have removed some paternall fears that accrued when you wrote first about it. I expect your brother will begin his progress the latter end of next week. He went home yesterday haveing a call upon business to day to Durham and, haveing taken leave of his friends at Newcastle and in these parts, proposes reaching Oxford in July, against your vacation and then you may choose whether [you] will continue some time longer at College or proceed with him on his travels or tour about England. Therefore weigh and consider well, and when comes to a resolution let me know it. I have been here all this week, but returns this morning notwithstanding it is excessive cold and windy. I brought fine weather with me here, the only good we have had, and made things begin to look pleasant and made rydeing about viewing the farms, &c., in this neighbourhood very agreeable till yesterday that it changed and now threatens winter over again. Cousin Rogers by all [*seal*]*s* in a very bad state, and fr[om] his obstinacy no prospect otherwise. Perhaps when too late [seal] sensible of his danger. Poor Robt. Hutchinson went off at last and it is 14 days tomorrow since he was buried. The Drake and Duck are here and send their service, as does likewise Mr. Goodchild,[560] who owns himself your Debtor. Pray mine to Mr. Thompson[561] and tell him his mother was well last week when I was to see her and that she expects him down early this year. I am your loveing father.

Ja. Clavering

To Mr. George Clavering at C[hrist] C[hurch] College in Oxford.

[560] ? John Goodchild of Pallion, 1699-1751. *Surtees*.

[561] ? Gustavus Thompson of The Queen's College, Oxford, B.A. 1740, M.A. 1743. He was later vicar of Penrith. *Foster*.

213. Greencroft. Tuesday, 24th June, 1740.

Son George,

It's not in my power to perform as mentioned in my last. There is such a stagnation in trade, by the severall disturbances and riseing of the mob. At Newcastle they are very outrageous and are obliged to keep the gates shut and guarded since Fryday when they threatned to burn the town and begun to raise contributions; so that when now I shall be able to send you a bill I cannot say, but it shall be done as soon as possible. I wish, by the advice of Mr. Thompson, you could find out some scheme, either to draw upon me or otherwise, could be supplyed for I should be sorry anything might hinder your proceeding with the travellers in their progress. I wrote your brother in my last that his misbehaviour and new ill treatment at Oxford had given me so great a distast, that I order'd him to acquaint you that it was my positive resolution you should return no more thither and what I now repeat to you, and charge you to order all your matters accordingly. The Newcastle mob above mentioned cheifly consist of the pit-men, waggon-men and keel-men, who all complain of hardships and I am truely afraid not without just reason. Yet had the grand allies performed their agreement with Alderman Ridley on Saturday they would have been entirely suppressed. He, the Alderman, raised upwards of an hundred men and headed them into town and dispersed numbers of the mob, whereas the courage of the other honourable gentleman failed, and none appeared. I expect some disturbance today from these oppressors about my boundary. The working my collierys give great offence yet my pit men does not joyn theres, but keep constant at work; they are not starved. Just now news is brought from Lanchester that the company who met at Lanchester were headed by Justice Whittingham and Sylvertop[562] and the retinue consisted of papists, Burtons, Bakers,[563] Whittinghams and the Pontop tenants.[564] What's designed time must shew. I had no letter from Oxford last post, from whence shall be glad to hear good news this. My service to Mr. Patrick and Mr. Thompson and love to your brother. I am . . .

562 See note 316.

563 The Rev. Thomas Baker, 1656-1740, celebrated scholar and non-juror. Uncle of George Baker M.P. for Durham City. *Surtees. Venn.*

564 The Swinburne family.

214. Durham. Tuesday, 14 July, 1741.

Son George,

In answer to your letters, [I] am glad the waters agree with you; as for bathing I can give no answer to it. You must write to Dr. Askew,[565] as you were directed when [you] left home, to have his advice and direction on any emergency or change. As for your stay, that's left to your own choise. When you write for the horses they shall come for you, but I must observe, that as I am going to Simonburn and shall not return till the latter end of next week, and only just to attend our assizes at Durham, being, as you may remember, after customary to attend Mr. Bootle on to the moors. Therefore when [you] want the horses [you] must write to Ja[mes] Raw for them. If you start early from Scarbrough [you] may with ease reach Long Newton that night, where I would have you stay two or three days and not longer if [you] designs goings with me into Cumberland, whether I propose going, if nothing intervene, after parting with Mr. Bootle. I was prevented geting to Richmond as [I] had promised by an affair of consequence, which hath kept me already here two or three days, but I hope I shall get away tomorrow. My service attends your uncle Yorke, who I hope received my letter wrote a post or two ago. When he leaves Scarbrough I fancy the place will not altogether be so agreable. I am in hast. Your loving father . . .

[P.S.] If your money fails [you] may draw upon me as I told you at parting.

Mr. George Clavering at Mr. Caterly's, an apothecary in Scarbrough.

[565] Dr. Adam Askew, the Newcastle physician and father of Dr. Anthony Askew, 1722-74. *D.N.B.*

INDEX